The ICSA

Corporate Governance
Planner

The ICSA
Corporate Governance Planner

VIVIENNE CASSLEY and DAVID MENSLEY

ICSA
PUBLISHING

Published by ICSA Publishing Ltd
16 Park Crescent
London W1B 1AH
© ICSA Publishing Ltd, 2006

Designed and typeset in 9.75 on 13 pt Goudy by Paul Barrett Book Production, Cambridge
Printed in Great Britain by TJ International Ltd, Padstow, Cornwall

British Library Cataloguing in Publication Data
A catalogue record for this book is available from the British Library

ISBN   1-86072-309-8
ISBN 13   978-1-86072-309-4

Contents

Contributors

Vivienne Cassley has over 20 years' experience in capital markets, gained initially as a sugar trader and then as a consultant with ICCH Financial Markets (IFM), advising equity and derivative exchanges across Europe.

From 1994 Vivienne spent six years with the London Stock Exchange's AIM Team and at EASDAQ, developing and promoting markets for smaller and fast growing companies. Her roles in both markets involved advising companies on their preparation for flotation, providing support and advice on continuing obligations and best practice as a quoted company.

Before co-founding EquityCulture in 2000, Vivienne worked as an independent consultant providing research and business development services to a wide range of organisations within equity markets.

As a director of EquityCulture, Vivienne has developed a range of services and tools for listed and quoted companies, and has worked with companies of all sizes to help them operate effectively in the areas of regulation and corporate governance.

Vivienne has an MA in Modern Languages from the University of Cambridge and an MBA from the Open Business School.

David Mensley has over 20 years' experience working with listed companies. His career has included relationship management roles with a number of key national organisations, including the CBI.

In 1997 David co-founded Catalyst Investor Relations Group plc to provide strategic Investor Management advice to a broad cross-section of companies.

Before founding Catalyst, David spent seven years as regional director of the Midlands area of the London Stock Exchange. During this time he advised companies on the practical application of the UK Listing Rules, including the handling of price sensitive information and issues surrounding corporate governance – a role he continues to undertake with EquityCulture clients.

On a regional basis David has created a number of influential listed company communities, which are supported and valued by local companies. He currently facilitates several long-standing company secretary discussion groups, some of which have been running since the early 1990s.

Samantha Griffiths has over 15 years' experience of capital markets gained initially as a credit analyst with the Bank of New York, a treasury dealer at GKN plc and in a relationship management role with the London Stock Exchange.

In 1997 she co-founded Catalyst Investor Relations Group plc to provide strategic Investor Management advice to a broad cross-section of companies.

Samantha has particular interest in and knowledge of developing key investor messages and identifying appropriate target audiences for effective investor relations programmes.

She is a qualified accountant (FCCA), and has a BSc (Hons) from City University Business School and a MBA with distinction from Manchester Business School. In 1995, she was awarded a Guardian Scholarship and in 1998 won the MBA Entrepreneur of the Year award, supported by the Association of Business Schools and the Observer Newspaper.

Julian Mathews is a senior associate corporate lawyer at DLA Piper Rudnick Gray Cary. He specialises in private and public M&A, private equity and corporate governance. Having spent time on secondment in the legal department of WorldCom EMEA during WorldCom Inc.'s chapter 11 filing, he has experienced the implications of recent corporate governance shortcomings first hand.

Nick Jeffrey qualified as an ACA in 1996, and worked in Grant Thornton's audit department until he transferred to the firm's national technical department in 2001. He has assisted the ICAEW (Institute of Chartered Accountants in England and Wales) on various committees, most recently the Reporting Accountants Panel. Nick advises Smaller Quoted Companies on corporate governance issues and runs Grant Thornton's listed company training days.

Alex Tamlyn is head of corporate finance at DLA Piper Rudnick Gray Cary. He specialises in UK and international securities offerings, schemes of arrangement, corporate governance and securities regulation. He advises companies and other forms of business organisation as to their formation, conduct, financing, reorganisation, acquisition and disposal. He also advises on financial services, securities regulations and practice, share transactions, capital reductions, minority rights, directors' duties and shareholder disputes. He is one of a small number of lawyers in the UK who are dually qualified as a solicitor and as a barrister. In addition to his transactional practice, Alex lectures to the legal and banking profession on domestic and cross-border corporate and business acquisitions and on topical issues in corporate finance related matters including corporate governance, IPOs and the reform of company law in the People's Republic of China.

List of abbreviations

ABI	Association of British Insurers
AGM	Annual general meeting
AIM	Alternative investment market
APB	Auditing Practices Board
CEO	Chief executive officer
CJA 1993	Criminal Justice Act 1993
CoMC	Code of market conduct
CRM	Customer relationship management
CSR	Corporate social responsibility
DB	Defined benefit pension schemes
DC	Defined contribution pension schemes
FSMA 2000	Financial Services and Markets Act 2000
IFRS	International financial reporting standards
IR	Investor relations
KPI	Key performance indicator
LSE	London Stock Exchange
MFR	Minimum funding requirement
NAPF	National Association of Pension Funds
NED	Non-executive director
OFR	Operating and financial review
PDMR	Persons discharging managerial responsibilities
PMI	Pensions Management Institute
RIS	Regulatory information service
SFO	Statutory funding objective
SIP	Statement of investment principles
SRI	Socially responsible investment
UK GAAP	UK accounting standards

Preface

There are many excellent publications available which address the complex subject of corporate governance. Our book takes a different approach and examines the topic from the perspective of key events and tasks in the board and Company Secretariat's calendar, such as board meetings, the annual report, and directors' training.

Our book approaches compliance issues from a more practical angle than is often the case. How *do* you establish an effective working relationship with your auditors, and how should you go about communicating with shareholders? What should be done to safeguard against breaches of the Model Code, and what are the key issues to consider when recruiting Non-Executive Directors?

The book is intended as a reference guide for those approaching a particular issue or event, to provide them not only with the relevant points of compliance, but also to offer best practice suggestions based on the experience of the authors in their work with listed companies. It is *not* intended as a definitive theoretical text on corporate governance, but instead sets out to show how compliance with best practice requirements can be approached in a practical and constructive way.

We are grateful to the ICSA for inviting us to produce this guide, and to our colleagues from DLA and Grant Thornton who contributed their time and specialist knowledge. We also thank those colleagues and clients who generously shared with us their experiences – both positive and not so positive! – in our preparation for this book. We hope that it will prove a useful tool.

Vivienne Cassley
David Mensley
March 2006

CHAPTER 1

Corporate governance
– where are we now?

Since the first joint stock companies were formed in the nineteenth century, the partnership between shareholders and management has been central to the sustainable growth of public companies and the prosperity of society as a whole. The success of this partnership is largely a question of balance: shareholders need to be assured that their investments are being managed prudently and will deliver a good return, whilst management needs the capital and freedom to run the company in the best interests of all concerned.

In the past this relationship was relatively simple. If a company made money and returned dividends to its shareholders, then it was assumed to be keeping its side of the bargain and everyone was content.

Now, though, the world is a far more complex place and a good set of numbers is not necessarily enough.

As the scale of public ownership increases, along with the dependence society places on the returns generated by public companies, so the management of those companies increasingly comes under scrutiny. As we have seen many times, corporate failure can have far-reaching consequences, not just for its own shareholders but other stakeholders such as employees, and for the broader financial community.

There is a global interdependence between the individual and the corporate entity which means that a company's responsibilities now extend far beyond its direct stakeholders to society as a whole. And society as a whole – whether through institutional shareholders, through environmental pressure groups, or as individuals – takes a much closer interest in the company's activities.

Issues such as excessive executive remuneration and well-publicised corporate accounting scandals have prompted successive reviews into the way in which companies are governed, and have led over time to the disclosure-based regulatory and governance regime we now have in the UK, which sets the standards for governance worldwide.

From the Cadbury Committee's work on internal financial controls, and Greenbury's Report on disclosure of directors' remuneration, through Turnbull, Higgs and other key reviews, we have arrived at the revised Combined Code which sets the current standards of best practice for UK companies.

For the board and company secretary this presents a real challenge – how to implement constantly evolving standards in a constructive and effective way and, most importantly, without stifling the entrepreneurial nature of their organisations.

Shareholders too have seen changes – in the expectations placed on them as owners. The obligation to be active owners, to exert a positive influence on the management of those companies in which they are invested, was formalised in the Institutional Shareholders' Committee statement of principles, 'The Responsibilities of Institutional Shareholders and Agents'.

For shareholders, the challenge is to be proactive in their relationships with management, to intervene where necessary but without interfering with the day-to-day operation of the business.

> One of the duties of owners is to allow Company Boards to manage the businesses which have been entrusted to their care without excessive interference. (NAPF)

There currently exists what could best be described as an uneasy tension between some UK public companies and their shareholders, with a sense that the optimum balance has yet to be achieved in the relationship between them. Both groups are endeavouring to work within a constantly evolving regulatory regime which makes increasingly broad and complex demands on them.

Many companies are overwhelmed by the sheer volume of regulatory change they have to implement and do not always feel confident that they know what is required of them. Companies are often criticised for adopting a box-ticking approach to compliance, yet many complain that investors themselves are guilty of this – and can be quick to criticise if all the boxes are not ticked. Other companies have found that despite the emphasis on engagement there are still instances of investors voting against the company without any prior discussion. The threat to corporate reputation is perceived to be very real.

This uncertainty and concern is reflected in attitudes towards compliance. According to research conducted by Ernst and Young, 90% of boards are spending as much as 40% of their time on compliance. However, a survey of attitudes towards corporate governance conducted by Price Waterhouse found that 70% of UK chief executives questioned (compared with 40% outside the UK) viewed expenditure on governance, risk management and compliance as a cost rather than an investment, and fewer than 50% believed that compliance could provide any competitive advantage.

Yet all the evidence indicates that a well governed company tends to be a successful company (there are of course well-known examples of the reverse not necessarily being the case!). McKinsey's *Global Investor Opinion Survey* is the most widely quoted research into the link between governance and share price. Of over 200 investors surveyed, 80% said they would pay a premium for shares in well-governed companies. For UK companies, that premium was 12%. A paper published by Hermes entitled

Corporate Governance and Performance points to a wide range of both qualitative and quantitative research which supports this link between good governance and performance.

There is another issue which affects the board's view of governance, and that is the difference between investor decisions to buy or sell, and their behaviour as shareholders. Whilst the fund manager will tend to focus primarily on the bottom line in making the initial investment decision, it is increasingly the corporate governance team who make voting decisions, and those decisions can have a significant impact on corporate reputation. Ultimately that is likely to impact on the share price too.

Perhaps the problem is not so much one of doing the right thing – by and large most companies do – but of having to demonstrate this in an increasingly detailed and apparently prescriptive way.

For their part, those institutions who gave their opinions for this book feel that progress has been made and that there is now a more open and constructive dialogue between them and management. They perceive most companies as being willing and eager to maintain a dialogue with shareholders, and there are very few doubts expressed about the general standards of governance within UK companies.

In general, investors are keen to see a more thoughtful approach to compliance reporting, which avoids 'box-ticking' or, at the other extreme, the 'information dump' – the tendency to throw in everything just in case! Companies are encouraged to expand on those areas which they feel are important and to explain more about how and why they approach aspects of governance – how procedures are actually implemented, how their effectiveness is measured, and how they impact on performance.

There are positive signs, but we should not underestimate the compliance burden. There is still progress to be made in achieving the balanced relationship between management and ownership and, with more change to come, this will take time. We hope this book will provide some help to those trying to navigate such turbulent waters!

Summary of key regulatory developments, codes and guidelines in corporate governance

The following table provides a quick reference guide to the evolution and current status of corporate governance in the UK. It sets out the key provisions of codes of best practice and related regulatory developments since the 1990s.

Further information regarding all reports and regulations can be found on the appropriate website, which is indicated in the table. All sources are also set out in the appendices.

Report/Title and source	Date	Authors	Main provision
FRC Review of the Combined Code www.frc.org.uk.	July 2005	FRC	The existing Combined Code (see below) is three years old. Formerly a part of the Listing Rules, it is currently maintained by the FRC. The FRC review is expected to result in changes of detail, not of overall substance.
City Code on Takeovers and Mergers www.thetakeoverpanel.org.uk	Current	Takeover Panel	The City Code applies to offers for the acquisition of shares in UK listed and unlisted public companies. When the EU Takeover Directive takes effect in 2006, the City Code will have statutory force. The overriding principles of the City Code are that all shareholders should be treated equally and that takeovers must be conducted in accordance with a strict timetable, on the basis of minimum prescribed levels of information.
Company Law Reform Bill www.dti.gov.uk	2006/7	DTI	The Bill represents the largest reform of company law in the UK since 1985. Its provisions are many and varied, but the guiding principle is that it is drafted according to the needs of the smaller companies which make up the largest proportion (by number) of corporate entities in the UK, with provisions relating to larger companies being described by exception. It includes a statutory statement of directors' duties, which will take the place of the current common law and equitable rights and obligations. Legislation was introduced in 2005 (through the Companies (Audit, Investigations and Community Enterprise) Act) ahead of the general company law reform which extended the ability of companies to indemnify their directors for breach of duty.

Report/Title and source	Date	Authors	Main provisions
Operating and Financial Review and Directors' Report www.dti.gov.uk	April 2005	Operating and Financial Review Working Group.	The introduction of a mandatory OFR was a key recommendation of the Company Law Review (2001). The OFR would require the directors of quoted companies to give a balanced and comprehensive analysis of their business as part of their annual reports and accounts to shareholders. This would include a company's objectives, strategies and key drivers of the business, focusing on more qualitative and forward-looking information than has traditionally been included in annual reports. At the end of 2005, however, the Government indicated its intention to remove the obligation to produce an OFR, announcing instead that companies would be required to provide a Business Review in line with the minimum requirements of the EU Accounts Modernisation Directive. At the time of writing, the precise requirements remain unclear.
EU Market Abuse Directive implemented in the UK by the Disclosure Rules www.hm-treasury.gov.uk	2005		The directive introduces a common EU legal framework for preventing and detecting market abuse and for ensuring a proper flow of information to the market. For listed and quoted companies, the key differences between this and the prior UK market abuse regime relate to the Model Code. Whereas the prior UK regime required directors and those closely associated with them to disclose dealings in shares of the companies for which the directors work, the directive extends the obligation to senior management and has a broader definition of those closely associated with the directors. For example, it includes relatives other than spouses and dependent children. Issuers are required to draw up a list of those individuals working for them who have access to inside information.

Report/Title and source	Date	Authors	Main provisions
Pensions Act 2004 www.dwp.gov.uk	Nov 2004		The Pensions Act 2004 received Royal Assent on 18 November 2004, following publication of the Pensions Bill, the Government's Green Paper 'Simplicity, security and choice: Working and saving for retirement' in December 2002 and 'Simplicity, security and choice: Action on occupational pensions' in June 2003. The Act is designed to strengthen and simplify the pensions industry. Key provisions relevant to this book include a requirement for minimum standards of trustee knowledge and understanding, increased emphasis on internal controls for pensions schemes, a new Scheme Funding Framework, and enhanced powers for the Regulator.
Revised Combined Code www.frc.org.uk.	July 2003	Published by the Financial Reporting Council	The revised Combined Code incorporates the key recommendations of the Higgs Report and the Smith Review, and continues to be enforced on a 'comply or explain' basis. Key revisions to the original code include: • a separation of the roles of the chairman and chief executive; • the board to comprise at least half independent NEDs; • candidates for board selection should be drawn from a wider pool; • the board, its committees and directors should evaluate their performance on an annual basis; • at least one member of the audit committee should have recent and relevant financial experience.

Report/Title and source	Date	Authors	Main provisions
Guidance on Audit Committees (The Smith Report) www.frc.org.uk	Jan 2003	Group appointed by the FRC, chaired by Sir Robert Smith	The report gives specific and detailed guidance on the role and responsibilities of the audit committee. In particular it recommends: <ul><li>there should be an audit committee comprising no less than three independent non-executive directors, with at least one of them possessing 'recent and relevant financial experience';</li><li>the audit committee should have principal responsibility for recommending an external auditor to the board and to shareholders;</li><li>the audit committee should develop and implement policy on the engagement of the external auditor to supply non-audit services.</li></ul> The report also gives guidance on the proper relationship between the committee and the board.
Review of the role and effectiveness of non-executive directors (The Higgs Report), www.dti.gov.uk	Jan 2003	DTI, chaired by Sir Derek Higgs	Published simultaneously with the Smith Report, the Higgs Report made recommendations regarding the role of the chairman and non-executive directors and also contained guidelines for the effective board. Recommendations are incorporated in the revised Combined Code, and are repeated here for convenience: <ul><li>the roles of CEO and chairman should be separated;</li><li>at least half the board should be 'independent' non-executive directors;</li><li>there should be a more rigorous selection process for non-executive directors, and selections should be made from a wider pool of candidates;</li><li>there should be a formal, annual appraisal of the board's collective and individual performance.</li></ul>

Report/Title and source	Date	Authors	Main provisions
Directors' Remuneration Report Regulations 2002 www.dti.gov.uk	2002	DTI	The Regulations are now enshrined in the Companies Act 1985. They apply to publicly quoted companies (not AIM companies) and in respect of financial years beginning on or after 1 January 2003 require those companies to prepare, submit to shareholders and publish a report on directors' compensation. The report must contain a detailed analysis of directors' compensation arrangements (on an individual basis) together with a graph comparing the company's performance with an index chosen by the board and also an indication of the board's proposed future strategy on pay.
The Responsibilities of Institutional Shareholders and Agents – Statement of Principles www.ifma.org.uk	Oct 2002	Institutional Shareholders' Committee	The document develops the principles set out in the Committee's 1991 statement 'The Responsibilities of Institutional Shareholders in the UK' and expands on the Combined Code on Corporate Governance of June 1998. It sets out best practice for institutional shareholders (the phrases 'shareholder activism' and 'shareholder engagement' are widely used in relation to the paper) and specifically recommends that they: • set out their policy on how they will discharge their responsibilities – clarifying priorities attached to particular issues and when they will take action; • monitor the performance of, and establish where necessary, a regular dialogue with investee companies; • intervene where necessary; • evaluate the impact of their activism and report back to clients/beneficial owners.

Report/Title and source	Date	Authors	Main provisions
Code of Market Conduct www.fsa.gov.uk	April 2001	FSA (UK)	The Code deals with three key aspects of market abuse: <ul><li>misuse of information – e.g. knowing of a forthcoming takeover and buying shares in the target company prior to general disclosure of that information;</li><li>creating false or misleading impressions – e.g. posting on a bulletin board an inaccurate story that an important deal had been secured by a major company in order to give a false or misleading impression;</li><li>market distortion – e.g., ramping the price of shares to a distorted level.</li></ul>
Financial Services and Markets Act 2000 (FSMA) www.hm-treasury.gov.uk	Came into effect Dec 2001		Under the FSMA the Financial Services Authority (FSA) was established as the UK's single statutory regulator for financial services. Some of the provisions of the Act impacted on disclosure of information and in particular the handling and dissemination of price-sensitive information. Under the Act a new, civil, offence of market abuse was introduced carrying a lower burden of proof than the existing insider dealing laws.
Review of UK Company Law and Modernising Company Law (Government White Paper July 2002) www.dti.gov.uk	June 2001	The Company Law Steering Group	The White Paper is a review of existing company law. It proposed a new regime for small and private companies, and also considered internal controls and external regulation of companies. Key governance-related proposals are: <ul><li>to modernise and simplify the ways in which companies take decisions, e.g. by removing the requirement for private companies to hold annual general meetings (AGMs) unless members want them;</li><li>to increase transparency, e.g. AGMs to be held within six months of the financial year-end for public companies and 10 months for private companies; shareholders to be able to require a scrutiny of a poll.</li></ul>

Report/Title and source	Date	Authors	Main provisions
Institutional Investment in the United Kingdom. A Review	March 2001	Chaired by Sir Paul Myners	Sir Paul Myners was commissioned by the government, 'to consider whether there were factors distorting the investment decision making of institutions'. The Review concluded that the current structures used by institutional investors to make investment decisions lack efficiency and flexibility, which often means that savers' money is not being invested in ways which will maximise their interests. In response to the issues raised, Myners outlined some basic principles of an effective approach to investment decision making. These principles are currently voluntary and to be adopted on a 'comply or explain' basis.
The Combined Code: Principles of Good Governance and Code of Best Practice, www.fsa.gov.uk	June 1998, updated May 2000	Committee on Corporate Governance	The Combined Code consolidated the work of the Cadbury Committee and the Greenbury Committee into a single code of practice. Within the Code, the Principles of Good Governance and Code of Best Practice were organised into guidelines for companies and also for institutional shareholders. Company guidelines relate to: • directors; • directors' remuneration; • relations with shareholders; • accountability and audit. The Combined Code embedded the concept of 'comply or explain' in UK corporate governance: listed companies were required to state in their annual report and accounts where they had complied with the Code and, where they had not, to explain why.

Report/Title and source	Date	Authors	Main provisions
Internal Control: Guidance for Directors on the Combined Code (Turnbull Report), www.icaew.co.uk	Sept 1999	Institute of Chartered Accountants in England and Wales. Chaired by Nigel Turnbull	The Turnbull Report required companies to identify, evaluate and manage their significant risks and to assess the effectiveness of the related internal control system. Boards of directors are called on to review regularly reports on the effectiveness of the system of internal control in managing key risks, and to undertake an annual assessment for the purpose of making their statements on internal control in the annual report. Specifically, the company's internal control system should: • be embedded within its operations and not be treated as a separate exercise; • be able to respond to changing risks within and outside the company; and • enable each company to apply it in an appropriate manner related to its key risks.
Hampel Report www.corpgov.com/	Jan 1998	Chaired by Sir Ronald Hampel. Sponsored by a number of institutions including the CBI, NAPF and IOD	The Report was commissioned following the recommendations of the Cadbury and Greenbury committees that a new committee should review the implementation of their findings. The committee drew up a set of principles which broadly reflected Cadbury and Greenbury and built on their recommendations (e.g. in recommending adoption of a formal procedure for appointments to the board, with a nominations committee making recommendations to the full board).

Report/Title and source	Date	Authors	Main provisions
Greenbury Report, Study Group on Directors' Remuneration www.ecgi.org	July 1995	Sir Richard Greenbury Commissioned by the CBI	Commissioned in response to concerns over excessive board remuneration. The group's key recommendations included: • that all listed companies registered in the UK should comply with the Code as far as practical and include a statement about their compliance in their annual reports and accounts. Any areas of non-compliance should be explained and justified; • that these recommendations be incorporated into the London Stock Exchange's continuing obligations for listed companies; • that all listed companies should set up a remuneration committee (the report gives guidelines for such a committee).
Cadbury Report (The Financial Aspects of Corporate Governance), www.ecgi.org	Dec 1992	Committee set up by the FRC, London Stock Exchange and the accountancy profession, and chaired by Sir Adrian Cadbury	The Report was commissioned in response to concerns about the working of the corporate system, highlighted by unexpected failures of major companies and by criticisms of the lack of effective board accountability for such matters as directors' pay. The Committee's recommendations focused on the control and reporting functions of boards, and on the role of auditors. The Report reviews the structure and responsibilities of boards of directors and summarises recommendations in a Code of Best Practice. It also considers the role of auditors and the rights and responsibilities of shareholders.

Effective board and committee meetings

- Scheduling board and committee meetings: the board's duty to meet regularly
- Organising board meetings – when, where, and how
- The role of the company secretary
- Setting the agenda
- Board papers – content and delivery
- Conduct and management of the meeting

Introduction

The regular meetings of the board and its committees are the central focus of the board's operations. The conduct of business at these meetings, the decisions taken and the processes governing those decisions lie at the heart of good governance – yet there are very few statutory provisions and very little specific guidance governing this area. The board must meet 'regularly', but directors may 'regulate their meetings as they see fit' (Companies Act 1985).

This chapter considers the purpose and objectives of board meetings and offers practical guidance on the key issues to be considered

The board's duty to meet regularly

The Combined Code requires the board to meet 'sufficiently regularly to discharge its duties effectively'. In practice this tends to be anywhere from six to 12 times a year depending on the size and complexity of the company and its operations, as well as its geographical spread.

For example, smaller companies may find that having fewer directors allows the board to meet on a less frequent and less formal basis. It may also be that those directors will be more in touch with day-to-day operations, which will further simplify the business of the board meeting.

The boards of larger and more complex organisations, where directors are more removed from the day-to-day operation of the business and where there are a greater number of non-executive directors (NEDs), will almost certainly find a more formal approach is necessary.

In general, most companies will schedule meetings of the board's committees on the same day as those of the main board to minimise travel requirements and time commitments for directors. The audit committee is likely to be the exception to this rule, especially around the time of the annual and interim reports when it may be necessary to schedule the committee meeting a few days in advance of the main board meeting. This allows committee members sufficient time to consider all relevant documents ahead of the meeting; it also allows time to deal with any issues arising from that meeting, so that the committee can report fully to the main board as required (Smith 2.9). In practice, this can present quite a challenge, given the tight schedule which generally surrounds the release of results.

Meetings are generally called by the company secretary on behalf of the chairman, but any board member has the right to request that a meeting be called. In practice, given the demands on directors' time, meetings will be generally be tabled in advance for the coming year, (in some cases, even further ahead) and skeleton agendas drawn up (see 'Setting the Agenda', later in this chapter).

Outside of the regular board calendar, there is also a requirement that there should be adequate procedures in place to address any urgent matters which arise between scheduled meetings. There are various acceptable methods of approaching this – these are considered in detail later in this chapter.

There is no statutory obligation for all members of the board to attend every meeting but it is clear that in order to be effective in their capacity as directors of the company, individuals will wish to be present at most, if not all, scheduled meetings.

The Combined Code (A.1.2) requires companies to set out in their annual report the number of meetings held by the board during the year (as well as by its main committees) and also to disclose directors' individual attendance records at those meetings. Where a director's attendance is consistently poor, the chairman is expected to take action and, if necessary, ultimately to remove the director concerned from office.

The quorum for the transaction of business of the directors may be fixed by the directors themselves (CA 1985, Table A), and must be recorded in the company's articles. If the board does not choose to set the quorum itself, Table A provides that it should be set at two directors.

To ensure independence in their decision-making, The Combined Code (A,1,5) also recommends that NEDs should meet regularly as a group without the presence of the executive. In addition, they should meet at least once a year without the chairman, and this meeting will be chaired by the senior non-executive director.

When, where and how should meetings take place?

The chairman, through the company secretary, should ensure that the frequency, scheduling and duration of meetings is appropriate to the company's business and the other commitments of board members. For their part, directors have an obligation to make themselves available for meetings and to dedicate sufficient time to prepare properly for all meetings.

Scheduling of meetings has become more complex for many UK companies as they become increasingly global in nature.

There is growing acknowledgement amongst many companies of the need to ensure that the composition of their board reflects the international nature of their business. In the course of evaluating their collective performance, many boards have identified the need to appoint additional directors from outside the UK.

Such changes to the composition of the board may also necessitate a change in venue for some meetings. Whilst some international boards continue to hold all meetings at the UK head office, others are increasingly taking a view that board meetings should be rotated around their key business centres. This has an added advantage of giving all directors regular exposure to senior management and operational practices at key sites other than head office. There are clear implications for input to succession planning across the organisation, as well as for employee motivation.

Scheduling of meetings has also been made more complicated for many companies by the increase in the number of NEDs on the board, all of whom are likely to have other external commitments. There is considerable incentive to schedule meetings as far in advance as possible to avoid clashes with other boards.

Non-scheduled meetings

We referred above to the importance of ensuring that procedures are in place to call non-scheduled meetings to discuss any matters of urgency which might arise. There may also be instances where, perhaps due to time constraints or unforeseen events, it is not possible for all the directors to meet in the same location for a board meeting.

There is no statutory provision for such circumstances but, in order to comply with the Combined Code, many companies have amended their articles to allow for:

- the use of written resolutions to record decisions taken by the board; their use should be limited to more routine issues or instances where it is impossible to convene a meeting by any other means. They should be signed by all directors. Some companies have made provision in their articles for occasions where it may not be possible for directors outside the UK to sign urgent resolutions. However, all directors will still have seen all relevant papers and will have had an opportunity to give their opinion.

- tele-conferencing or video-conferencing. The evidence points to a certain antipathy amongst directors towards telephone and video conferencing as a means of conducting a meeting, but most will accept them 'in extremis'. The logistics of arranging such meetings will be the responsibility of the company secretary.

Whatever the mechanism, the primary objective must be to ensure that all directors have an opportunity to participate in extraordinary meetings, so that the board as a whole is best able to respond to any urgent events which may arise. Even in circumstances where it proves impossible for all directors to participate in person, they must all be equally informed about the matter for consideration and have the opportunity to make their views known to the chairman ahead of the discussion.

There may be situations when a decision is required, and where the matter is so urgent that there is no time to convene a full meeting or to arrange a teleconference with absent directors. This is likely to be where the matter in question is of a price-sensitive nature and the board needs to make an announcement to the market without delay.

The FSA will *not* accept the need to convene an emergency board meeting as a valid reason for delaying such an announcement.

The board should ensure that there are processes in place to deal with such urgent or extraordinary events. It is good practice to establish an emergency sub-committee of the board which has the appropriate delegated authority to handle such matters. Membership of the committee would be whichever directors are available at the time.

Scheduling of committee meetings

Many, if not most, companies will typically schedule meetings of board committees on the same day as main board meetings.

Whilst this is convenient, and efficient in terms of minimising travel time, many boards are finding that time pressure may result in agenda items being hurried through – whether in the main board meeting or those of the various committees.

This appears to be especially true of the audit committee. Some companies have found that the volume of board papers now required to allow the committee to comply with best practice has increased to the extent that meetings are now scheduled on a separate day from those of the main board.

The role of the company secretary

Whilst the chairman is ultimately responsible for the board's performance, in practice much of the responsibility for preparation and organisation of its meetings falls to the company secretary, who is generally accountable for the proper administration of the board and its committees.

The company secretary's role has expanded greatly in recent years, for the most part as a direct result of changes in corporate governance. He or she may justifiably be viewed as the 'keeper of the corporate conscience'!

The company secretary, under the direction of the chairman, is responsible for ensuring that proper processes are in place and that there is a good flow of information within the board, and within its committees (CC A.5).

Specifically (though not exhaustively), this involves:

- drawing up meeting agendas with the chairman and/or the chief executive;
- providing advice to management on the content and format of papers or presentations to be submitted to the meeting, as well as the required length of any presentations;
- collecting, organising and distributing all documents and papers required for the meeting;
- ensuring that appropriate tools and technology are in place for the meeting – e.g. audio-visual equipment, conference links;
- ensuring that all board and committee meetings are fully and accurately minuted and that certified copies of the minutes are maintained;
- ensuring that all board committees have appropriate membership and that they are provided with clear terms of reference;
- ensuring a good flow of information between the NEDs and senior management;
- giving feedback as appropriate to management on decisions taken by the board.

The company secretary should, and normally will, be present at all board and committee meetings. We are aware of instances where the company secretary has not been permitted to attend committee meetings, and this has proved a considerable obstacle to the proper functioning of the committee and the objective recording of its business.

What should be on the agenda?

The regular items on the board's agenda will for the most part be driven by the schedule of matters it has reserved for its decision. The Combined Code (A.1.2) states that there should be a formal schedule of matters specifically reserved for (the board's) decision, and the regular items on the board's agenda will – for the most part – be driven by that schedule.

This schedule should be documented formally so that the division of responsibility between board, management and committees is clear. The board should also publish in its annual report a high level statement of which decisions are to be taken by the board and which are to be delegated to management.

It is for the board to decide which specific matters it wishes to bring under its own remit, and which matters it wishes to delegate to committees or to management. These may change from time to time in line with the strategic direction and priorities of the company. The precise content of the schedule will depend on a number of company-specific factors, such as the size and complexity of the company, the nature of its activities, and the environment in which it operates.

A study of actual published schedules confirms that there is indeed great variance in the content, length, structure, and level of detail of these, reflecting the nature and priorities of each organisation concerned.

However there are certain core matters which most, if not all, listed companies will place on their schedule and ample guidance is available on this issue. The ICSA has produced a guidance note, *Matters reserved for the board* (Dec 2003).

CHECKLIST Sample schedule

This sample illustrates one possible approach and incorporates most of the matters which the directors of listed companies might generally wish to include in their schedule.

Finance, controls, and risk management

1   Approval of:

- the annual report and accounts;
- interim and preliminary financial statements;
- other significant statements to shareholders/the Stock Exchange/the press;
- any interim dividend, and recommendation of the final dividend;
- financial policy;
- all material capital projects;

- major acquisitions and disposals;
- the annual operating and capital expenditure budget;
- any significant change in accounting policies or practices;
- Treasury policies (e.g. foreign currency exposure and use of financial derivatives);
- any purchase by the company of its own shares;
- insurance, including directors and officers' liability insurance.

2   The establishment and annual review of the effectiveness of the company's systems of internal control and risk management processes.

Corporate structure

1   Approval of changes in the capital structure of the company.

2   Changes to the company's status as a public limited company or as a listed entity.

3   Appointment, re-appointment and removal of the chairman and directors and the recommendation to shareholders of their election or re-election under the articles of association, following recommendations of the nominations committee.

4   Changes to the management and control structure.

Delegation of authority

1   Approval of the division of responsibilities between the chairman and chief executive.

2   Changes to the authority delegated to the CEO or FD.

3   Documentation of the division of responsibility between chairman and chief executive as Terms of Reference.

4   Establishing Terms of Reference and membership of board committees.

5   Reviewing the activities of and decisions taken by board committees.

6   Recommendation to shareholders for the appointment, re-appointment or removal of the auditors.

Strategy

1   Establishment of the company's overall strategic direction and strategic plans.

2   Establishment of the company's key business and financial objectives.

3   Review of company performance against objectives.

Corporate governance matters

1   Approval of material changes to the company's pension schemes rules, any change of trustee or material changes to funding and management arrangements.

2   Approving the remuneration of non-executive directors.

3   Approval of all listing particulars and circulars.

4   Determining the remuneration of the external auditors for audit related work (subject to recommendations of the audit committee).

5   Appointments to the board (subject to the recommendations of the nomination committee).

6   The appointment and removal of the company secretary.

7   Ensuring adequate succession planning for the board and senior management.

Policies

1   Approval of company policies, including:

- share dealing code
- code of conduct
- health and safety
- environmental policy
- communications
- corporate social responsibility
- whistle blowing.

Setting the agenda

It is common practice for the chairman and company secretary to agree a 'rolling agenda' of regular items on the board's agenda – at least a year in advance, and possibly more. This outline agenda may be circulated in advance to give directors ample notice of the timetable of events. For example, the board of a company whose year end is in March will always approve figures at its June meeting. This can be 'hard-wired' into the agenda. Certain matters, such as pensions, might be discussed annually while others, such as health and safety could be discussed twice a year. These and other similar matters can be scheduled well in advance.

The final agenda will usually be agreed between the company secretary and the CEO after discussion with other directors, before being submitted to the chairman for his approval.

Achieving balance

The board's remit, and consequently the matters on its regular agenda, continues to grow significantly, both in size and complexity. As a result, a challenge is emerging, which seems to be shared by a significant number of boards, and this is the difficulty in dedicating sufficient time to strategic issues – which should lie at the heart of the board's business.

One of the principal causes of this is the increase in regulation and compliance. A survey by Ernst and Young published in early 2005 found that over 90% of the participating directors were spending up to 40% of their time on compliance issues.

Many boards also find that discussion at meetings becomes too focused on operational issues. Often this may have begun in response to a particular corporate development, such as a major acquisition or a series of bad results, but often it appears that the board has found it difficult to rebalance its agenda away from operations and to refocus on strategy.

There is no simple solution to this. However, the board should ensure that it regularly reviews the schedule of matters reserved for its decision, together with the levels at which authorities are delegated to committees and management to ensure that they remain appropriate to the company's current situation.

It can be beneficial to move routine items to the end of the agenda to ensure that key strategic issues receive sufficient time and attention.

The company secretary has a key role to play in freeing directors to focus more on strategic issues, by ensuring that for each agenda item they are provided with relevant, high quality briefing papers, in a format which is clear, concise and which clearly highlights key points and priorities.

The chairman, of course, also plays a key role in directing the business of the meeting so that sufficient time is allowed for the full consideration of *all* agenda items.

Additionally, the board should consider whether the number of meetings and the length of time allocated to meetings remains appropriate. The scheduling of main board and committee meetings may again be an issue here.

Finally, the agenda must also allow for any director to raise any matter for consideration and discussion by the board, even if it has not been placed formally on the agenda.

Board papers – content and delivery

The documents circulated to the board ahead of meetings should include (but are not limited to):

- an agenda of items to be covered, with references to any supporting papers;
- the minutes of the previous meeting;
- regular reports such as monthly accounts, sales figures, operational reports;
- papers in support of specific agenda items. These might include new business proposals, or draft contracts;
- draft of the annual and interim reports.

Other useful reports include:

- regular copies of analyst reports;
- reports of any underperforming areas of the business;
- reports on the performance of recent acquisitions measured against the original business case;
- details of any regulatory or governance developments since the previous meeting. This will help to ensure directors' continuing education in this area;
- a report of any regulatory or compliance breaches which might have occurred;
- a regular IR report to the meeting. This should set out details of all shareholder contact since the previous meeting, and include details of any presentations give to shareholders, any concerns raised, the key questions put and the answers given to those questions. This would ensure that directors are aware of communication with shareholders and any issues arising from this.

CHECKLIST Meeting preparation

There are some basic principles of best practice – and general housekeeping – which will assist directors to prepare for board meetings. The board, with the company secretary, should review these matters regularly to ensure that the it's information requirements are being met:

- Do all directors receive sufficient information to prepare for board meetings?
- Do all directors receive the same information, at the same time?
- Do all directors receive information in sufficient time to prepare for meetings?
- Are existing procedures for the preparation and dissemination of board papers appropriate? For example, directors may find electronic delivery helpful where previously, papers have always been delivered by post.
- Are the systems currently in place for organising and collecting papers appropriate and are they functioning properly?
- Are there processes in place to facilitate discussion and clarification of issues ahead of the meeting?
- Are papers submitted to the board:
  - relevant to the agenda;
  - of appropriate length and content;
  - of good quality;
  - clear;
  - in the most appropriate format (e.g. could more information be presented diagrammatically or graphically?)

- Do papers make clear what decision is required?
- Is there any unnecessary overlap between the papers submitted to the board (e.g. content of reports from the CEO and finance director)?

Are board presentations always necessary and, if so, is their purpose clear?

Is the quality and nature of external advice provided to the board's committees appropriate?

Conduct and management of the meeting

In addition to the Schedule of Matters, it may be helpful to draw together in a single document the board's written guidelines and procedures for matters such as:

- the role of the chairman;
- the role of the CEO;
- the quorum for meetings of the board and its committees;
- the general order of business for board meetings – including approval of the minutes of the previous meeting, matters arising from previous minutes;
- procedures for voting on formal resolutions.

This document will provide directors with a general guide to the principles underpinning the conduct of board meetings.

The emphasis on procedure should not detract from the central purpose of the board meeting, which is to allow the directors to reach a collective and well informed decision on the matters put before them through open and constructive debate and discussion.

It is the chairman's role to ensure that all directors have an opportunity to express their opinion, and that no individual or group is allowed to dominate.

The board has collective responsibility for its decisions, and all directors must therefore be willing to challenge – and to listen to the views of – others when necessary.

Once a majority decision is taken, however, individual board members should be prepared to unite behind that decision. Should it happen that an individual has genuine and lasting concern regarding the correctness of a particular decision and is unable to persuade follow directors, he/she should ensure that the dissenting view is recorded in the minutes and, if necessary, should put the concern separately in writing to the chairman.

After the meeting

It is a requirement of the Companies Act that all board discussion and decisions should be clearly documented, providing a complete audit trail of its business. The company secretary will normally be responsible for producing and circulating minutes to all board members.

In some companies, draft minutes will be circulated to all those who attended the meeting for their comments. As the minutes constitute an official record of proceedings it is important that any amendments should seek only to correct inaccuracies rather than to add or change the meaning of what was actually said at the meeting. To avoid this issue, in most cases, the company secretary will discuss draft minutes only with the chairman and with individual directors as necessary to clarify any issues of complexity.

Detailed minutes should also be produced to record the meetings of board committees and to give relevant background to those decisions – including any papers presented to the committee in support of any particular topic.

The circulation of committee minutes, especially those of the remuneration committee, can sometimes pose problems for committee members, who may feel uncomfortable about the details of their discussions being available to all directors.

Best practice is quite clear on this issue. Whilst the board has delegated authority to its committees, the board as a whole remains responsible for the decisions taken by those committees. Therefore all committees of the board should circulate minutes to members of the committee and to the chairman, and should make available to other board members either full minutes or a written summary of the proceedings.

Board decisions should be promptly and clearly communicated to management, and there should be procedures in place to verify that management implements those decisions.

The board should also have procedures in place to follow up on any areas of concern between meetings.

CONCLUSION

- Successful board meetings are a combination of:
  - preparation;
  - dissemination of information;
  - effective leadership from the chairman; and
  - the personalities of directors themselves.
- The company secretary's role is pivotal in achieving the first two of these, and this aspect of the role is increasingly significant in helping the board to achieve its own remit. However, regular review by the directors themselves of many of the issues discussed in this chapter will help to ensure that meetings remain focused and effective.

Recruiting non-executive directors

Introduction

In its simplest form a non-executive director (NED) is a director who does not have day-to-day operational responsibility for the company. However, it is important to remember that the law makes no distinction between the duties of a full-time executive director and a non-executive director. All directors (both executive and non-executive) have individual responsibility arising through their position and cannot hide behind the collective responsibility of the board.

The basic duties owed to a company by its directors are primarily based on case law rather than the Companies Act. Common law duties of directors include fiduciary duties and duties of skill, care and diligence. Directors can be personally liable for any 'torts' committed, including negligent misrepresentation. Directors may also be prosecuted for corporate manslaughter in health and safety matters. As a result, there is some anecdotal evidence that concerns about legal liability are affecting the behaviour of directors and creating a further barrier to accessing talented individuals who are discouraged from seeking or accepting directorships because of the law relating to directors' liability. As a result, the law relating to directors' liability has been changed by ss 19 and 20 (Audit, Investigations and Community Enterprise) of the Companies Act 2004, particularly in relation to the relaxation of those rules covering indemnification and payment of directors' defence costs.

In the years following the Cadbury Code, the role of non-executives has strengthened significantly – they are no longer seen as 'Christmas tree decorations' (pretty but useless) or as 'positions of pomp and circumstance'. In particular, the provisions of the Combined Code have put a new emphasis on the professionalism and effectiveness of NEDs.

The role of the non-executive director

NEDs have a number of broad responsibilities:

- Provide advice and direction in respect of strategy – '*Should we?*'
- Monitor the effectiveness of strategy implementation throughout the business – '*Did we?*'
- Keep in check the company's legal, moral and ethical position – '*Could we?*'
- To validate the robustness and adequacy of company information supplied to investors and other stakeholders – '*We did/will do this!*'

From this stems a requirement to be able to appoint, evaluate and, where necessary, change the top team and in this respect NEDs provide an important role in helping to shape and deliver effective succession planning.

Why are NEDs needed?

The recent emphasis on the role of NEDs is based on the premise that they contribute heavily to strengthening and improving boardroom effectiveness, which in turn promotes and fosters improvements in overall corporate performance. The evidence to support this link appears to be weak, although intuitively, the scope for NED contribution appears to be great.

However, there have been some notable critics of the role and expectations being placed upon NEDs – Lord Young following the Higgs Report suggested it was hopeless to expect them to supervise executives whose company insight was greater. This argument is open to criticism in that it misses the objectivity, independent reason and fresh perspectives that truly talented NEDs can bring to the boardroom table. Is there a mismatch between what NEDs are expected to do and what they can reasonably do? This very much depends upon the perceptions of the role and will to some extent be reconciled by more rigorous selection processes.

The Tyson Report indicates that the adoption of broader, more rigorous searches for NEDs 'will not only enhance board talent and effectiveness but will also foster greater diversity in knowledge, skills, experience, gender, race, nationality and age of board members'.

What type of NED do you need?

This depends on the type of signals the business is trying to give to its various stakeholders. Whilst board diversity (as measured by background, skills and experience) is seen as a positive element in enhancing board effectiveness, with it comes the softer challenges of managing such diversity and ensuring the board's decision-making ability is not diluted but remains focused on the performance of the underlying business. This means building cohesiveness and trust amongst the board. Benefits of enriching board composition through perspective and knowledge enhancement can provide positive messages to the company's stakeholders likely to have some bearing on future success, including: customers, shareholders, employees and competitors.

CHECKLIST NED requirements

In addition to having the requisite core knowledge, experience and skill base, corporate governance literature indicates a number of personal attributes required to discharge the responsibilities of the NED role effectively and to make credible contributions to the board:

- *integrity and high ethical standards* – without these the confidence of investors and the credibility of the entire board and company will be undermined. Ultimately NEDs should be prepared to resign over matters of principle if necessary.

- *sound judgement* – based on knowledge about the company and its operating environment. A valuable NED will be one that is able to raise potential problems and risks and highlight flaws in the assumptions underlying the decision-making process. The quality of an NED contribution will be in his/her ability to judge correctly how and when to raise issues.

- *the ability and willingness to challenge and probe* – this is recognised as a key characteristic of an effective NED. It is important that NEDs are comfortable confronting their peers on difficult and challenging issues.

- *strong interpersonal skills* – will ensure that a NED is able to participate fully, irrespective of the balance of power within the boardroom. NEDs must have 'sufficient strength of character to seek and obtain full and satisfactory answers within the collegiate environment of the Board.' (Higgs, 6.15)

- *'independence of mind'* – the ability of NEDs to test and challenge boardroom thinking, foster fresh perspectives and raise issues that concern them on the basis of their experiences elsewhere. In addition, as well as being independent thinkers, it will be necessary for them to have no relationship or circumstances that could create or appear to create a conflict of interest with their decision-making role on the board. However, whilst requiring an independent mindset it will be important that the work of the NED and co-directors should be seen as interdependent – board members need to work together.

- *high levels of engagement and commitment* – NEDs need to actively engage through formal and informal initiatives to understand the nature of the business that they oversee – it is not enough just to turn up to board meetings and take the fee. There must be a willingness to learn and continue to learn. Principle A.5 of the Revised Combined Code formalises the requirement for directors to undergo continued training and education. (See Chapter 4 for guidance on the areas which should be covered.)

The NED climate

The Higgs Report on the *Role and Effectiveness of Non-Executive Directors* (published 20 January 2003) contained a number of proposals to improve corporate governance and enhance corporate performance linked to the role. In particular, the Report made a number of recommendations to improve board quality and performance which required improvements to the ways in which NEDs were traditionally identified, recruited, selected, and trained for the role. Building on this, the Tyson Report put forward a number of suggestions on how companies might draw on broader 'pools of talent' to increase board diversity, leading to enhanced board effectiveness.

Traditionally, previous board or top-team experience was sometimes the only competence companies looked for when assessing potential candidates. However, it is increasingly recognised that this is not the only relevant experience required for effective NEDs.

A typical NED profile at the time of the Higgs Report has been well documented – homogenous boards tended towards homogenous performance and were traditionally based on informal selection and recruitment processes with heavy reliance upon personal networks of people who shared common experiences, perspectives, careers and backgrounds. Whilst there has been considerable debate about the independence of NEDs, the real issues are more specifically about personal integrity, access to information and commitment of time.

Multiple directorships

The demands placed upon NEDs by their companies will vary enormously depending upon the particular needs of the business at a given time. However, the Revised Combined Code (A.4.7 and A.4.8) states that if a NED is offered an additional appointment elsewhere, the chairman should be informed before any position is accepted, and the board as a whole should subsequently be informed. A full time executive director should not take on more than one non-executive directorship, nor become director of a FTSE 100 company. The NAPF has also issued guidelines which encourage full-time executive directors to consider taking on only one outside directorship. In the case of a NED holding a portfolio of non-executive positions, the guidelines require him/her to justify how he/she can take on more than five posts (including boards of charities etc) and contribute effectively to each of them.

Embarking upon the recruitment process

Selection needs to be based on the particular needs and challenges facing each company/organisation. Indeed, the Combined Code emphasises the need for board appointments to be made on merit and against objective criteria relating to the specific requirements and circumstances of the company. This requires a full assessment of the incumbent board to be made and will be further shaped by factors such as the company's size, maturity, customer, supplier and employee profiles, market and geographic penetration, future objectives, strategic paths and an assessment of the rate of change impacting the business going forward.

To ensure real value is added to the effectiveness of the board, the recruitment of NEDs has to be underpinned by broader and transparent selection processes. Because the searches are broadening and the board's decision-making processes are under the spotlight; the approach adopted by boards in this area needs to be robust and rigorous.

Achieving greater board diversity whilst ensuring there is a positive cultural fit requires effort and can be time-consuming, as well as requiring commitment from the top, with a chairman able to bring the different elements of the board together into a cohesive and effective top team. There is no such thing as the perfect board and each company will have its own distinct opportunities and challenges.

CHECKLIST A step- by-step approach to recruitment

- *Determining the board's specific needs*: Selection best practice should be based on a careful assessment, and an understanding of the relative importance of skills, knowledge, experience and attributes of existing board members. This will include taking into account the existing composition of the board, the likelihood of future board turnover, the opportunities and challenges facing the businesses and an assessment of the incumbent skill set to meet these challenges. Having identified gaps or shortfalls, a profile of what characteristics would make the ideal NED should be compiled.

- *Determine approach to find the NED*: Agree on process and timing. It will be necessary to consider what sources of supply can be accessed and the best ways of doing this.

- *Screen applicants*: Identify who meets essential requirements and wants the job.

- *Compare and assess candidates*: This needs to be done with particular regard to those factors considered to be the most important for the role. Having decided upon the assessment process, including approach to be taken during the interview, a decision as to who will need to conduct the interview will have to be made.

- *Make the choice*: Ensure you select the best talent available, taking into consideration factors such as emotional intelligence as well as more traditional yardstick assessments.

- *Establish and maintain positive relationships*: This includes those who were not successful in the final stage – consider building a waiting list for future board appointments.

- *Communicate approach*: Communicating in this area with investors, employees and other stakeholders will demonstrate commitment at the top, enhance the credibility of the board and build trust around the NED appointment.

In line with best practice, the majority of listed companies will have nomination committees to oversee the selection of executive directors. It will be the role and responsibility of this committee to filter proposals and recommend candidates to the board. In respect of non-executive director appointment, this is reserved as a matter for the whole board, based on a formal and transparent process. An independent approach to selecting a suitable NED may involve the use of an external third party such as a specialist search firm or a register comprised of suitably qualified individuals. See also Chapter 5 on conducting board appraisals

Using a third-party specialist

Going it alone or deciding to use a search firm will depend upon the competencies of the nomination committee and internal staff supporting the process as well as having the in-house ability and resource to identify and target potential candidates. Whilst opting to use a search firm will involve cost, the possibility of limiting the scope of the search and therefore limiting access to the best talent available may prove to be a false economy in the long run. The Revised Combined Code (A.4.10) requires the nomination committee to set out in the annual report the process it has followed to make appointments and, if it has not taken external advice or made use of open advertising, to explain why it has not done so.

In opting to use a search firm it would be wise to consider the following issues:

- size v capability;
- geographical reach;
- industry knowledge and specialisation;
- conflicts;
- track record;
- guarantees and liabilities;
- qualities of the search team.

Size v capability

The company as a client initiating a search assignment may already have a preferred relationship or choose to opt for a different search firm depending on the needs of the assignment and the experience and capability of the search firm. The search industry is driven by talented individuals and therefore the number of offices and consultants may not be an appropriate indicator of ability to get the job done. Many single-office firms relying on star players operate comfortably on both a national and international scale, whilst some multi-office firms will be purely regional in their focus and unlikely to deliver an international search effectively. Instead an assessment of the firm's capability overall should be made, including the resources available to the search professional to reach and identify the best possible candidates. It is important that the search professionals engaged on the assignment have a thorough understanding of the candidate required to work in the role effectively. As the client, the company should ensure it has a full understanding of the resources available to the search and which staff will be leading and supporting the assignment.

Geographical reach

In those instances where the search is aiming to attract an international element it will be important to understand the extent of the international network the search firm can draw upon. It will be important to understand the working relationship underpinning the overseas offices if the firm is not represented by a single office. Other issues to address include:

- The scope of sourcing meaningful candidates in different markets.
- Who will conduct the screening of candidates?
- Will it be necessary to involve video conferencing?

- Will there be a lead consultant?
- Who will meet with all short-listed candidates?
- Will travel on the part of the candidate or the company be necessary?

Once these issues have been addressed the company will have a much better insight into the service levels to expected, which is particularly important in the case of complex international searches.

Industry knowledge and specialisation

The executive search industry has become increasingly specialised over recent years and at times it may seem that the process in selecting a search firm suited to the needs of the company is just as involved as the candidate search process itself. Although the search process itself is generic to all sectors and functions, clients increasingly require the search firm to have in depth knowledge of an industry or a function.

In the case of NED searches, there are numerous organisations available to assist in the selection process, including traditional trade associations, business organisations and professional bodies. Client choice will depend on the in-house capability to resource and execute a successful search assignment.

Conflicts

In an attempt to build board stability it will be important that the company ensures an agreement is in place with any external search organisation that it works with not to recruit from the client company where they have previously placed a client until a sufficient amount of time has lapsed. It is therefore also important to understand from the search firm if any existing limitations (e.g. clients or individuals that are 'off-limits') which will impact upon the scope of the overall search assignment.

Track record

Approach your choice of search firm as you would your choice of candidate. Ensure references relating to the search firm are taken up and make an assessment of both the firm and the individual handling the search assignment. Positive indicators of a sound track record include endorsements of past performance from other clients, completion rates, completion times and evidence of repeat business.

Guarantees and liabilities

Firstly, the search firm should demonstrate a commitment that any information gained during a search assignment is confidential and will not be disclosed outside the search assignment. Whilst a search consultant cannot guarantee to fill the position, they can provide quality assurance regarding the way the search is conducted.

Qualities of the search team

The following qualities are important to identify with the search consultant (ensure the search professional engaged is the actual person executing the search and not just a figurehead rolled out for business development purposes of the search firm):

- professional communication, presentation and interpersonal skills;
- sufficient industry and role knowledge to make informed recommendations;
- perceptive and well-developed assessment skills;
- persuasive, determined and tenacious;
- demonstrates honesty and integrity.

The dynamics between the client (often the nominations committee) and the search firm are dependent upon trust, chemistry and professional respect. It is important for the client to understand how they can ensure the search assignment is successful in delivering a candidate who meets the future needs of the board. It is essential that a candid relationship exists between the company and the search firm engaged on the assignment. It is important that the company delivers a substantial brief – a search firm can only be as good as its brief. Get this wrong and expectations on both sides will be damaged and frustrated. Ensure the consultant meets with the key decision makers involved in the selection process. As with investors, ensure there are no surprises or skeletons in the cupboard.

Due diligence

Getting the top team wrong can hinder not enhance board and ultimately corporate performance. The stakes are high and need to be taken seriously by the whole board, not just the nominations committee (or, on smaller boards, the individual allocated the task of recruiting a fellow member).

CHECKLIST Due diligence to be undertaken

The board: Before making an offer to a candidate, the board should satisfy itself:

- Why does the candidate want to become a NED?
- What does the candidate have to offer? What difference would they make to the board and how they can best contribute?

- How will the appointment fit in with their existing work/personal commitments?
- Does the candidate understand the implications of the appointment including legal responsibilities and liabilities?

The candidate: Before accepting an appointment, a prospective NED should carry out some basic due diligence on the company/organisation whose board they are about to join. Questions to consider before taking on a non-executive role include:

- Does he or she have the necessary time?
- Would the appointment give rise to any conflict of interest?
- Would resignation from the post materially impair the individual's personal financial position and thus compromise independence?
- Is the relationship between the candidate and the executive team sufficiently detached to enable the role to be executed objectively?
- Would serving on the board compromise personal credibility and reputation?

In addition to the above, the potential candidate should take the opportunity to request informal conversations with other directors and officers of the board and senior management as well as taking time to talk with the company's auditors. Where possible, the candidate, in the case of appointments involving publicly-traded companies, should discretely try to understand prevailing shareholders' perceptions of the company, whether this is by reading analysts' notes, reviewing financial press coverage or where possible talking to investors/market participants.

Making the offer

It is important to set clear expectations from the outset.

Formal terms of appointment

NEDs are usually appointed to a board under a letter of appointment, rather than having formal terms of engagement set out in a service contract. The Higgs Report recommended that the nomination committee should set out in a letter of appointment the time and responsibility envisaged (including if relevant, involvement in board committees and/or in performing the role of the senior independent director).

In addition, the appointment of a NED will also be subject to the company's articles of association, and as such should be detailed in the appointment letter.

CHECKLIST Additional core elements to be included within the
terms of appointment

These include:

- the role the non-executive director is to undertake, both in general and specific terms;
- the length of term for which he should be appointed (subject to approval of or re-election by shareholders);
- remuneration to be paid;
- requirement to attend minimum number of board meetings;
- requirements as to confidentiality and non-competition;
- an obligation to undertake further training and development initiatives.

A specimen letter of appointment for an NED is set out in the Combined Code and is reproduced in Appendix 2.

The learning curve

Induction

Key to the success of a new recruit's ability to add value to the board's effectiveness as soon as possible is to ensure that a well-tested and documented induction process is in place for all new board members. Establishing NEDs in their role as quickly as possible will maximise their contribution to the board, ensure they get to grips with the dynamics of the board and enable them to understand where they can potentially add value to the board's agenda. Having established an effective induction procedure it is important that it is documented not only for future use but also to ensure that working knowledge of the board is captured and not lost should significant turnover take place. Directors' training is covered in greater detail in Chapter 4.

CHECKLIST Induction for new directors

Some basic induction rules before the new board member commences their role:

- Ensure both internal and external communications surrounding the appointment have been considered and the necessary actions put in place, e.g. stock exchange announcements, internal announcements and contact arrangements.

- Provide the new appointee with a comprehensive information pack including all site locations, key suppliers and customers.
- Prepare a tailored induction checklist including areas to be covered and timescales for delivery.
- Ensure the board has been fully briefed.
- Ensure the individual is integrated into board information circulation/distribution lists.

Initiatives to ensure new recruits get up to speed as quickly as possible include:

- A 'buddy' system where non-executives are partnered with executive or senior managers in areas of joint interest. This allows informal relationships to be developed whilst getting a feel for the business issues driving the business.
- A fostering/adoption system where non-executives are encouraged to adopt an area of the business (e.g. a group company, plant or store) or a business theme/issue (e.g. CSR or new product development). This opens up channels of communication, increases direct access and exposure to the board and sends strong commitment signals to both those working in the company at lower levels and shareholders.

Ongoing development

Induction will be only the first stage of meeting a new director's development plan. A director should be willing and able to commit to a tailored development programme that enables their knowledge and capabilities to continuously evolve. Just as in their professional capacity they are likely to have to maintain their own professional development so the role of NED should be treated as a profession, with high standards of conduct and a focus on improving their knowledge, skill and core qualities – this may be company-specific learning, an evolving awareness of the environment within which the company operates (e.g. legal, regulatory and competitive factors) or personal effectiveness (e.g. influencing, communication and decision-making skills). Establishing ongoing personal development plans will be linked closely to the formal evaluation of the board and making an assessment of skill, knowledge and experience gaps.

Evaluating contribution to the board

A key input to any training and development plan will be the chairman's regular evaluation of each director's contribution to the board. A number of possible approaches to evaluating the performance of individual directors are set out in Chapter 5.

Compensating non-executive directors

Non-executive remuneration is based on the principle that NEDs should be rewarded commensurate with their responsibilities.

It should be noted that a NED (unlike an executive director) is not considered to be an employee. As a result, a NED will typically receive fees, but none of the benefits associated with employment (e.g., share options, pension, health cover or company car). However, the usual position is that NEDs should be treated as employees for tax and national insurance purposes, and have deductions made at source via the PAYE scheme.

Where the NED appointment differs from common practice, the tax treatment may alter. For instance, some NEDs will charge a fee to the company (possibly including VAT). Alternatively, other NEDs may contract with the company via a service company which is used to charge the fee. In both these cases, the NEDs will be liable to tax calculated under Schedule D. The company should ensure that before it pays its NEDs in this way the individual has received advance clearance from HMRC.

Surveys indicate that a range of fees are paid to NEDs. There is a general perception amongst commentators and participants in the markets that in many cases, the fees may now be too low given the significant increase in expectations regarding NED contribution to the board including the:

■ level of time commitment;

■ expertise expected of the individual;

■ expansion of the role and increased responsibilities;

■ potential risks and liabilities associated with carrying out the role.

However, some concerns have been raised that payment of higher fee levels could compromise NED independence, as it could put short-term gain above the long-term development of the company.

Given the well-documented changes to the role of the NED, recent debate has centred upon value-added contribution, and how this should be reflected in compensation packages. This has raised questions about fee levels and whether it is desirable to link remuneration to performance in the same way as their executive counterparts. This was one of the conclusions within the Cadbury Report (1992) and was further accepted as part of the conclusions of the Hampel Report. The potential benefits arising from share options were perceived as inappropriate for the remuneration of non-executive directors.

Whilst using share options to compensate NEDs is overwhelmingly opposed, many believe that a mixture of cash and shares should not be problematic, as long as shares are held for a minimum 'respectable' period. In this way, the use of shares as part of an overall payment mechanism is seen as a useful and legitimate way of aligning NEDs' interests with those of shareholders. This view was initially expressed in the Hampel Report and continues to be included within the Combined Code which does approve payment of NEDs partly in shares. The ABI does not object as long as there is no element of performance-related pay to the provision.

There is substantial external resistance to paying NEDs in the form of share options or providing performance-linked bonuses. It should be noted that these restraints do not apply to private companies which have a greater degree of flexibility in structuring their NEDs' remuneration packages, although this coincides with a recognition that those performing the NED role within the private arena are likely to be more 'hands on' and have different motives for being involved with a private company (e.g. such as an investor representative).

Where shares are a part of the remuneration package

Where shares are to be used as a straight exchange for some of the fees as part of the overall remuneration package there are some technical issues to be considered:

- Most NEDS are not employees of the company and are more likely to be regarded as service providers in their own right. As a result, exemptions from the provisions on financial assistance and the financial services acts for employee share schemes would not be applicable to any arrangement providing non-executive directors with shares.

- Foregoing fees to which the NED is entitled in exchange for shares should be made clear, so as to avoid the shares being identified as a 'gift'.

- The company may wish to impose holding requirements in respect of the shares provided to ensure accusations of short-term trading cannot be levied against the NED.

- The company's articles must allow for the directors to be paid in shares.

- Any limits on how remuneration can be provided must be checked.

- The company must have sufficient net assets and the use of shares must not materially reduce the company's assets.

- The statutory and disclosure requirements in respect of companies whose shares are publicly traded apply equally to non-executive and executive directors as do the restrictions imposed during 'close periods'.

- Contracts for services held by NEDs may need to be amended to provide for payment of fees in the form of shares.

when things don't work out

As NEDS do not carry out full-time managerial roles on behalf of the company they will not usually be subject to post-termination restrictions on their activities.

If a NED is denied full access to the facts of the business despite having raised issues with the board and/or has placed pressure on investors, resignation should be the ultimate sanction. This will be particularly true where the company is in financial difficulties. The decision to resign is not without risk, however, and it is always advisable to seek legal advice before taking such action.

If following an appointment it appears that there are still gaps on the board and training/further development cannot improve the situation, then steps should be taken to re-evaluate board composition and to make such changes as are necessary to ensure continued board effectiveness. Any changes to the board, and in particular the benefits derived from those changes, should be communicated to shareholders in accordance with the Listing Rules to ensure they continue to have full confidence in the board.

CONCLUSION

- In the years following the Cadbury Code, the role of NEDs has strengthened significantly. The Combined Code puts a new emphasis on their professionalism and effectiveness.

- These changes mean greater responsibilities not only for the NED but also for the company. The recruitment process must be rigorous and transparent; remuneration must strike an appropriate balance between motivation and reward, and governance concerns such as maintaining independence and aligning the NED's interests with those of shareholders.

Information and professional development

- The Higgs Report and subsequent Revised Code have focused the spotlight on the training needs of all directors, both when they join the board of a company and during their tenure in office

- Boards need to ensure that there are comprehensive induction programmes, relevant on-going training courses and probing performance evaluations put in place for their directors

- Boards should appreciate that access to independent advice for directors may also be appropriate in certain situations and should provide accordingly

Introduction

Main principle A.1 of the original Combined Code states that listed companies should be headed by an effective board which should lead and control the company. It would therefore seem logical to conclude that directors' training needs, performance evaluation and induction needs would all be prioritised within the general culture of a company upon a new director joining the board. However, the Higgs Report found that this simply was not the case. Although the Combined Code included a code provision that 'every director should receive appropriate training on the first occasion that he or she is appointed to the board of a listed company, and subsequently as necessary', it became clear that many companies were not complying with such requirements. In response to a telephone survey undertaken for the purposes of the Higgs Report of executive directors, non-executive directors (NEDs) and Chairmen of UK-listed companies, it was found that:

- less than one-quarter of participating NEDs had received a formal briefing or induction after appointment;

- two-thirds of NEDs and chairmen had not received any training or development;

- over one-third of boards never formally evaluated their own performance;

- over three-quarters of NEDs and over half the chairmen had never had a formal personal performance review.

Against the backdrop of such perceived shortcomings, the Revised Code brought induction, training needs and performance evaluation much more into focus on a board's agenda, by strengthening the emphasis placed upon them.

This chapter examines not only induction, professional development and performance evaluation, but also examines the additional Revised Code provisions regarding access to independent advice and to the company secretary.

Induction

The objective of induction is to 'inform the director such that he or she can become as effective as possible in their new role as soon as possible'. As Higgs noted: 'to be effective, newly appointed non-executive directors quickly need to build their knowledge of the organisation to the point where they can use the skills and experience they have gained elsewhere for the benefit of the company'.

It is with such thoughts of enabling a newly appointed director to 'hit the ground running' that the Revised Code raised the profile of induction. The Main Principle contained in section 1, paragraph A5 of the Revised Code simply states that 'all directors should receive induction on joining the Board'. However, the subsequent Code Provision elaborates upon this requirement to state that 'the Chairman should ensure that new directors receive a full, formal and tailored induction on joining the board. As part of this, the company should offer to major shareholders the opportunity to meet a new non-executive director'.

Higgs highlights that a company should set aside adequate resources and ensure sufficient time is allowed for a thorough induction for directors. In practice this will mean that a suitably comprehensive programme is compiled which is relevant to the company's business and which combines presentations, meetings and the provision of information in an induction pack. The induction must also be specific to the director in question, taking into account whether the individual:

- is executive or non-executive;
- has prior experience or no experience as a director; and
- has prior experience within the industry sector of the company.

Higgs also commented that non-executive directors who were interviewed highlighted that visiting company locations and attending company events 'significantly developed their knowledge of the business and its people'.

An induction checklist is provided as an annex to the Higgs Report and is reproduced in Appendix 3. This establishes that the induction process should build:

- an understanding of the nature of the company, its business and the markets in which it operates;
- a link with the company's people; and
- an understanding of the company's main relationships.

In addition, the need for an induction pack is identified to provide a new director with certain basic information about the company. In this regard the ICSA produced a Guidance Note setting out comprehensive details of the materials that should be considered for inclusion. The ICSA devised a three-part approach consisting of:

- the essential material that should be provided immediately;
- the material that should be provided over the first few weeks following the appointment; and
- items which the company secretary might consider making the director aware of.

Irrespective of splitting the information in such a way, the director should be provided immediately with a comprehensive list of all the material which is to be made available to him.

CHECKLIST Sample material for induction pack

(a) Essential information

    The following information should be given to the director before the first board meeting:

- Information on directors' duties such as a memorandum on responsibilities and obligations under legislation, regulation and best practice, a copy of the UKLA Model Code and a schedule of matters reserved for the board.

- Information on the company's business such as its business plan, budgets, last annual report and accounts, a comprehensive corporate structure, insurance details including a copy of the D&O insurance policy, details of major litigation, the company's funding position and appropriate corporate brochures.

- Board and constitutional issues such as a copy of the company's memorandum and articles of association, copies of the last three to six board minutes, timetable of future board meetings, details of the company secretary and all fellow board members and the details of all board committees.

(b) Material to be provided during the first few months

    Although not necessary for his commencement with the company, the following are examples of the information the ICSA considers to be crucial for a director to develop his knowledge of the company:

- details of the company's advisers, together with contact details;
- details of the company's risk management procedures;
- a brief corporate history;
- copies of all management accounts since the last accounts date;
- details of the company's largest customers and suppliers;
- details of all other company policies such as health and safety and environmental.

(c) Additional information to consider

The last category suggested by the ICSA covers such matters as procedures for the signing off of accounts and the expenses policy. The nature of such information depends upon the nature of the company itself and what may be relevant to it. The responsibility for selecting what is appropriate falls in practice on the company secretary.

The above is drawn from the ICSA's *Guidance Note* (Reference No. 030214) on this subject.

In terms of overall responsibility for compiling the induction programme, Higgs suggested that the chairman should take the lead in providing a properly constructed induction programme and should be facilitated by the company secretary. This approach was subsequently reflected in the Revised Code.

Higgs also suggested the use of site visits. Commentators have subsequently suggested that an intensive three-day programme of meetings with senior management and other crucial employees of a company ensures that the director is suitably informed from the start of his tenure.

Updating and refreshing skills and knowledge

When considering the training needs of NEDs, Higgs noted his belief that there 'should be a step change in training and development provision so that it is suited to the needs of boards'. He emphasised that what he envisaged is continued professional development tailored to the individual.

In the context of the results of the Higgs Report telephone survey, where two-thirds of NEDs and chairmen stated that they did not receive any training or development, Higgs also noted that demand for formal training was very low. He highlighted the relatively limited supply of training specifically aimed at NEDs by business schools and other providers, but went on to note that such provision as there was had been reduced because of poor uptake. It was suggested that providers of MBA courses should consider courses on the behaviours and skills needed in the boardroom, amongst other relevant issues, so the board members of tomorrow know more precisely what is expected of them.

He concluded that an entrenched boardroom culture tends to regard NEDs as being fully equipped for the role without requiring further personal development or training, and noted that in most cases such a presumption is not justified. Refreshment and, where appropriate, extension of knowledge and skills should be what the chairman and company secretary are concerned with when considering the training needs of their directors and the board as a whole.

So what are the training issues which the chairman and the company secretary need to consider? Higgs underlines the importance of the performance evaluation process to the formulation of a training schedule and also states that NEDs themselves should regularly appraise their individual skills, knowledge and expertise to determine whether further professional development would 'help them develop their expertise and fulfil their obligations as members of the unitary board'. It is with this sentiment of self-responsibility that Higgs sums up his view that 'non-executive directors should be prepared to devote time to keeping their skills up-to-date'.

Examples of training for potential directors are:

- understanding the role of the board;
- understanding the obligations and rights of directors of listed companies;
- understanding the behaviours needed for effective board performance.

For existing directors these are:

- updating knowledge of strategy, management of human and financial resources and audit and remuneration;
- legal and regulatory updates;
- revisiting board behaviours.

As with induction, Higgs laid overall responsibility for director training at the door of the chairman, who should lead in identifying the development needs of individual directors. As before, the company secretary would play the crucial role in facilitating provision.

The Revised Code provides, at Main Principle A.5, that 'all directors should regularly update and refresh their skills and knowledge'. Higgs' view that the chairman should take overall responsibility for training is delivered by a supporting principle as follows:

> The Chairman should ensure that the directors continually update their skills and the knowledge and familiarity with the company required to fulfil their role both on the board and on board committees. The company should provide the necessary resources for developing and updating its directors' knowledge and capabilities.

Sources of training and information for directors

Induction

Companies will normally be expected to provide company-specific training and information to new directors in-house, generally through a combination of visits, meetings and written briefings.

More general training for new directors is provided by a number of sources including:

- professional bodies and associations;
- professional advisers;
- business schools;
- specialist commercial providers.

Ongoing training and education

Continued training may take the form of briefings and seminars designed to maintain up-to-date knowledge of relevant developments in:

- regulation and legislation affecting companies;
- accounting practice and requirements;
- corporate best practice.

Directors are less likely to require formal courses, but should have briefings or seminars on specific issues. Best practice might be to add a 'training session' into board meetings on a regular basis. Again, such information may be provided by:

- professional advisers (perhaps through regular in-house briefings, newsletters or seminars), including corporate brokers, sponsors or nominated advisors (as applicable), lawyers or accountants;
- professional bodies and associations;
- regulatory or governance specialists.

The company secretary may also update the board at its regular meetings on any key developments and their implications for the board. For this purpose, a standing agenda item may be recommended.

Access to independent advice

The Revised Code sets out the principle that 'directors, especially non-executive directors, have access to independent professional advice at the company's expense where they judge it necessary to discharge their responsibilities as directors'.

Although the Revised Code aims to ensure that directors are suitably equipped with the necessary knowledge via professional development to discharge their duties, by making suitable provision for access to independent professional advice, the Revised Code acknowledges that training cannot cover all eventualities. For directors, especially NEDs, to discharge their duties to the company, and for NEDs to demonstrate independence of thought, they may require independent advice and guidance from time to time.

In implementing this Code Provision, both the chairman and the company secretary will need to devise and implement a policy for directors to obtain independent advice. The basis for obtaining such advice should be considered, including:

- whether there should be a prior authorisation procedure;
- generally speaking, precluding the company's existing professional advisers from time to time from providing such advice due to the requirement of independence; and
- whether a specific professional firm should be allocated to such role or whether the director in question should be able to choose the source of advice.

The chairman must ensure that the spirit of the provision is given its true worth whilst ensuring that a balance is struck so that the company is not incurring excessive professional fees without some form of check and balance.

Once the process has been devised, all directors should be briefed on how they may gain access to such advice, the guidelines on usage and full contact details for such independent advisers. Finally, the process should be formalised and adopted by resolution of the board.

Access to the company secretary

The company secretary's role as facilitator of information as well as training is underlined in the Revised Code, which provides that 'all directors should have access to the advice and services of the company secretary, who is responsible to the board for ensuring that board procedures are complied with'.

Higgs noted the importance of the company secretary, particularly in the role he plays 'in the provision of information and more widely in supporting the effective performance of non-executive directors'. He identifies the 'facilitation of good information flows, provision of impartial information and guidance on board procedures, legal requirements and corporate governance, together with best practice developments' as being key responsibilities of the company secretary to aid enhancement of director performance.

Higgs also notes the role played by the company secretary in all governance matters. As a result he observes that 'although there may be certain matters on which the company secretary reports to the chief executive, this should not undermine their overall responsibility to the board on all matters of corporate governance'.

It is the emphasis which Higgs places on the company secretary as being, ideally, a provider of independent impartial guidance and advice which has, quite rightly, led to the provision in the Revised Code and to the company secretary being viewed increasingly as a key player in the overall issue of directors having sufficient information and resources to discharge their duties.

Board evaluation and individual director evaluation

In an age where performance and accountability have become increasingly important, it was inevitable that the lack of provision for formal performance evaluation in the original Combined Code would be addressed. Higgs observed that a board performance appraisal gives the chairman the information and confidence to manage the board effectively. He noted that it helps the chairman to identify and address the strengths and weaknesses of the board and to consider whether the board has the right balance of skills for the future. Finally, he went on to propose that the Revised Code should provide that the performance of the board as a whole, of its committees and of its members should be evaluated at least once a year and that the annual report of the company should state whether such performance evaluation is taking place and how it is conducted.

The Revised Code embraced the conclusions of the Higgs Report on performance evaluation and provides for a 'formal and rigorous annual evaluation' of the board, the committees and the individual directors alike. The Supporting Principle goes one step further and provides as follows:

> Individual evaluation should aim to show whether each director continues to contribute effectively and to demonstrate commitment to the role (including commitment of time for board and committee meetings and any other duties). The Chairman should act on the results of the performance evaluation by recognising the strengths and addressing the weaknesses of the board and, where appropriate, proposing new members be appointed to the board or seeking the resignation of directors.

In recommending that resignations should be sought from under-performing directors, the principle was established that a performance and results-led culture should prevail in the boardroom, as it has amongst the general workforce of the company.

The chairman is tasked by Higgs with selecting an appropriate and effective process and acting on its outcome. Although not going so far as to suggest it should be compulsory, Higgs indicates in the performance evaluation guidance to his Report that the 'use of an external third party to conduct the evaluation will bring objectivity to the process'.

In such guidance, the questions set out in the following checklists are examples of the questions, which in themselves are not meant to be definitive or exhaustive, which may form the basis for considering what should be included in a performance evaluation. The processes by which such an evaluation may be undertaken are dealt with in detail in Chapter 5.

CHECKLIST Performance evaluation of the board

- How has the board performed against performance objectives?
- How has the board contributed to testing and developing strategy?
- How has the board ensured robust and effective risk management?
- Is the composition of the board and its committees appropriate and effective?
- Is the board as a whole up-to-date with latest developments in the market of the company?

CHECKLIST Performance evaluation of the non-executive
director(s)

- How well prepared and informed are they for board meetings?
- Do they attend the board meetings?
- Do they demonstrate willingness to devote time and effort to understand the company and participate outside the boardroom?
- What has been the quality and value of their contributions at board meetings?
- How effectively have they probed to test information and assumptions?
- Have they refreshed their knowledge and skills?

Although group appraisals of the board as a whole have, to a degree, been commonplace, the idea of individual director appraisals, particularly for NEDs, is a relatively new concept.

The results of the performance evaluations should help to reveal the respective training needs of the board as a whole and the individual directors. The chairman will need to act on such findings, whether by ensuring suitable training is provided, finding new directors or possibly seeking the resignation of under-performing directors. Irrespective of such findings, the results of performance reviews of individual directors must always remain confidential.

CONCLUSION

● Where appropriate, a company should ensure that a comprehensive induction programme is established and maintained for new directors so that they may become effective in their new role as soon as possible.

● Continued professional development for a company's board should be tailored to specific needs and should cover both refreshment and extension of knowledge and skills.

● Access to independent advice at should, in certain circumstances, be acknowledged as a legitimate entitlement of directors, especially NEDs. The rules of access should be devised by the chairman and company secretary and should be formally adopted by the board.

● Performance evaluation should be used to help establish the training needs of directors, to monitor the strengths and weaknesses of both the board as a whole and of individual directors, and also to address under-performance.

CHAPTER 5

Conducting board appraisals

KEY ISSUES

- The role of the nomination committee
- Why conduct an evaluation?
- What to evaluate?
- In-house process v using external third parties
- Appraisals: 'processes' and 'people'
- Conducting an appraisal: Questionnaires, interviews or facilitated discussion?
- Evaluating the chairman
- Handling outcomes

Introduction

When Derek Higgs and his committee published their report in January 2003, it started a prolonged and high profile debate about the role of the chairman in listed companies – in particular whether the chairman was to be regarded as independent, how many companies he could act for, and which (if any) of a boards' committees he could serve on – let alone chair!

The Higgs Report also contained the five words: 'Boards should evaluate their performance'. The phrase originally appeared in annex A to the Higgs Report as part of the suggested rewording of the Combined Code. At the time of publication it did not immediately give rise to discussion and debate – however, the impact of these five words has far outlasted the initial debate generated over the role of the chairman.

By the time the revised Combined Code was published and adopted in July 2003 these five words had been transformed into a requirement under the Code which now reads:

A.6 Performance evaluation

Main Principle

The Board should undertake a formal and rigorous annual evaluation of its own performance and that of its committees and individual directors.

Supporting Principle

Individual evaluation should aim to show whether each director continues to contribute effectively and to demonstrate commitment to the role (including commitment of time for board and committee meetings and any other duties). The Chairman should act on the results of the performance evaluation by recognising the strengths and addressing the weaknesses of the board and, where appropriate, proposing new members be appointed to the board or seeking the resignation of directors.

A.6.1 Code provision

The Board should state in the annual report how performance evaluation of the Board, its committees and its individual directors has been conducted. The non-executive directors, led by the senior independent director, should be responsible for performance evaluation of the Chairman, taking into account the views of executive directors.

Board, committee and individual evaluations are now a part of the reporting requirement placed on companies by the Combined Code. Although the responsibility to ensure that this task is undertaken lies with the chairman; in practice this will probably fall to the company secretary to organise.

The Code does not prescribe the way in which an evaluation – whether for board, committee or individual – should be completed (see Appendix 4). The requirement is to undertake a formal and rigorous evaluation every year and to state in the annual report how the performance evaluations have been conducted. The chairman is required to act on the evaluation by recognising strengths and addressing any weaknesses identified.

The inclusion of this principle into the Combined Code did not have the high profile of the earlier debates about the chairman's role. It has, however, contributed to a wide debate amongst company secretaries as to how to implement a performance evaluation process to achieve these objectives.

Role of the nomination committee

Whilst it is ultimately the chairman's responsibility to oversee the process of a board evaluation, in this, he (and the company secretary) should be supported by members of the company's nomination committee.

In his report, Higgs acknowledged that less than one-third of smaller listed companies have a nomination committee. No explanation was offered for this, but one suspects that smaller companies consider that there is insufficient demand, or work, for such a committee (see also Appendix 5).

However, with the introduction of the Combined Code and the requirement for an annual evaluation of the board's performance there is now a much clearer argument that the nomination committee's terms of reference should include involvement in, and some responsibility for, the appraisal process.

The hints are contained in the Higgs Report itself and, subsequently, in the Combined Code where, under the summary of the principal duties of the nomination committee is the requirement that it should '…be responsible for identifying and nominating for the approval of the Board, candidates to fill board vacancies…'.

The Combined Code goes on to list a number of areas which fall under the remit of a nomination committee, including the general requirement to undertake evaluations which a properly conducted board, committee and individual assessment process would encompass.

These include:

- evaluating the balance of skills on the board;
- performing an annual evaluation of time spent in their role by non-executive directors (NEDs);
- considering the succession planning requirements of the company;
- reviewing the structure, size and composition (including the skills, knowledge and experience) of the board.

Furthermore, the Code is clear that it is the responsibility of the nomination committee to make recommendations to the board concerning the re-election by shareholders of any director under the retirement by rotation provisions.

Principle A.7.2 of the Code is also explicit:

> The chairman should confirm to shareholders when proposing re-election that, following formal performance evaluation, the individual's performance continues to be effective and to demonstrate commitment to the role.

By extension it appears logical that if a chairman is to give assurances to his shareholders – and he in turn is to receive recommendations from the nomination committee – that an individual director is suitable for re-election, the nomination committee should be in a position to support their recommendations by overseeing the evaluation procedures.

Why evaluate?

What then are the company's drivers for undertaking an evaluation process? Clearly for many it has been the desire to comply with the requirements of the Combined Code in terms of reporting to shareholders – and to demonstrate best practice in the corporate governance arena. However, although these are clearly valid reasons, they should not be the only reasons for persuading a company to embark on the exercise.

The ultimate motivation for a company should be the expectation of improved functionality; this could be improved performance of individual directors through identifying potential weaknesses which can be addressed through additional training; or it could be an improvement in the way in which the board or a committee operates, by a change in administrative procedures.

With such a clear mandate for and the wide-ranging implications of overseeing the evaluation process, the profile of the nomination committee should increase. Shareholders will also want to know how the committee can properly discharge its responsibilities unless it can report that it has in place and oversees a formal and rigorous annual evaluation of its own performance, that of the board, the other committees and the individual directors.

What to evaluate

Wherever the responsibility ultimately sits, the question arises 'What to appraise?' The Higgs Report is marvellously vague on this matter and it is left to the individual company to define how it should meet its obligations in this regard.

The only clue the Combined Code provides is to define the three roles that require evaluation: board, committee and individual; and perhaps this provides a solution as to how companies might approach this matter. In simple terms, what is being asked of companies is to evaluate 'process' and 'people'.

Collective bodies like the board and its operating committees will want to assess the feedback from an evaluation of their processes on a collective basis. However, when assessing strengths and weaknesses from an individual evaluation, the chairman will wish to give individual, personal feedback to each director.

Whilst there can be a degree of overlap between the two processes – and indeed some companies will attempt to undertake an all embracing single evaluation – there is a view that board and committee evaluation should be separate from directors' evaluation, since both the approach to undertaking the exercise and the feedback methods are likely to be different. (Pages 193–195 provide checklists of some of the areas that might be evaluated.)

For companies new to the concept of undertaking an evaluation it is probably easier to start with the less intimidating task of a board and committee 'process' evaluation before tackling what might be seen as a much more personal and subjective 'people' review of an individual director's performance.

Points to consider

The rest of this chapter will discuss some of the points companies should consider when undertaking a performance evaluation.

Many companies may choose to keep the appraisal process in-house and there are indicators of the amount of work to be carried out if this is the chosen route. However, we will also discuss selecting and working with independent external advisors, detailing the areas which should be appraised, some of the methods which might be adopted and the importance of providing feedback – particularly on individual assessments.

Internal v external evaluation

The arguments for and against using external consultants for this exercise are the same as for any other project and there are a number of external advisors who are offering assistance to companies in this area to help them meet their reporting requirements under the Combined Code.

While some companies approach what can be a sensitive issue by asking independent external organisations to help, it is probably fair to say that so far, the majority of UK-listed companies have elected to undertake some degree of evaluation using their in-house resources. If you have appropriate HR support there are advantages to adopting this approach.

The primary advantage – at least initially – will be the budget, although there will still be internal cost implications. Other key advantages are that in-house staff will have a greater degree of familiarity with the organisation and knowledge of the individuals involved. It must be a given that the persons managing the project will be sufficiently senior to have the respect of the participants. A further advantage to running the exercise entirely in-house is that it avoids any potential conflict of interest with competitor organisations.

Bringing in external consultants to assist with a performance evaluation also has a number of advantages:

- they can provide a resource which may not be available in-house and this alone could represent a significant time saving in completing the project;

- the evaluation process can be undertaken as a discreet assignment where the cost is known and fixed in advance; any additional work involved is immediately out-sourced and there is little or no impact on the company secretariat to help the company to meet its commitments in this area;

- the wider experience external consultants bring to the evaluation process should bring a greater degree of structure to the process, and will also enable a company's results to be put into a broader corporate context;

- the independence of external consultants will be a key factor in ensuring that the process remains objective;

- and, of course, any potentially unpalatable messages can be blamed on the messenger!

When selecting external advisers to help in this area, probably the most important factor is the experience they have gained through having conducted similar exercises elsewhere. In this regard companies should satisfy themselves that the work they have done for previous clients has been satisfactory. As ever, reputable consultancies will be more than happy to provide senior level references from client companies who have already used their services.

Who leads the process?

As we have seen, the Combined Code is clear on this issue; it is the chairman's overall responsibility to ensure that an evaluation of the board, its committees and individual directors is undertaken on an annual basis. In this, he should be assisted by the nominations committee, supported by his board and company secretary, but in the final analysis it is the chairman who will be responsible for identifying the skills base against which the board is to be judged and it is for him to set the agenda to ensure that this objective is achieved.

However, before commencing an evaluation process it is important for the chairman to ensure that there is a good degree of 'buy in' from all participants. He should obtain general consent for the specific areas of operation/skills to be appraised and a general agreement of the criteria against which these subjects are to be measured.

If the exercise is being undertaken internally, a nominated lead board member (the senior NED?) could also be proactively involved, as could the director of human resources and/or the company secretary.

If external assistance is sought to help complete the process, whoever is leading the project will need to demonstrate a good degree of objectivity, understand the objectives of the chairman and help to set an appropriate agenda. Key to the process will be an appreciation of the seniority of the individuals being appraised and an understanding of the hierarchy within the board; they will need to engender a good degree of trust from all participants to ensure full value is derived from the exercise.

CHECKLIST Leading the process

- Is the process being driven by the chairman? If the company secretary is simply 'spoon-feeding' a solution without proper buy-in from the chairman or the board, the exercise will not deliver optimal results.
- Is this to be an internal exercise – or can value be added by using external agencies?
  - If the former, will the board be satisfied their responses will be treated confidentially?
  - If the latter, what is their experience and are references available?

What to appraise: 'processes v people'

If we assume that companies will distinguish between the appraisals of 'process' and 'people' it becomes much easier to examine the various methods of running an evaluation of the board.

Process

Any evaluation of the board or a committee should be as objective as possible; the overall purpose should be to assess current (or proposed) processes, to invite commentary and suggestions with a view to improving the running of the board or committee.

This part of the appraisal should include areas such as: the structure of the board, the administration and conduct of meetings, corporate governance, and relationships with senior management.

It would be appropriate to canvass each board/committee member's views on how well they believe they are discharging their duties – but unless there are already some easily-measured objectives in place it is difficult (at least initially) to do anything but ask for observations.

The opportunity should also be used to obtain some constructive feedback from the participants as to how well they perceive the board/committee to be operating as a whole. This feedback could be fashioned into measurable objectives, thereby providing a baseline for future evaluation.

At this point it would be appropriate to review Chapter 2. All the processes highlighted there could be the subject of a general evaluation. The areas covered should incorporate the running of the meetings themselves (e.g. frequency and length), the content (e.g. are we covering the correct topics?), the administration surrounding them including the quality of the agenda and supporting papers/presentations and the adequacy of minutes.

In looking at the operation of the board/committee it would also be important to seek opinions about its structure and composition – including the suitability of members.

Because the questions asked here will tend to centre on some skill sets (is there appropriate knowledge of relevant markets?) and some personal attributes (is the age profile of the board correct?) there is likely to be a degree of cross-over between this and the individual evaluation process. If handled positively, the responses to some of these questions will highlight matters that could be investigated in greater depth as part of an individual assessment programme.

People

Due to its very nature, evaluating individuals is likely to be a significantly more subjective exercise than discussing processes.

Inevitably the questioning will touch on individual contribution – and this can be an extremely sensitive issue, particularly when it is perceived that judgements are being made about personal 'performance'; it will require a very open approach from participants and a good degree of skill in conducting the assessment to gain any commitment to change.

As important as the qualities and contributions of individual directors, however, is the chairman's ability to achieve an effective balance of skills and experience on his board, which when brought together, contribute to the efficient and effective running of the company.

What the chairman should be seeking is a team which can operate within a culture of open exchange, constructive dialogue and an environment of mutual trust and respect.

The individual appraisal is likely to focus more on relationships, particularly between board members but also between the board and senior management. It will tend to centre on skill sets – some of which may be generic (good communication skills) while others will be company specific (understanding the business and its sector).

The individual evaluation will invariably need to address personal attributes in addition to assessing an individual's professional performance and contribution. Again, it will be the job of the chairman to explain that he is looking for a balanced board rather than one where every member excels at everything. It is also an opportunity to measure existing skill sets against the long-term objectives of the business to identify any particular gaps which could be addressed through the appointment of an additional board member.

There is almost bound to be a degree of crossover between this exercise and the board/committee 'process' evaluation. However both processes will, over a period of time, build to give an overall view of the specific strengths of the board and the contributions made by individuals.

One facet of undertaking individual evaluations which exercises the minds of those involved is how to reduce the 'subjective' aspect. Here it might be helpful to involve a degree of self assessment which will allow the director to identify his own strengths and areas for further development.

Individual self appraisal can work well if the purpose is clear and well communicated, and the emphasis is on the identification of positive contributions. Under these circumstances, with a positive approach towards identifying problem areas and with the support of appropriate remedial action, it can be very successfully incorporated as part of the personal evaluation process.

The chairman may also wish to consider the advantages of obtaining a wider view of each director's contribution by inviting a 360 degree, or peer group, contribution to the process to supplement his own observations. The advantage of drawing views from a wider grouping will be that any individual subjective bias will be diluted and a truer picture of the perceived contribution made to the group by each individual can be allowed to emerge.

How to conduct the evaluation

Broadly speaking there are only two basic approaches that can be adopted by companies in undertaking an evaluation: use either a questionnaire-based methodology or arrange a meeting or a series of meetings with all members of the board. Some companies attempt a combination of the two!

A questionnaire

The main advantage of basing the evaluation on a standard questionnaire is that the chairman knows that (once identified and agreed) the same question is being addressed in the same way by every member of the board/committee. There is no room for misinterpretation – and he can be sure that everybody is addressing the same issue.

Most questionnaires offer a 'multiple choice' of responses (e.g. strongly agree to strongly disagree) which can be perceived as a box-ticking exercise. It is the responsibility of the chairman to ensure that this does not happen.

We have seen instructions from a chairman requiring all board members to explain their choice of box ticked! While this approach certainly worked, it is often sufficient to allow individuals the flexibility to add some commentary to the replies they give. It is also true to say that the additional commentary provided by a respondent can go some considerable way towards adding 'depth and colour' to the bare responses.

Providing hard copy questionnaires will also allow individual directors to complete the exercise at their convenience – allowing the process to be fitted around other business commitments. It is certainly a less intrusive means of conducting an evaluation.

In this option, the key lies in collating the various replies and providing a comprehensive report by interpreting the range of answers received. Collating all replies into a single document can highlight very clearly the areas where there is broad agreement – and where little or no alteration to the status quo is needed. The converse is also true; a great divergence of opinions is immediately obvious and highlights any areas requiring attention. Careful analysis of the completed questionnaires can further help to identify whether the point of disagreement is truly 'across the board' or whether, in fact, it is exposing a divide between non-executives and executives.

Interviews

An alternative to using a questionnaire is for the chairman to identify a series of questions or issues for discussion and to schedule time with every member of the board to undertake a one-on-one interview.

This can be a very time-consuming process, particularly if the board is large, and is probably an unnecessary exercise when addressing 'processes' – however the one-on-one interview should form an essential part of the feedback process for individual evaluations.

The main disadvantage of this approach is that while the broad direction of a meeting can be agreed at the outset (and even where there is a pre-defined list of questions) it is impossible to control with any degree of predictability where a conversation will lead, and this could invariably open discussions of unscheduled areas.

If an external third party is appointed to undertake this exercise, unless he or she knows the board extremely well or is very well briefed, the disadvantages of one-on-one interviews can only be compounded – it would be a very disciplined individual who would refuse to explore all avenues that might be thus exposed!

A further disadvantage of conducting interviews is that objectivity can be compromised. Personalities will inevitably be a factor in the interview process, and there is scope for interpretation of the interviewee's replies to be rather subjective, and even to be coloured by existing perceptions of a particular individual.

Facilitated discussion

A third approach, and one adopted by some companies, particularly when undertaking a full evaluation of the board, is to have a round-table discussion as part of a board meeting when all aspects of the board's processes can be openly debated. If this process is to be effective, a degree of preparation is necessary (as with one-on-one interviews), but an experienced facilitator can act as observer and help the chairman to guide the meeting to ensure that everyone is encouraged to express an opinion and that all opinions are recorded. The success of this type of approach may well depend upon the board's willingness to have 'strangers' participating in board meetings – and commenting upon their contributions!

Evaluating the chairman

The Combined Code makes it the responsibility of the NED to undertake a performance evaluation of the chairman:

> ...the non-executive directors, led by the senior independent director, should be responsible for performance evaluation of the chairman, taking into account the views of executive directors.

The performance of a chairman will invariably incorporate questions on his leadership and leadership style and the relationships he has with management, shareholders and other stakeholders. In addition, his style of board management and the role he plays in developing his team should be reviewed.

Many of these evaluation points could just as usefully be applied to the chairman of board committees. The same observations made concerning subjectivity in the section (above) about 'people appraisal' can be applied to the chairman's evaluation; the larger the number of contributors into this review, the more objective it becomes.

Again, the least threatening and most objective approach to this may be to issue a questionnaire to at least the NEDs, and possibly to the whole board and for the senior independent director to use these responses as the basis for a private discussion with the chairman.

CHECKLIST Which approach to evaluation?

- Does the chairman wish to conduct an all-embracing appraisal – or would it be easier and more constructive to differentiate between a 'personal' and 'process' evaluation?
- Would the individual board members prefer to schedule time for one-on-one interviews to cover board/committee issues – or can these matters be covered via a questionnaire?
- Would the board be inhibited by the presence of an external facilitator?
- In conducting individual evaluations, would the chairman find it helpful to seek 360 degree input from all board members and provide feedback to individuals taking into account a wider body of views?
- Use the results from the evaluations to set targets and performance indicators for future years.

Handling outcomes

Providing comprehensive feedback is an essential – indeed perhaps the most important component of undertaking an evaluation and this part of the process should not be overlooked.

The results of a 'process evaluation' of the board or a committee can be relatively easily identified and tend to be apparent to all. The assessment may have been undertaken using a fairly standard template but the outcome of the exercise should at least merit time on a subsequent board and/or committee agenda. There should be an objective presentation of findings and any recommendations for change debated.

Where appropriate, specific actions should be agreed and a timetable drawn up for their implementation. Some action points might be used to feed into the board's objectives for the coming year (e.g. to strengthen the board's collective knowledge of the US market), and all should be highlighted in the following year's evaluation process to allow the board to monitor its progress.

An individual appraisal needs to recognise that the process will be looking at development and performance improvement. It is essential to provide constructive personal feedback to individual directors and to agree what actions, if any, need to be taken to help the individual improve in any particular aspect of his performance. This is the responsibility of the chairman and can only be undertaken on a one-to-one basis.

CONCLUSION

- Many companies new to the process of evaluating board performance have questioned whether there is any value to be derived – or whether it is in fact just a 'box-ticking' exercise.

- There is evidence that companies which have undertaken a board evaluation have often been pleasantly surprised at the outcome; they have tended to see positive changes coming as a result of the exercise. Asking what may seem to be fairly straightforward questions can tease out issues that can easily be addressed and remedied.

- Experience has shown that the majority of companies and their boards tend to follow internal procedures that have not changed for some time; historical systems may still be perfectly acceptable but it can be remarkable how minor amendments to procedures, arising from suggestions made by members of the board and/or its committee can improve the way in which these organisations operate.

- Results have been as extreme as identifying the need for a new boardroom table (!) or (more commonly) an acknowledgement that the composition of the board no longer reflects the international nature of the company's business, and subsequently remedying that position.

● Undertaking a successful board evaluation will involve:

– the active co-operation of the chairman and the board;

– the expectation that the procedure will be confidential; and

– the anticipation that process and skills will improve.

Working with auditors

- The role of the audit committee
- Appointing an external auditor
- Provision of non-audit services by the auditor
- What makes a successful audit
- The auditor and the interim statement

Introduction

In the current climate 'corporate governance' makes headline news. Now more than ever the audit committee – and the individuals who sit on it – find themselves in the spotlight: 'While all directors have a duty to act in the interests of the company the Audit Committee has a particular role, acting independently from the executive, to ensure that the interests of shareholders are properly protected in relation to financial reporting and internal control' (Smith).

Investors and other interested parties are now far better educated about how public companies are run. The audit committee for a listed company must report to shareholders on the work it has carried out in the year, and must make its terms of reference available to the public. When things go wrong, these statements will be re-visited with the benefit of hindsight.

This chapter looks at the role of the audit committee and, in particular, considers the importance of the relationship between the committee and its external auditor. This relationship has a vital role to play in the preservation of both personal and corporate reputations.

One of the key aspects of the committee's role is to recommend to the board the appointment of the auditor and to subsequently monitor the terms and effectiveness of that appointment in an objective and transparent way.

Smith emphasises that the most important features of the relationship between the audit committee and the board, internal and external audit functions are a 'frank, open working relationship and a high level of mutual respect'. In this chapter we focus on how the audit committee might achieve this and, in particular, how the audit committee might best communicate and interact with the company's independent auditor.

This chapter does not focus in great detail on published codes or rules for audit committees but instead is intended to be a practical guide. It is difficult, however, to look at the work of the audit committee without first looking briefly at the Smith *Guidance on Audit Committees* (reproduced in Appendix 6).

The key terms of reference for an audit committee, as defined by Smith are:

- To monitor the integrity of the financial statements of the company, reviewing significant financial reporting judgements.

- To review the company's internal financial control system and, unless expressly addressed by a separate risk committee or by the board itself, risk management systems.

- To monitor and review the effectiveness of the company's internal audit function.

- To make recommendations to the board in relation to the external auditor's appointment; in the event of the board's rejecting the recommendation, the committee and the board should explain their respective positions in the annual report.

- To monitor and review the external auditor's independence, objectivity and effectiveness, taking into consideration relevant UK professional and regulatory requirements.

- To develop and implement policy on the engagement of the external auditor to supply non-audit services, taking into account relevant ethical guidance regarding the provision of non-audit services by the external audit firm.

Appointing an external auditor

In many ways the appointment of the external auditor is the most important decision that the audit committee and the board will make. It is vital to take time to understand what the auditor will do and how they will do it. Take time and make the right choice. This will not just be a matter of skills and experience. Your auditor must be someone you can deal with, someone who will be approachable, but also someone who will reciprocate in a frank and open manner.

Independence, objectivity and effectiveness

'Independence, objectivity and effectiveness' is a phrase that is often used when looking at the role of the auditor. Elsewhere in this chapter we consider this in relation to the provision of non-audit services by the auditor, but most experienced audit committee chairmen know that 'independence and objectivity' is also very much a state of mind.

The auditor should be prepared to challenge management assertions. During the course of its work, the audit committee should be able to observe the auditor using a healthy level of scepticism. The auditor should be able to demonstrate to the audit committee that where possible he/she is obtaining third-party evidence to support management representations. The auditor should tell the audit committee what is being done and why.

Does the auditor take time to understand the business?

Some audit committees are very keen to employ auditors who have detailed knowledge of their industry. This can be helpful, but is not absolutely necessary in all cases. There may be an element of industry practice, but the most important thing is that the auditor gets to know how the company runs its business.

The auditor should understand:

- the pressure points in workflow; in cash flow; in management information streams; and in the financial reporting function;
- the risks facing the industry in which the company operates but, more importantly, the risks facing the particular business; and
- the controls in place to mitigate those risks.

But the auditor should not rest there. The auditors should get to know what is actually happening in the business, not what the accounting records say is happening. They should speak to people throughout the organisation. They should do all this so that when the auditor comes to report their findings to the audit committee (and ultimately give an opinion in their audit report) they have a real feel for how the business has performed and where the business is going.

No third party gets to know the business like the auditor does – the audit committee should make sure that they get the most out of that knowledge. In fact 'annual audit' is really an out-dated term, as your auditor should be:

- in constant contact with the audit committee and with management throughout the reporting cycle; and
- fully briefed by the audit committee or management on the board's business plans.

The auditor often formally reports only once during the year, but they should be offering business advice every step of the way. The auditor should be providing briefings on new developments, seeking out news, communicating throughout the year. Your auditor should not be hindered on grounds of 'independence' from giving you sound business advice, whenever you need it.

Does the auditor have sufficient resources to do the work?

It is tempting to assume that an audit is just an audit and so the audit committee is doing the right thing by the shareholders in appointing the auditor who undertakes to complete the engagement for the lowest fee.

This is not necessarily the case. Financial reporting rules are becoming ever more detailed. Auditing standards are going through unprecedented change, which mean that the statutory audit will need more manpower. The audit committee is charged with ensuring that the audit process is sufficiently robust and has the appropriate resources to carry out the level of work required.

Remember that the work of the audit committee is under scrutiny from investors. A robust audit process reflects well on the audit committee. By ensuring that the auditor does all that they should do and has the resources to do it, the members of the audit committee are taking appropriate steps to uphold their own personal reputation.

In the past the auditor may have had to justify a fee increase for the audit, or an audit fee at a higher level than that of its competitors. Increasingly the more enlightened audit committee chairmen are asking 'We want more than just an audit so how can our auditor do all this work for such a low fee'?

Non-audit services and the auditor

Understanding the professional guidance for auditors

Auditors of public companies in the UK must comply with the ethical standards issued by the Auditing Practices board (APB). In general, the standards say that an auditor should not audit their own work and that auditors should implement suitable controls (such as partner rotation) to safeguard independence. The audit committee should at least be familiar with the ethical requirements, available from the APB section of the Financial Reporting Council's (FRC) website (www.frc.org.uk).

The audit firm will have its own ethical procedures in place and the audit committee will want to know how those procedures have been applied to their particular relationship. Those procedures will include but not be restricted to:

- ensuring that no employee holds shares in your company;
- restrictions on how non-audit services are provided to your business, who can do that work (see 'Chinese walls' below);
- rotation of senior members of the audit team such as the audit and review partner;
- client acceptance procedures.

The audit committee should talk to the auditor and understand how the audit firm ensures compliance with the APB's ethical requirements. If the audit committee wishes, it is perfectly justified in seeking additional or alternative procedures to be applied by the audit firm to its particular circumstances.

Chinese walls

In certain circumstances the auditor and/or the audit committee could put in place specific measures to safeguard the independence of the audit team. We return here to our theme of communication – in many cases the company will want the auditor to perform additional services because of their knowledge of the business. The auditor and the audit committee must work out an arrangement which satisfies both the auditor's ethical requirements and the audit committee's reciprocal desire to ensure the independence and objectivity of the audit team, ensuring that the audit opinion is and is seen to be free of outside pressures (pressures external to the audit team).

A long-used practice among professional firms, not just audit firms, is the imposition of 'Chinese walls'. In the context of the audit this might mean for example, that corporate tax planning and corporate finance advice is given to the business by members of the audit firm who are never utilised as part of the audit team.

The audit committee could seek other controls over the quality and independence of the audit. For example, the audit committee might seek assurances that the remuneration of the audit partner is in no way affected by fees received by the audit firm for non-audit services.

Policy on non-audit services

Some commentators consider that payments for non-audit services in excess of the audit fee show that auditor independence has been impaired. Re-appointment of the chair of the audit committee has, on occasion, been opposed by shareholders on the grounds that the chairman has at least tolerated 'excessive' non-audit services.

This is an example of a 'box-ticking approach' by shareholders to non-audit fees and is unhelpful to the company. Often the investor appears to take no account of the controls put in place by the audit committee and/or the auditor to ensure the independence of the audit team. There is scant regard for the nature of the services provided.

An easy way to address many of the misgivings of investors on auditor independence is for the audit committee to draw up a policy on non-audit services. This should be made available to the public. The policy could draw a distinction between services that the auditor:

- should provide;
- could provide, but only at the discretion of the audit committee; and
- should not provide.

CHECKLIST Specimen policy on non-audit fees

Work which can be carried out by external auditors has been split into three categories:

Category A

The external auditors are excluded from providing services where the threat to their independence is considered to be too great to be mitigated by any safeguards. The auditor will not be engaged to provide services where that could lead to them having to audit their own work at some point in the future. Prohibited services include internal audit, systems design and implementation, accounting assistance (other than with technical advice on the implications of and implementation of financial reporting standards and related disclosures), legal services including resolution of litigation, actuarial services, management functions or human resources, investment advice or services, investment banking and appraisal or valuation services.

Category B

This comprises those services where the company would expect to use the external auditors. Such services include due diligence, reports on historical financial information, taxation compliance and routine tax planning and consulting services.

Category C

This includes other services to be decided on a case-by-case basis taking into account the perceived impact on independence and the skills and experience of the people proposed for the assignment.

Any work proposed to be carried out under category C would normally be expected to be competitively tendered unless for reasons of historical knowledge, timing or confidentiality, it was considered by the company to be in its interests to appoint on a single tender basis.

The company will remain free to seek competitive tenders for any particular assignments but would expect to work within these guidelines. Where it is proposed to appoint auditors on a single-tender basis for category C work, the prior consent of the audit committee chairman is required. The audit committee will review annually the level and nature of non-audit services provided by the external auditors in the previous financial year.

This disclosure could be supplemented by an explanation of how the policy has been implemented during the year, together with numerical breakdown of the fees for non-audit services, which should be described. Disclosure of the controls to ensure independence of the audit team requested by the audit committee and/or implemented by the auditor would also be useful.

The key point here is that the audit committee should clearly and concisely tell the investors about the arrangements they have in place for assurance services other than the statutory audit.

The audit process should be more than just an audit

The most important period of interaction between auditor and audit committee is the statutory audit. The audit process should not be something to be feared – the audit should be eagerly anticipated by the management. A good working relationship between the two parties will result in an efficient, challenging and productive process.

The audit committee must understand what the auditor plans to do

The best processes always start with a plan!

The audit committee should meet with the auditor to agree the scope of the work that they plan to carry out. It must understand which audit areas the auditor perceives to be of greatest risk and to have the greatest potential impact on the financial statements. The audit committee should critically analyse the evidence that the auditor will seek on those risk areas.

During the course of its work, the audit committee may identify its own concerns about certain of the company's procedures, or perhaps about how a specific business segment or geographical location is managed and controlled. The nature of these concerns will drive how the committee responds. It might be appropriate to give direction to the auditor, or to request certain procedures to be carried out in addition to the main audit.

The audit committee would normally expect to receive and be asked to comment on, an audit strategy memorandum, or similar document.

Strategy memorandum

A standard strategy memorandum might address:

- the audit approach and scope of work;
- an assessment of the accounting function, systems and internal controls – and impact on the nature and focus of the audit work;
- a preliminary assessment of materiality;
- the work of others – the auditor might seek to use the work of other specialists such as other group company auditors; actuaries; property valuers; share option valuers; or internal audit;
- a timetable – with key dates and responsibilities.

The audit committee should receive updates during the audit

Not every audit proceeds according to the plan. The audit planning is based on draft figures and the auditor's understanding of systems derived from preliminary discussions with management. Often the auditor will commence work and discover that something has changed, or something does not happen or has not happened as expected. Occasionally, this will mean that the auditor has to redirect the focus of the audit.

Having agreed the plan with the auditor, the audit committee will want to be kept abreast of these changes and be able to raise queries or request additional work as necessary. The audit committee would normally expect to receive an audit progress memorandum to facilitate this which might address:

- progress of work by reference to the audit timetable;
- significant issues identified so far and proposed resolution including nature of audit evidence obtained/required;
- significant changes to planned audit work with explanation.

A productive closeout meeting is key to the audit process

It is for the mutual benefit of the auditor and the audit committee to sit down at the end of the audit and discuss the major issues. This meeting should be an integral part of the audit process for both parties. The audit committee should meet with the auditor when the audit of the financial statements is all but complete, but prior to release of the preliminary announcement. Many firms require a technical review of the financial statements and key audit judgements by staff that have no contact with the company – any technical review should also be completed prior to the closeout meeting.

The efficiency of the meeting is best facilitated by a clear briefing document prepared by the auditor for the board as a whole and for the audit committee in particular.

Briefing document

The briefing document and subsequent closeout meeting should address:

- major issues arising during the audit;
- review of key accounting and audit judgements;
- review of errors identified during the audit;
- variations from the planned audit work and additional procedures performed;
- potential or imminent changes in financial reporting or other standards relevant to the company.

The audit committee should also seek the opinion of the auditor on the quality of accounting policies and financial reporting. This brings us neatly on to the next point – the audit committee might ask the auditor what would change if the auditor were selecting accounting policies.

If the auditor was the chief executive...

A key area of judgement for the board is how to talk about corporate performance in the annual report. The board will want to give certain messages to the market.

The auditor will read the 'front end' to ensure that it is not misleading in the context of the financial information that is published alongside it. However, the audit committee could seek more constructive input from this 'review of the front end' and from the results of the statutory audit and could ask the auditor: 'What would you [the auditor] change if you were writing the annual report?'

There are other questions that the audit committee could ask the auditor, which will help bring to life the auditor's opinion of the financial statements and provide a framework from which it will be able to ascertain the auditor's opinion of the accounting function and of management.

Further questions that might be put to the auditor

- If you [the auditor] were our chief executive, actually writing our financial statements, would the judgemental items in our accounts look different to what management is proposing?
- What is your impression of our finance function?
- How would you categorise management's approach to financial reporting – prudent? aggressive? well-balanced? biased towards the positive? reporting choices influenced by impact on share price? high regard given to quality reporting procedures?
- Given your overall impression of our business obtained during the course of your audit would the annual report be written with a different slant, give a different flavour, or highlight different areas?

In light of these discussions the audit committee might ask itself:

- Are there differences between how management conclude on judgemental areas and what the auditor would say?
- What would our shareholders think of management's presentation?
- What would shareholders think if they were party to the closeout meeting?
- Would their investment decisions change?

The audit committee is in part responsible for ensuring that the board gives a balanced view in its public statements. Putting the auditor in the 'shoes' of the chief executive is often an enlightening way to help the audit committee to form its own opinions on what the board should be saying and how it should be saying it.

The auditor must discuss the preliminary announcement with the audit committee

Before the annual report is sent to shareholders, a listed company must make a preliminary announcement of results. In common with all public statements by the company of a financial nature the audit committee should be involved prior to release.

The Listing Rules do not allow the company to make a preliminary announcement of annual results without first having had clearance from the auditor to make that announcement. The auditor should give clearance in writing, but the audit committee should first ensure that the audit is all but complete and that the auditor is satisfied that all significant outstanding issues have been resolved.

Information the auditor will want to see prior to release of financial information:

- the press release;
- the chairman's statement;
- financial highlights;
- management commentary;
- accompanying financial information;
- any other information that is released at the same time.

AIM and Ofex companies might wish to implement similar procedures voluntarily.

The auditor and the interim statement

The interim statement can cover a three-month but more often a six-month period. There is no requirement for the interim statement to be audited.

However, the audit committee can engage the auditor to perform one of:

- an 'interim review';
- an 'interim audit'; or
- 'agreed upon procedures'.

The level of assurance that the audit committee seeks from the interim work will to a large extent depend on what the shareholders of the company expect to see. It might seek guidance from the company's broker in this regard.

Many smaller quoted companies choose to engage the auditor to perform an interim review. The auditor signs a standard 'review report' and the review work is conducted in accordance with guidance issued by the APB. The level of assurance provided by a review report is not as high as a full audit, but it is generally considered to be a cost effective way of obtaining at least a degree of third-party assurance. The auditor's review report must be published as part of the interim statement.

An alternative method used by the audit committees is to engage the auditor to perform 'agreed upon procedures'. The auditor is engaged to perform specific work, perhaps on specific areas of the accounts. The auditor will normally report to the board informally on the results of that work. In this case no report is published alongside the interim accounts.

CHECKLIST Key responsibilities of the audit committee

(The Smith Report, reproduced in Appendix 6 sets out in full the responsibilities of the audit committee.)

Financial reporting

- To review the significant financial reporting issues and judgements made in connection with the preparation of the company's financial statements, interim reports, preliminary announcements and related formal statements.

- Taking into account the external auditor's view, the audit committee should consider whether the company has adopted appropriate accounting policies and, where necessary, made appropriate estimates and judgements.

- The audit committee should review the clarity and completeness of disclosures in the financial statements and consider whether the disclosures made are set properly in context.

Internal controls and risk management systems

- The audit committee should review the company's internal financial controls and unless expressly addressed by a separate board risk committee or by the board itself, the company's internal control and risk management systems.

- Except to the extent that this is expressly dealt with by the board or the board risk committee, the audit committee should review and approve the statements included in the annual report in relation to internal control and the management of risk.

Whistle blowing

- The audit committee should review arrangements by which staff of the company may, in confidence, raise concerns about possible improprieties in matters of financial reporting or other matters.

The internal audit process

- The audit committee should monitor and review the effectiveness of the company's internal audit function.
- The audit committee should review and approve the internal audit function's remit. It should ensure that the function has the necessary resources and access to information to enable it to fulfil its mandate in accordance with appropriate professional standards for internal auditors.
- The audit committee should approve the appointment or termination of appointment of the head of internal audit.

The external audit process

- The audit committee should have primary responsibility for making a recommendation on the appointment, reappointment and removal of the external auditors.
- The audit committee should assess annually the qualification, expertise and resources, and independence of the external auditors and the effectiveness of the audit process.
- The audit committee should approve the terms of engagement and the remuneration to be paid to the external auditor in respect of audit services provided.
- The audit committee should review and agree the engagement letter issued by the external auditor at the start of each audit.
- The audit committee should have procedures to ensure the independence and objectivity of the external auditor annually, taking into consideration relevant UK professional and regulatory requirements.
- The audit committee should seek from the audit firm, on an annual basis, information about policies and processes for maintaining independence and monitoring compliance with relevant requirements, including current requirements regarding the rotation of audit partners and staff.
- The annual report should explain to shareholders how, if the auditor provides non-audit services, auditor objectivity and independence is safeguarded.
- At the start of each annual audit cycle, the audit committee should ensure that appropriate plans are in place for the audit.
- The audit committee should review, with the external auditors, the findings of their work.
- At the end of the annual audit cycle, the audit committee should assess the effectiveness of the audit process.

Communication with shareholders

- The terms of reference of the audit committee, including its role and the authority delegated to it by the board, should be made available. A separate section in the annual report should describe the work of the committee in discharging those responsibilities.

The chairman of the audit committee should be present at the AGM to answer questions, through the chairman of the board, on the report on the audit committee's activities and matters within the scope of its responsibilities.

CONCLUSION

- The role and responsibilities of the audit committee are more extensive and onerous than in the past.

- There is increased scrutiny of accounting procedures by shareholders and regulators.

- One effect of this has been to change the nature of the relationship between company and auditor. A successful relationship with the auditor depends on effective communication, rigorous planning and a clearly-defined service provision.

- The directors should use the auditor as an independent sounding board and the audit process should help to inform management. The audit is more than just an annual visit and directors should use the audit process to get more value from their auditor.

Preparation of the annual report and accounts

- The purpose of the annual report
- Achieving a balanced and understandable assessment
- Content of the annual report
    - Financial: International Financial Reporting Standards (IFRS)
    - Non-financial
    - The Combined Code
    - Social, environmental and ethical reporting
- Operating and Financial Review (OFR)

Introduction

Preparation of the annual report and accounts is a key event in the annual corporate timetable, requiring immense amounts of planning and coordination.

There are many sources of guidance regarding the detailed content of the annual report, and many external advisers whose role is to guide companies through its production.

This chapter will not attempt to duplicate such guidance, although it will refer to statutory and best practice requirements. Instead, it will focus on the wider objectives and potential of the annual report as a means of communicating a full and balanced view of the company to its shareholders and the broader community. Reporting to shareholders should not be seen simply as a box-ticking exercise, but as a positive investment of time and effort.

Where applicable, the views of institutional investors on current reporting practices will be given, but it is recommended that companies should consult their own key shareholders to find out what they are looking for from the annual report.

Purpose of the annual report

End of term report and manifesto

The annual report and accounts has the potential to be an extremely powerful document. For most listed companies it is the most detailed means of communication with their full shareholder base during the financial year. This is where they will give shareholders a formal and detailed assessment of the company's current financial position and the way in which directors are managing its affairs on their behalf.

All companies will communicate periodically with their shareholders during the year – whether through the interim report and preliminary results announcement or through regulatory market announcements. Many will also undertake a programme of investor relations activities, though this will often be directed primarily at key institutional shareholders.

For most *individual* shareholders the annual report remains the primary means of assessing the current state of a company's affairs.

Equally, the report and accounts remains a key investor communication event for many smaller companies, who find access to larger institutions more difficult. A strong report can thus provide an initial opportunity to put themselves onto the institutional radar.

For larger companies, the annual report is an opportunity to consolidate and reinforce messages which will have been communicated throughout the year, especially to their larger institutional shareholders.

The importance of the document is therefore not only as a regulatory report; it is also a key marketing tool. The annual report is the company's opportunity to publicise its strengths and achievements in every aspect of its business – financial, management and governance – not only to its shareholders but also to its wider stakeholders, including employees, clients and suppliers, as well as to society at large.

Certainly this is an 'end of term report', measuring achievements and progress in the previous year, but it is also (within the constraints of the UK regulatory system) a 'manifesto' of the company's intentions and capabilities for the coming year and beyond.

A balanced and understandable assessment

The board should present a balanced and understandable assessment of the company's position and prospects.   *cc D.1 Financial Reporting*

This sounds simple, but as these views given by the institutions and company secretaries interviewed for this chapter illustrate, it is not always easily achieved in practice.

Institutional view of reporting	Corporate view of reporting
'Too many companies are still making boiler plate statements' 'Many companies are incapable of or not interested in thinking beyond compliance' 'The further you get into the report, the more anodyne it becomes' 'Every year it's the same words, the same paragraphs....People don't bother to read it' 'Companies need to understand more what shareholders want – this is happening more' 'Reports should be shorter and more meaningful – more fun to read!' 'In my experience, companies are willing and eager to have a dialogue'	'We see other companies receiving criticism for what they say, which discourages us from making meaningful statements in our own report' 'Some of our investors take a box-ticking approach so in seeking to avoid criticism why shouldn't we take a box-ticking approach?' 'Every year we set out with the intention of writing everything from scratch but then there's never enough time and we have to just focus on the numbers' 'We want to write what *we* think is important and will add value, but it gets used with the benefit of hindsight to criticise the company's management' 'We have spent a lot of time talking to our shareholders, and it has been very positive'

Concerns are often expressed that the annual report, with its traditional emphasis on the annual financial statements, is unlikely to provide investors with an assessment which is truly 'balanced and understandable'.

Several factors have contributed to this. There have been several well-publicised corporate scandals in recent years that have uncovered inappropriate accounting practices in companies whose published accounts appeared to show them to be in excellent financial health.

A rules-based interpretation of accounting standards by some has meant more detailed rules for all. The breadth and depth of non-financial information required in the report, and the level of qualitative disclosure and analysis that directors are now expected to provide has increased greatly.

However, more disclosure is not necessarily more useful to the shareholder. Investors often complain either of a box-ticking approach or of companies not exercising critical judgement in what they choose to include.

Even where accounts are perfectly correct, there is often a tendency to over-use technical language and jargon. This runs the risk of producing a document which is dry and inaccessible for many investors.

The key directive for directors should be to tell shareholders how the company has performed and where the company is going.

Content of the annual report

The annual report of a UK quoted company must comply with the Companies Act 1985 and with the rules of the market on which its shares are traded (OFEX, AIM or the full list of the London Stock Exchange). This section gives an overview of the basic rules, but the reader should refer to the main sources for the detail.

Much of the following text is written with listed companies in mind. That should not deter other public companies. Rules for listed companies are often seen as good practice for others, particularly when it comes to non-financial reporting.

Financial reporting

The annual report and accounts of a quoted company must contain as a minimum, a profit and loss account, a balance sheet, a cash flow statement, a statement of accounting policies used to compile those financial statements, and notes to support the primary statements.

For accounting periods commencing on or after 1 January 2005 listed companies must prepare their group accounts using International Financial Reporting Standards (IFRS). This is an EC requirement for EC-regulated markets. Individual listed companies may continue to use UK Accounting Standards (known as UK GAAP) although UK GAAP is converging with IFRS.

The London Stock Exchange (LSE) has announced that the AIM will mandate IFRS in group accounts with effect from 2007. OFEX has said that it does not intend to mandate IFRS for the foreseeable future. AIM and OFEX companies may still wish to adopt IFRS voluntarily, especially if they see themselves competing with listed groups (reporting under IFRS) for investment funds.

IFRS is a huge change for EU markets

It is intended that IFRS will be used by markets across the world. It is hoped that a common basis for producing financial information will aid comparability and reduce the world's cost of capital.

First time adoption of IFRS

IFRS 1 '*First-time adoption of International Financial Reporting Standards*' sets out rules for disclosures and treatments in an entity's first set of IFRS accounts. In the short term, the conversion process from UK GAAP to IFRS is a significant project, requiring considerable planning and management time. It is not a process that can, or should be, completed at the same time as the annual audit, particularly since the interim report for the year should also be in IFRS.

A rough rule of thumb is that balance sheets under IFRS will show more liabilities than under UK GAAP. Companies must communicate clearly to shareholders and lenders where gearing is a key ratio, for example on bank covenants.

Recent standards issued in the UK have taken into consideration international developments. In certain areas IFRS are similar in *principle* to those in the UK. However this is not always the case and, where it is, the devil is often in the detail.

Here are some basic rules to follow with IFRS adoption:

- the conversion process should be led by a named individual who will both oversee the process and drive it forward;
- there will probably be training needs for the finance function;
- IFRS requires more detailed disclosure in certain areas – the company's accounting systems must be updated in sufficient time to enable data capture.

Other than first-time adoption of IFRS, here are five potential problem areas under IFRS:

Financial instruments
This is a large and highly complex topic.

- The most likely areas where the impact will be significant are carrying values of financial assets and reclassifications between liabilities and equity.
- Equity is more narrowly defined than shareholders' funds in UK GAAP, such that some instruments that are classified as non-equity shares under FRS 4 will be financial liabilities under IAS 32 (e.g. most redeemable shares).
- Convertible debt instruments are often split into a debt element and an equity element on initial recognition, with the equity element representing an option to subscribe for equity.
- The disclosure requirements for financial instruments are more extensive than UK companies have been used to.
- Many of these rules are becoming part of UK GAAP, so strictly this is not simply an IFRS issue.

Deferred taxation

- IAS 12 requires full provision to be made for deferred tax on most temporary differences.
- Temporary differences are differences between the tax base of the asset or liability and the accounts carrying value.
- Discounting is not permitted.
- Deferred tax is provided on revaluation surpluses and fair value adjustments.
- Deferred tax is usually provided on the undistributed profits of associates, and may be provided on profits of subsidiaries and joint ventures.
- Deferred tax principles under IFRS are not that different to those that we have been used to in the UK, but on deferred tax more than anything else the devil is in the detail.

Business combinations and goodwill

- From the date of transition to IFRS all combinations are acquisitions or reverse acquisitions (there will be no mergers other than group reconstructions).
- Intangible assets need to be recognised separately from goodwill to a much greater extent than is currently the case under UK GAAP – separability will no longer be a requirement.
- Companies with significant goodwill may face searching questions from shareholders such as 'If you have not bought intangible assets, what have you paid this money for?'
- Goodwill is not amortised but instead is subject to annual impairment review.

Share-based payment

- If the company has issued, or plans to issue, shares or share options as part of employee remuneration packages (or otherwise in return for goods or services) then profits will almost certainly be affected by these rules.
- The rules also apply to amounts calculated by reference to share price changes, but which may be settled in cash (e.g. phantom option schemes).
- IFRS 2 is virtually the same as FRS 20 in UK GAAP so that, again, strictly this is not just an IFRS issue.

Leases

- IFRS is similar in some respects to UK GAAP.
- The basic definitions of operating and finance leases are similar and the principle remains that a lease is a finance lease if it transfers substantially all the risks and rewards of ownership.

- However, the detail on lease classification differs, which may result in different classification under IAS 17 compared to SSAP 21.
- In IAS 17, there is no '90% test'. Instead, IAS 17 lists factors normally indicating a finance lease.
- Leases of land and buildings have to be split into their component parts.
- Reclassification of operating leases as finance leases will increase gearing.

Non-financial reporting

The directors' report

The Companies Act 1985 requires the report and accounts of all public companies to include a report by the directors covering a range of issues designed to give shareholders a more complete picture of the company's current status and the way in which it is governed by the board.

The statutory content of this depends in part on the size of the company. However, the report should always include:

- the principal activities of the company during the year, and any changes in those activities;
- the names of directors who held office during the year, details of their interests in the company's shares, including share options;
- details of any purchases of its own shares made by the company during the year;
- any political or charitable donations made by the company in excess of £200;
- any additional disclosures such as payments to the auditors for non-audit work.

The reports from directors of medium and large companies must include additional information such as:

- a fair review of the business of the company and its subsidiaries during the year, the position at the end of the year, and any likely future developments;
- the amount of any dividend recommended by the directors;
- significant post-balance-sheet events;
- details of any research and development conducted by the company;
- the company's policy on trade creditors;
- an explanation of the company's policy on the employment of disabled people;
- a statement of employee involvement in the company (e.g. employee share schemes or employee consultation processes);
- exposure of the company and its subsidiaries to price risk, credit risk, liquidity risk and cash flow risk;

- financial risk management objectives and policies, including hedge transactions.

The UKLA listing rules set out additional disclosure requirements. These include:

- *Commentary on forecasts.* An explanation of the difference if the results for the period under review differ by 10% or more from any published forecast or estimate by the company for that period.

- *Interests in contracts.* Particulars of any significant contract in which the company is involved and in which a director of the company has a material interest.

The annual report must also include a statement by the directors that the business is a going concern, together with any supporting assumptions or qualifications.

UKLA *requirements for disclosure relating to directors' remuneration*

Company law requires the directors of UK listed companies to include a Directors' Remuneration Report in their annual reports (see Appendix 7). This information includes:

- a statement of the company's policy on executive directors' remuneration, such as basic pay, performance-related bonuses, share options and retirement benefits;

- details of each director's remuneration package, including basic salary and fees, the estimated value of benefits in kind, annual bonuses, deferred bonuses;

- information on share options, for each director by name and details of any long-term incentive schemes, other than share options.

The question of directors' remuneration has become the subject of considerable scrutiny not only by shareholders but also by the general public. 'Fat cat pay' makes front page news, and 'Rewards for failure' was the title of a DTI consultation on the subject. Some shareholders however are now saying that perhaps the public uproar has gone too far. They are worried that talent is not rewarded and that talent in certain sectors is lost overseas or to the private market.

This remains a difficult and sensitive issue. Many companies believe that this is the most difficult part of the report to produce in a way which will be satisfactory to all shareholders.

The following factors are some of those which shareholders are most likely to consider in assessing a company's remuneration policy:

- the overall quality of disclosure;

- comparability;

- consultation with shareholders;

- service contracts;

- significant changes in remuneration packages;

- annual bonus arrangements;
- structure of share schemes;
- adequacy of performance linkage;
- non-standard pension arrangements;
- dilution.

Corporate governance

The annual report of a full listed company must also contain a detailed statement setting out how the company has applied the recommendations in the Combined Code and, where it has failed to do so, giving the reasons for its non-compliance.

It is this area which has proved difficult for some companies and where there is still some distance between shareholder expectations and the statements made by directors.

In most instances it is a question of focus. For example, Principle C2 of the Combined Code D.2.1 requires the company to maintain a sound system of internal controls to safeguard shareholders' investments and the company's assets. shareholders do not wish simply to be told that such a system exists: they wish to know how it is applied, what are the processes surrounding it, and how effective it is in practice.

Similarly Code Provision 3.4 requires a statement from the audit committee setting out its role and responsibilities and the actions taken by the committee to discharge those responsibilities. This might usefully be achieved by summarising the minutes of committee meetings during the year.

The shareholder view is generally that company reporting should go beyond a statement of procedures, and should explain in a meaningful way the risks facing the business, and the controls in place to mitigate those risks.

The directors should talk to their shareholders and try to understand what they are looking for. Similarly, if shareholders do not like what they see or hear they should be prepared to enter into open dialogue with the company before embarking on a course of public criticism.

Schedule C of the Combined Code sets out the provisions of the Code that must be addressed in the annual report.

As with many elements of the annual report, on matters related to corporate governance and risk management the directors should state not only how the company approaches such issues, but also why it takes that approach.

Areas of corporate governance where companies can set themselves apart from their competitors will include:

- assessment of business risks, and statement of controls in place to mitigate those risks;

- a statement of performance evaluation – how the performance of the board, its committees and individual directors has been assessed;
- disclosure of a policy regarding on engagement of the auditor to perform non-audit work;
- discussion of bonus allotments in the light of performance targets and policy on performance-related pay;
- description of what skills were missing from the board where there is a new appointment, and of why the new director is the right person for the job.

Social, environmental and ethical reporting

Whilst there are currently no statutory requirements for companies to report on their approach to social or environmental issues, public concern regarding corporate social responsibility has grown to a point where this is now part of the standard disclosure expected by shareholders.

The level of disclosure will, of course, depend on the nature of the company's business, but the ABI has published some general guidelines setting out the sort of information institutional shareholders expect.

The guidelines recommend that the annual report should:

- include information on social, environmental and ethical-related risks and opportunities that may significantly affect the company's short and long-term value, and how they might impact on the business;
- describe the company's policies and procedures for managing risks to short and long-term value arising from SEE matters. If the annual report and accounts states that the company has no such policies and procedures, the board should provide reasons for their absence;
- include information about the extent to which the company has complied with its policies and procedures for managing risks arising from SEE matters;
- describe the procedures for verification of SEE disclosures. The verification procedure should be such as to achieve a reasonable level of credibility.

The guidelines also recommend that companies consider the following questions in compiling their report:

- Has the company made any reference to social, environmental and ethical matters? If so, does the board take these regularly into account?
- Has the company identified and assessed significant risks and opportunities affecting its long and short-term value arising from its handling of SEE matters?

- Does the company state that it has adequate information for identification and assessment?
- Are systems in place to manage the SEE risks?
- Are any remuneration incentives relating to the handling of SEE risks included in risk management systems?
- Does directors' training include SEE matters?
- Does the company disclose significant short and long-term risks and opportunities arising from SEE issues?
- Are policies for managing risks to the company's value described?
- Are procedures for managing risk described? If not, are reasons for non-disclosure given?
- Does the company report on the extent of its compliance with its policies and procedures?
- Are verification procedures described?

The operating and financial review and the business review

There has been considerable confusion surrounding the implementation of the Operating and Financial Review (OFR). In the latter half of 2005, many companies had been preparing to publish their first OFR, which was at the time mandatory for those listed companies reporting on accounting periods commencing on or after 1 April 2005.

However at the end of 2005, the Government announced its decision to remove the statutory requirement on quoted companies to publish an OFR. This was replaced with a requirement to provide a Business Review in line with the EU Accounts Modernisation Directive, which became effective from 12 January 2006.

The Business Review retains the emphasis on narrative reporting central to the OFR, but is generally less prescriptive. Key differences between the OFR and the Business Review are:

- *Trends and forward-looking statements* – this way was a mandatory requirement for the OFR, but only to be included 'where necessary' in the business review. However, the Business Review does require an indication '…of likely future developments in the business of the company'.
- *The principal risks and uncertainties* – to be reported on 'where necessary' in the business review.

- *Key performance indicators* – information on environmental, employee, social and community matters should be included 'where necessary' and this should be complemented by KPIs. However, medium-sized companies are not required to include non-financial KPIs.

- *Auditors* – must state whether or not the information contained in the business review is consistent with that in the accounts (as for the OFR). However, auditors are not required to raise any issues that they have observed in the performance of their work that are inconsistent with information given in the business review. In practice, they may well choose to identify any such instances to protect their own reputations.

Early indications are that many companies still intend to go ahead with an OFR-style report, and that this may become the industry accepted best practice over the next few years. We have therefore included the key content for an OFR set out by the Accountacy Standards Board (ASB) in its Reporting Statement 'The Operating and Financial Review'. Companies should, of course, monitor any subsequent guidance published by the DTI on this subject.

ASB reporting statement

Background

In 1993, the Accounting Standards Board issued its 'Operating Financial Review'; a reporting framework for directors, based on prevailing best practice at the time. This was revised in January 2003 to reflect improved reporting practices by listed and quoted companies.

The Statement was intended to have 'persuasive rather than mandatory force' and was recommended by the Financial Reporting Council, the Hundred Group of Finance Directors and the London Stock Exchange.

In 2004 this statement formed the basis of Draft Regulations under s. 257 of the Companies Act 1985 introducing a statutory Operating and Financial Review (OFR) for quoted companies. The OFR was intended to extend the fair review of the company's business required in the Directors' Report under the EU Accounts Modernisation Directive.

In January 2006, following the change in the law, the ASB reissued the standard as a Reporting Statement 'The Operating and Financial Review', a statement of best practice on the OFR. This statement can be downloaded from the ASB's website: www.frc.org.uk/asb/publications/documents.cfm.

The objectives and key content of the OFR

The objective of the OFR is to reflect the directors' view of the business and to provide a 'balanced and comprehensive analysis, consistent with the size and complexity of the business', of:

- the development and performance of the business of the entity during the financial year;
- the position of the entity at the end of the year;
- the main trends and factors underlying the development, performance and position of the business of the entity during the financial year; and
- the main trends and factors which are likely to affect the entity's future development, performance and position.

The ASB's framework is intended to be adopted to suit the particular circumstances of each company, for example:

- the industry or industries in which it operates;
- the range of products, services or processes it offers;
- the geographical markets that it serves.

The framework sets out the key content that should be addressed by the OFR:

- the nature, objectives and strategies of the business;
- current and future development and performance;
- resources;
- principal risks and uncertainties;
- relationships;
- financial position;
- key performance indicators (KPIs).

KPIs are defined in the standard, but a rough rule of thumb is that KPIs are the key ratios, figures or indicators that the board uses to manage and drive the business. A KPI might be a key figure from the regular management accounts, although it need not necessarily be a financial measure.

Some practical considerations in producing the annual report

Timing, coordination, contingency

The most common advice given to anyone planning an annual report is to allow time at the end of the process for quality control. An annual report containing errors gives a bad impression of the company. The planning and coordination involved is immense, and the process can rarely be relied upon to proceed smoothly.

Company secretaries tell us of critical meetings involving the chairman of the audit committee which have to be rescheduled at the last moment as a result of a diary clash, and of photographs selected for the report cover which, on closer inspection, turn out to be totally inappropriate for the purpose. There will always be factors which are beyond the control of the board and the company secretary and, with the best planning, there is always the possibility of last-minute hitches.

Dissemination of the annual report

It is not currently a regulatory requirement that companies should put the annual report on their corporate website but it is considered best practice to do so. This should ideally be in a pdf format to allow book-marking and ease of navigation around the document, but also to safeguard the integrity of any financial information published on the website.

It is also considered best practice to include any supporting analyst presentations on the web-site, together with related speakers' notes so that this information is available to all shareholders.

CONCLUSION

- The annual report serves many purposes and many different audiences.

- It is first and foremost a legal and regulatory requirement, but it is also potentially a powerful marketing and communications tool. It takes a huge amount of company time and effort to produce, so the company should derive corresponding benefits from it. It is an opportunity to tell a compelling story about the company – its talent, its successes, its strengths, its plans and its potential.

CHAPTER 8

The Annual General Meeting

KEY ISSUES

- The importance of the AGM in a company's annual calendar should not be underestimated and the opportunity to communicate effectively with shareholders should not be missed
- Preparation is always key for successful AGMs, be it in relation to administrative preparation or for anticipating problematic AGMs. This includes:
  - The venue
  - The agenda
  - Notice of the meeting
  - The key players
  - Conduct of the meeting, including anticipation of shareholder questions and preparation of a chairman's script.

Introduction

A company has various means of communicating with its shareholders during a financial year, whether by its annual or interim report, by circular or by public announcements, but the annual general meeting (AGM) remains the one meeting which a company is generally required to hold during each financial year with its shareholders.

As such, the AGM should not be seen solely as a legal requirement but also a forum for the board to engage with shareholders on the company's performance and for shareholders to raise questions with the board about any issues they may have regarding the company, its business and its management. Although many formal reviews by committees and by commentators point to the fact that the AGM continues to be an opportunity missed, the Revised Code underlines the importance which the AGM should have by emphasising that the board 'should use the AGM to communicate with investors and to encourage their participation'.

What is not disputed is that considerable effort is required by a company to ensure that the AGM is both effective and complies with all current requirements. This chapter aims to set out those requirements for companies registered in England and Wales, to highlight potential problems that may arise and to make practical suggestions to ensure the AGM passes smoothly and efficiently.

CHECKLIST   Core requirements when planning an AGM

When planning for an AGM the following fundamental requirements should be borne in mind:

- With the exception of private companies whose members have passed an elective resolution dispensing with the requirement to hold AGMs, every company must hold an AGM in each calendar year. CA 1985, s. 366(1).

- AGMs should not be more than 15 months apart. CA 1985, s. 366(3).

- For a company which has been recently incorporated, its first AGM must be held within 18 months of the date of its incorporation. CA 1985, s. 366(2).

- The notice convening an AGM must specify the meeting to be an AGM. CA 1985, s. 366(1) and Table A, reg 38.

- Although the required statutory notice period given to shareholders by the company of the AGM is 21 clear days, the Revised Code provides that, for listed companies, the notice and related papers should be sent to shareholders at least 20 working days before the meeting. CA 1985, s. 369(1) (a) and the Revised Code Section 1, paragraph D.2.4 respectively.

- The notice must state the time and place at which the AGM is to be held.

- The notice must state with reasonable prominence that a member entitled to attend and vote at the meeting has the right to appoint a proxy, or, where it is allowed, one or more proxies, to attend and vote instead of himself and that such proxy need not be a member of the company. CA 1985, s. 372(3).

- For listed companies, all directors should attend the AGM (Revised Code, section 1, paragraph D.2.3) and the chairmen of the nomination, remuneration and audit committees should be available to answer questions. Revised Code, section 1, paragraph D.2.3.

- For listed companies, the service contracts of directors and the terms and conditions of appointment of non-executive directors must be made available for inspection by any person at the place of the AGM for at least 15 minutes prior to the AGM and during the meeting itself.

- The register of directors' interests must be produced at the commencement of the AGM and should remain open and accessible during the continuance of the meeting to any person attending the meeting. CA 1985, s. 325(5) and CA 1985, Sch 13, Part IV, para 29.

- Although there is no specific requirement that the accounts are laid before the members at an AGM, as opposed to an extraordinary general meeting, the customary practice is that the AGM is the forum which is used.

- A quorum of members must be present at the time when the meeting proceeds to business.

  If a company fails to hold an AGM in accordance with the statutory requirements, the company and every officer in default will be liable to a fine. CA 1985, s. 366(4).

  For a more detailed examination of best practice suggestions of ICSA, the reader is referred to 'A Guide to Best Practice for Annual General Meetings' published by the ICSA.

Preliminary preparation

As a general rule, companies tend to have their AGMs at or around the same time of year each year, unless there is a specific reason for change, such as a change in accounting reference date or difficulties in getting the accounts signed off by the auditors. This means it should be possible for all those concerned with the preparation for, and implementation of, the AGM to have sufficient time to plan correctly.

The following issues should initially be considered:

- venue availability;
- avoiding clashes of dates with other companies' AGMs in the same sector;
- suitable input from the company's professional advisers, if appropriate, should be built into the timetable and attendance of key advisors at the AGM requested in advance;
- the availability of all directors of the company on the proposed date of the AGM;
- consideration of likely shareholder questions which may be asked; and
- if it is envisaged that the AGM may be controversial, consideration should be given to what security arrangements are necessary.

Once a date and time has been set, it is important to ensure that all other likely attendees are given sufficient warning. However, since the accounts often drive the timetable, the planning begins during the audit process itself.

Agenda

The starting point for a company when deciding upon the agenda for its AGM is its articles of association, since the Companies Act 1985 does not set out any provisions as to what business should occur at the AGM. Table A is now silent on this issue, compared with the Companies Act 1948 edition of Table A which distinguished between ordinary and special business.

Under Art 52 of the 1948 edition of Table A, ordinary business constituted the declaration of a dividend, the consideration of the company's accounts, balance sheets and the reports of the directors and auditors, the election of directors in the place of those retiring, the appointment of auditors and the fixing of auditors' remuneration.

Although the current edition of Table A merely requires the general nature of the AGM business to be identified, the distinction between ordinary and special business remains under common practice.

Ordinary business

Ordinary business usually constitutes the following:

- consideration of the directors' report and the accounts;
- approval of a final dividend (if any) recommended by the board;
- re-election of those directors who are retiring by rotation;
- appointment of the auditors;
- authorisation of the directors to fix the auditors' remuneration.

For listed companies, the Directors' Remuneration Report Regulations 2002 require the following resolution to be added:

- to approve the directors' remuneration report for the immediately preceding financial year end.

Report and accounts

Although there is no specific requirement that the company's annual report and accounts need to be laid before the members of the company in AGM, as opposed to at any other meeting of the members, in practice that is generally the case and as a result AGMs are timed to enable those accounts to be so laid. The accounts do not need to be read or accepted. The resolution often provides that they be 'received'.

Dividend payment

If a dividend is to be paid, shareholder approval is usually sought for the declaration of a final dividend at the AGM. The meeting may reduce the dividend recommended by the directors, but it may not increase it.

Directors retiring by rotation

If a company's articles of association provide that directors shall retire from office by rotation, then such retirement and, if appropriate, re-appointment is usually undertaken at the AGM. Table A provides that all directors shall retire from office at the company's first AGM and at subsequent AGMs one-third, or a number nearest to one-third, of the directors who are subject to retirement by rotation shall so retire. The directors to retire by rotation are those that have been in office longest since their last appointment or re-appointment.

Although s. 292 of the Companies Act 1985 envisages that multiple appointments of directors of public companies may be made under a single resolution if a resolution that it shall be so made has first been agreed to by the meeting without any vote against, the provisions of the Revised Code that separate resolutions be used at AGMs for each sub-stantially separate issue is the better practice. Consequently, each appointment or re-appointment should be made by separate resolution.

Appointment of auditors

Every public company, and every private company which has not elected to dispense with the laying of accounts, shall, at each general meeting at which accounts are laid, appoint auditors to hold office from the conclusion of that meeting until the conclu-sion of the next general meeting at which accounts are laid. Consequently auditors are usually appointed from one AGM to the next.

Section 390A of the Companies Act 1985 provides that the remuneration of auditors appointed by the company in general meeting shall be fixed by the company in general meeting or in such manner as the company in general meeting shall determine. The normal procedure is for the proposed resolution to resolve that the directors should fix the auditors' remuneration.

Directors' remuneration report

Finally, for listed companies, the Directors' Remuneration Report Regulations 2002 introduced a compulsory annual shareholders' vote on directors' remuneration pack-ages at the meeting before which the company's accounts for the relevant financial year are laid. The company is required to:

- prepare and publish a report on directors' remuneration for each financial year. The report, parts of which must be reported on by the company's auditors, must disclose details of, amongst other things, the remuneration package of each individual direc-tor, and must be sent to shareholders with the notice of the AGM; and

- lay the report before shareholders at the company's AGM, and to put the report (notably, not the company's remuneration policy, or the remuneration packages of the individual directors) to the vote of shareholders.

Failure to comply with the regulations results in every director committing an offence and as such, liable to a fine.

It should be noted, however, that the shareholders' vote is only advisory — no entitle ment of a person to remuneration is conditional upon the resolution being passed. Nevertheless, a vote against the remuneration report (or, for that matter, shareholder disapproval that falls short of defeating the resolution) can produce significant adverse publicity.

Special business

Where a company's articles of association distinguish between ordinary and special business, all AGM business which is not specifically defined as ordinary business will constitute special business.

Unlike ordinary business, which may be transacted at the meeting irrespective of whether it is referred to in the notice of AGM, special business must be set out in full in the notice.

Special business often entails matters for which the company seeks specific authorisation from shareholders to undertake, such as a special resolution to disapply statutory pre-emption rights on an issue of shares for cash or an ordinary resolution authorising the directors to allot a specified number of shares or to make a political donation.

In respect of special business, it is considered best practice for a company to include an explanation of the resolutions proposed as special business, since the text of the resolutions are often in legalistic language. Such explanation should be in plain English and should explain fully the context, purpose and effect of each resolution. This is in fact a requirement for a listed company, which must send out an explanatory circular with any notice of a meeting that includes any business other than routine business at an AGM. Where the special business is to be considered at or on the same day as the AGM, the explanation may be included in the directors' report and in practice that is the approach taken, with the AGM notice usually incorporated into the back of the company's annual report and accounts.

Also for listed companies, the Revised Code provides that a company 'should propose a separate resolution at the AGM on each substantially separate issue and should in particular propose a resolution at the AGM relating to the report and accounts'. However, this requirement is arguably good practice for any company, irrespective of whether it is listed.

Shareholder resolutions

In addition to the resolutions constituting ordinary and special business which the company will propose in the agenda of the AGM, the notice of meeting must also include any resolutions that are submitted by shareholders. One hundred or more members with shares on which an average of not less than £100 has been paid up, or members with 5% or more of the total voting rights, can require a company to circulate a resolution for discussion at the company's AGM.

Such shareholders may also require the company to circulate a statement of no more than 1,000 words with respect to the matter referred to in the proposed resolution or business to be dealt with at that general meeting.

The company must circulate such a resolution or statement either at the same time that notice of the meeting is given or, if that is not practicable, as soon as practical thereafter.

The costs of circulating the resolution or statement will be borne by the member, unless the company resolves otherwise.

Notice

Entitlement to notice

Every member of the company is entitled to notice of a general meeting unless the company's articles provide otherwise. Table A provides that notice must be given to all members and to all persons entitled on the death or bankruptcy of a member, but notice is not required to be given to a member who does not have a registered address in the United Kingdom and has not given the company an address within the United Kingdom where notice may be sent.

Even if a shareholder does not have the right to vote, unless the company's articles of association provide otherwise, that shareholder must be given notice of the AGM.

It should not be forgotten that the company's directors and auditors must also receive notice of the AGM.

If the company is listed on the Official List of the UK Listing Authority, then the company must forward two copies of the notice to the UK Listing Authority at the same time as the notice issued. If the company is listed on AIM, then three copies of such notice should be sent to the London Stock Exchange.

Failure to give notice

If the company fails to give notice to all those entitled to receive it, such failure will, in the absence of provision to the contrary in the company's articles of association, invalidate the meeting. However, Table A provides that the accidental omission to give notice of a meeting to, or the non-receipt of notice of a meeting by, any person entitled to receive notice shall not invalidate the proceedings at that meeting.

Content of notice

The notice convening an AGM must specify the meeting to be an AGM and must state the time and place at which the AGM is to be held.

The notice must state with reasonable prominence that a member entitled to attend and vote at the meeting has the right to appoint a proxy, or, where it is allowed, one or more proxies, to attend and vote instead of himself and that such proxy need not be a member of the company.

Table A provides that the notice should set out the general nature of the business to be transacted at the AGM. However, for extraordinary or special resolutions, the notice must state the intention to propose a resolution as an extraordinary or special resolution and it must set out the text or the entire substance of such resolution.

The Revised Code provides that companies should propose a separate resolution for each substantially separate issue so that shareholders can vote separately on each proposal.

Length of notice

Although the required statutory notice period given to shareholders by the company of the AGM is 21 clear days (i.e. excluding the date of the notice and the date of the meeting), the Revised Code provides that, for listed companies, the notice and related papers should be sent to shareholders at least 20 working days before the meeting.

The company's articles of association should be checked to ascertain the deemed time that notice is given if the notice is sent by post. Table A provides that the notice is deemed to be given 48 hours after it is posted or sent electronically.

Although unlikely to be relevant to listed companies, or indeed companies with a wide shareholder base, it is possible for an AGM to be held on short notice provided that all members entitled to attend and vote at it agree to that.

Method of giving notice

The articles of association of a company will set out the method by which the notice may be given. Table A (as amended by the Companies Act 1985 (Electronic Communications Order) 2000) provides that notice may be served personally or by post to the member's registered address or by electronic communication to an address notified to the company by the member.

For notice by electronic communication, both the company and the member must have agreed that notices of meetings may be given to that person electronically or by publication on the company's website and such member has been sent the notice electronically or has been notified of the publication of the notice on the company's website, where it may be accessed and how it may be accessed.

For further details of electronic communication with shareholders, the reader is referred to ICSA's best practice guide entitled '*Electronic Communications Order 2000 – ICSA's Guide to Recommended Best Practice*', as updated in 2001.

The players

Inevitably the company secretary will be the person taking the lead in preparing for an AGM, but on the day the chairman will be the primary person responsible for the successful conduct of the AGM. Other important players on the day will be the respective chairmen of the remuneration, nomination and audit committees, the other directors of the company, the auditors and the shareholders themselves.

Company secretary

One key function of a company secretary is to undertake all the practical preparations for the AGM. This not only includes arranging for the notice to be circulated in a timely and efficient manner to all those entitled to receive it, but will also include arranging for an appropriate venue to be booked and ensuring that the chairman is fully prepared for meeting.

The company secretary will need to liaise with external professional advisers, such as the auditors and lawyers, to ensure that they provide their respective input to the AGM as and when required.

The typical matters which the company secretary will need to have in mind are as follows:

- preparing the agenda;
- preparing the notice of AGM;
- ensuring the notice is sent out, allowing for the requisite period of notice, to all those entitled to receive it;
- booking an appropriate venue;
- arranging for suitable catering;
- ensuring that suitable audio and visual support is available;
- drafting the chairman's script;
- ensuring that proxies are correctly counted, be it by the secretary or by liaising with the registrars;
- ensuring that the registrars are present so that a poll (if demanded) can be easily conducted;
- preparing suitable replies to anticipated shareholder questions;
- collating a file of relevant information for the chairman to have to hand during the meeting.

The chairman

Unless the company's articles of association provide otherwise, the chairman of the board of directors will generally be the chairman of any general meeting. If the articles do not provide for the appointment of a chairman, the members present may elect any member present. However, the articles usually provide that the chairman of the board of directors shall be the chairman at general meetings.

If the chairman is not present within a designated time, or if he is unwilling to act, the directors are usually permitted to choose one of their number to act if willing. Failing that, the members may choose any member present to be chairman.

The duties and powers of the chairman include the following:

- determining that the meeting is properly constituted and that a quorum is present;
- ensuring that the meeting is conducted in an efficient manner and in accordance with the law and the company's articles of association;
- if possible, ensuring that all opinions are given a fair hearing and that the views of the meeting are ascertained;
- accepting all legitimate resolutions and amendments;
- controlling the meeting;
- adjourning the meeting;
- arrangements for the taking of a poll;
- receiving or rejecting proxies;
- giving a casting vote;
- declaring the results of voting.

Chairmen of the remuneration, nomination and audit committees

For listed companies, the chairmen of the nomination, remuneration and audit committees should be available to answer questions, as provided for by the Revised Code.

The directors

For listed companies, all directors should attend the AGM, but it should be considered good practice for all directors of private companies with a large shareholder base to be present also.

The auditors

In addition to the auditor's entitlement to receive notice of and attend the AGM, the auditors are entitled to be heard on any part of the business of the meeting which concerns them.

The registrars

If a company has appointed registrars then it is advisable that they are present so that a poll (if demanded) can be easily conducted.

The shareholders

As previously indicated, the Revised Code highlights the importance of the AGM to the company in communicating with shareholders, and as such the shareholders themselves must be seen as principal players at an AGM. They will be the ones, subject to the articles of association, who are entitled to attend, speak and vote. Since the Revised Code also discusses encouraging their participation, the shareholders' willingness to become involved will often be the other required component for a successful AGM, in addition to a meeting which is well presented by the company's directors.

The position of institutional shareholders has recently come under a greater spotlight in the context of shareholder activism. The UK government commissioned Paul Myners in the 2000 Budget 'to investigate whether there were factors distorting institutional investment in the UK, resulting in inefficiency and inflexibility in capital markets'. Although Mr Myners chose not to go down the route of an express statutory duty as has been seen in the United States (e.g. the Employment Retirement Income Security Act 1974 (ERISA)), in his report 'Institutional Investment in the United Kingdom: A review' published on 6 March 2001, he suggested that the 'beneficial owners should be responsible for ensuring that there is a clear chain of responsibility for voting their shares in the companies that they own'. Further 'each participant should be clearly accountable to those on whose behalf they act and should be required to explain how they have discharged their obligations with regard to voting'.

Proxies

Any shareholder who is entitled to attend and vote at a meeting may appoint a proxy, who need not be a member. This right must be communicated to the member in reasonable prominence in the notice convening the meeting.

A proxy may attend and vote on a poll and, in the case of a private company, a proxy may also speak at the meeting.

A shareholder may appoint more than one proxy to attend the same meeting and appointing a proxy does not prevent that shareholder from attending and voting in person at the AGM. A shareholder may appoint a proxy by electronic communication sent to such address as provided for by the company.

A company's articles of association often require that proxy forms must be lodged with the company within a specified period of time before the time of commencement of the meeting. Table A provides that this is not less than 48 hours before the time for holding the meeting, but it should be noted that s. 372(5) of the Companies Act 1985 provides that the articles of association of the company may not extend the time for lodgement to a time more than 48 hours before the time of the meeting, otherwise the provision is void.

Although a proxy does not have the right to speak at a public company meeting, in practice, the chairman often permits a proxy to speak. Irrespective of law and practice, the chairman must ensure he is consistent in how he treats proxies.

For listed companies, a two-way proxy form must be sent with the notice of AGM to all those members entitled to vote at the meeting, to enable those members to direct the proxy to vote for or against each resolution.

Corporate representatives

A corporation which is a shareholder may appoint an individual to act on its behalf at general meetings. The individual's appointment must be authorised by a resolution of the corporation's directors or other governing body. The individual is entitled to exercise the same powers on behalf of the corporation as that corporation could exercise if it were an individual shareholder.

Others

Although the above persons are strictly the only persons entitled to attend a company's AGM, other categories of individual are likely to want to attend, particularly with larger quoted companies. Such categories include journalists, stockbrokers and general members of the public.

The question of whether such individuals may attend falls to be decided by the chairman with the agreement of persons entitled to be present (*Carruth* v *ICI* [1937] AC 707). The basis of such decision should be that priority must be given to the members of the company and if a potentially disruptive meeting is envisaged, it may be prudent to adopt a strict approach.

Conduct of meeting

Commencement of meeting

If a quorum is present, the chairman should aim to start the meeting on the time allocated for in the notice. However, this may not always be possible if, for example, there have been problems in members gaining admission due to security measures. In such a situation, the chairman will need to manage expectations and also ensure that all member's interests are considered equally.

The quorum for general meetings of a company is usually two members present in person or by proxy, who are entitled to vote upon the business to be transacted. However, a prior review of a company's articles of association is required to understand both this and what is to happen if a quorum is not present within the specified time after the time provided for the meeting to commence.

Order of business

The chairman should ensure that the meeting is informed as to the order in which business is to be transacted. An AGM normally opens with a presentation by the chairman about the company, and then will progress on to the formal business set out in the notice.

However, consideration should be given as to any element of the business of the AGM which may be problematic, since it may be prudent to consider that later on in the meeting to ensure that the non-contentious business passes without incident.

Discussion, debate and questions

Other than in circumstances where it is believed in good faith that disclosure would not be in the interests of the company or where information is price sensitive, the general approach to shareholders' questions and discussion should be one of openness. Indeed, for listed companies, the Revised Code underlines the sprit of cooperation which should be demonstrated at the AGM and provides that the chairman should ensure that the chairmen of the audit, remuneration and nomination committees are available to answer questions and that all directors are present.

If the chairman declines to answer a question on the basis that, say, it is not in the company's best interest to answer, he should give good reason for doing so, to manage shareholder expectations.

The chairman must permit debate on the resolutions under discussion and he cannot simply obstruct this from happening. He has a duty to ascertain all the views of the meeting, if possible.

However, the chairman must balance having full discussion with keeping discussion relevant to the proposed business and keeping the AGM efficient and effective. This entails having to take a view of when to end discussion on one matter (and, if relevant, take a vote) and then move to the next item of business.

It should be noted that it has become general practice to permit more wide-ranging discussion of the business activities of the company when the resolution proposing adopting the company's annual report and accounts is considered. Consequently, the chairman should be more willing to permit such discussion on this form of resolution.

Amendments

The chairman must take great care when deciding upon whether to accept or reject a proposed amendment to a resolution set out in the notice, since a mistake will result in the resolution which is passed being invalid, even if he or she acted in good faith (e.g. *Henderson v Bank of Australasia* (1890) 45 ChD 330).

An amendment may be validly proposed to an ordinary resolution if:

- it is within the scope of the resolution set out in the notice convening the meeting;
- it is no more onerous on the company than the resolution set out in the notice;
- it does not have the effect of negating the original proposed resolution.

The crucial test is whether the amendment would affect a shareholder's decision as to whether to attend the AGM or not.

Other grounds for rejecting a proposed amendment are if it tries to re-open previously decided issues or if the proposed amendment is obstructive or irrelevant.

A special or extraordinary resolution may only be amended in very limited circumstances (see *Re Moorgate Mercantile Holdings Ltd* [1890] 1 All ER 40). It is a statutory requirement that at least 21 days' notice must have been given of a special resolution, specifying the intention to propose 'the resolution' as such.

The company's articles of association may also make specific provision as to amendments and this has the benefit of giving more certainty to the chairman as to the decision he will need to make.

When considering an amendment, the chairman should, if he deems it possible to put the proposed amendment to the vote, take the following course:

- put the proposal to the meeting as to whether the amendment should be accepted or not;
- assuming the amendment is voted to be put, then put the amended resolution to the vote;
- if the amended resolution is rejected, put the original resolution to the vote.

Voting – show of hands

Subject to any contrary provision in a company's articles of association, each resolution put to the vote at the AGM will be decided by a show of hands unless a poll is demanded. Only shareholders present in person are entitled to vote on a show of hands, unless the articles provide otherwise.

A body corporate present by a duly authorised representative is the equivalent of a shareholder present in person and may vote on a show of hands. Proxies are not entitled to vote on a show of hands unless the articles provide otherwise.

On a show of hands, every ordinary share carries one vote. However, in practice and contrary to voting on a poll, on a show of hands each shareholder present in person has one vote regardless of the number of shares held by him.

If the voting is exactly equal, usually the chairman will have a casting vote in addition to any other vote he may have.

A declaration by the chairman of the result of the show of hands is conclusive evidence of the fact without proof of the number or proportion of the votes in favour or against the resolution. Such a decision is only ever likely to be investigated if there was evidence of fraud or manifest error.

For listed companies the Revised Code requires the company to count all proxy votes and, except where a poll is called, to indicate the level of proxies lodged on each resolution and the balance for and against the resolution, after it has been dealt with on a show of hands. The company should also indicate the number of abstentions and should ensure that votes cast are properly received and recorded.

The announcement of the level of proxies lodged may be dealt with as follows:

- The chairman declares the proxy count after each resolution;
- The proxy count is displayed by slide projection after each resolution; or
- The chairman announces that the proxy counts for all resolutions will be available for inspection at the end of the meeting.

The reader is also referred to ICSA's guidance note entitled 'Disclosing Proxy Votes'.

Voting – on a poll

Although the articles of association of a company determine who has the right to demand a poll, the Companies Act 1985 provides that the articles must at least provide for the following:

- five members present in person or by proxy and entitled to vote; or
- any member or members present in person or by proxy with either not less than one-tenth of the total voting rights or not less than one-tenth of the total sum paid up on all shares giving rights to attend and vote.

Table A also permits a poll to be demanded by the chairman and by two members rather than five.

On each resolution upon which a poll is demanded, every ordinary shareholder present in person or by proxy has one vote for every ordinary share held.

The chairman will often be appointed proxy. On a poll, the chairman's votes can be dealt with by the secretary providing him with two correctly completed voting cards for signature:

- one will be marked to show a vote in favour 'for self and ordinary shareholders for whom I am a proxy except where the form of proxy requests a vote against';
- the other will show a vote against 'only for those ordinary shareholders for whom I am a proxy where the form of proxy requests a vote against'.

A poll demanded on the election of a chairman or on a question of adjournment must be taken straight away. However, a poll on any other question can be taken either immediately or at any time, place and date within the next thirty days directed by the chairman.

The reader is also referred to ICSA's guidance notes entitled 'Polls – Chairman's Obligations' (Reference Number 020228) and 'Voting At General Meetings' (the latter being reproduced in Appendix 8).

Adjournment

A meeting may be automatically adjourned pursuant to the company's articles of association if the quorum is not present within a specified time. The meeting stands adjourned to a time, place and date, within a specified period determined by either the articles of association or the chairman.

In relation to other adjournments, the chairman must adjourn a meeting if he is requested to do so by the meeting or he may adjourn a meeting with the consent of that meeting. Similarly the company's articles of association may make specific provision for other circumstances in which the chairman may adjourn the meeting.

No business can be transacted at the adjourned meeting other than business which could properly have been transacted at the original meeting.

CHECKLIST   Tips for problem meetings

1   Consider whether security is required and if so, how visible it should be.
2   Consider what issues are likely to be problematic and arrange the order of business around them.
3   Prepare thoroughly for anticipated questions.
4   Ensure that the company's lawyers are fully briefed and suitably prepared.
5   Ensure that the chairman is briefed in how to manage difficult shareholders, particularly regarding those matters he is expected to adjudicate on, e.g. when to reject proposed amendments to resolutions.

Post-meeting business

Minutes of the AGM must be kept and they should be signed by the chairman and placed in the company's minute book. Preparation of the minutes is usually undertaken by the company secretary or a member of the legal team, or failing that, by the company's professional advisers, such as its lawyers.

If special resolutions have been proposed and passed, then they will require notification to the Registrar of Companies. Similarly, certain ordinary resolutions will also require notification.

Certain other matters of housekeeping should also be considered, e.g. up-dating the company's investor relations website to ensure that the outcome of the AGM is reported and that the resolutions passed are noted.

CONCLUSION

- The Combined Code emphasises that companies should view the AGM as a constructive opportunity for communication with shareholders, and with private investors in particular.
- Early planning and thorough preparation by the company secretary is essential to ensure that a company's AGM not only complies with relevant legal, regulatory and best practice requirements but is also a positive occasion for a company's board of directors to deliver the correct messages to its shareholders.

Investor management

Introduction

This chapter focuses on the relationship between investors and companies whose share capital is traded publicly. However, many of the fundamental principles apply equally to those companies who are backed by private capital providers, namely venture capitalists and business angels.

High profile corporate failures have increased the pressure for companies to provide transparent information in a timely manner, whilst pressures on investors to exercise their voting rights and to engage with companies proactively rather than reactively have raised the tempo and the stakes within the investor relations arena.

What are investor relations?

Managing shareholders is part of the evolving discipline of investor relations, a multifaceted role combining financial, communication, marketing and business acumen skills. Investor relations (IR), encompasses a broad range of activities that involve on one level direct engagement with both existing and potential investors, whilst simultaneously engaging indirectly with a diverse range of key influencers. Shareholder relationship management is further challenged by the rare opportunities that companies have to be close to their investors (for fear of making them insiders), the intermediaries that come between the company and the investor to form capital markets that are almost perfect from an economist's perspective, and the dislocation between investor and company that occurs through the operation of secondary markets to trade ownership rights (shares/stock) in the company.

From a company's perspective, it will be important to encourage a realistic market value, as this will assist in lowering its weighted average cost of capital, whilst also protecting it from a takeover on unfavourable terms and therefore disadvantaging incumbent shareholders. This is likely to be best achieved by ensuring that a proactive rather than reactive investor engagement plan is put into place to ensure the company's market value is sustainable and not subject to the whims and vagaries of a misinformed market place. This in turn will help create healthy liquidity levels (the ease with which investors can buy and sell shares) and ensure that investor appetite is on demand for the stock rather than its supply.

Together these factors assist in creating positive signals about the current and likely future performance of the company. Such support for the company should be further translated from the secondary market to the primary market should the company find itself in a position where it needs to raise/access future capital – be it equity or debt. Hopefully, such situations will arise for positive reasons rather than because the company is in distress. However, even within a distressed situation, those companies who have a track record of positively engaging with investors and ensuring that they are constantly informed of material developments within the business will be in a stronger position to win the hearts, minds and wallets of its investor base.

The ultimate goal of any shareholder relationship activity is to ensure investors and potential investors are put into a position where they can make informed investment decisions – be it to buy for the first time or to increase, hold or sell out of their position. In a market both buyers and sellers are necessary otherwise trade could not take place – the trick is to ensure that a company fosters an investor climate where the market pressure is more on the buyer than the seller. Where sellers have the upper hand, an effective and sustainable IR strategy will be one that stems the flow of sellers quickly and stabilises the market for its shares. The difficulty however is that a company has little control of the market and market sentiment may ebb and flow on many other external factors including the outlook for the wider economy, attitudes towards other players in the sector or simply time of the month. This is where it is important to build dialogue (not one-way communication flows), trust and track records based on robust business models, driven by talented top teams that the market can believe in.

From an investor's perspective, informed investment decision making will lead to an active investment strategy. This depends upon having the requisite skills to differentiate competing investment opportunities based on the provision of clear, transparent, accurate and timely information from a variety of sources based on both quantitative and qualitative data. In order to position the company's 'investor appeal' it will be important for the company to have a clear understanding about its key investment drivers and the needs of its shareholder base.

Investor relationship management

Shareholder relations are fundamentally no different from the much-written-about world of customer relationship management (CRM) – responsible for spawning an entire industry dependent upon technology, metrics and 'marketing savvy'. At the core of CRM and pertinent to the world of investors is the 'get to know your customer, get your customer to love you' mantra, building a relationship so that the bond between you is difficult to break. The importance of maintaining positive relationships with your customers is that retained customers cost less to acquire and service than new customers. Building relationships helps you to understand the needs of your customers, should help you evolve your product/service offering and help to keep you one step ahead of your competitors. Overall, loyal customers are valuable customers. Investors are no different.

Investor relationship management (IRM) involves knowing and understanding your investor base. It is equally important to understand what their current and future needs are, their purchasing patterns, and their engagement patterns. Companies need to understand what drives investor turnover in their stock and have in place realistic investor retention strategies. Using value added engagement initiatives (e.g. 'teach-in' sessions where investors and market influencers are separately bought together to help them understand the key drivers and differentiators within the business, sector and industry) can help to build a bond based on knowledge, transparency and trust.

Developing a sustainable IRM culture within the business requires commitment from the top and a willingness to commit time and resources to the cause. Time spent profiling and segmenting your investor base reaps rewards in terms of building investor appetite and establishing dialogue. It is never too late to start but requires an understanding of the various roles played by both investors and market influencers and enablers. The frustration will arise because ultimately the company will be removed from the physical share transactions and will have no absolute control over its buyers or sellers of its stock – this is not a feature of traditional CRM.

Investor segmentation

The market is made up of many players – the most obvious will be the investors – a company's prime audience group. However, investors are influenced in their investment decisions by information obtained from sources independent of the company itself. Influencers will include analysts, media, market commentators, pressure groups, auditors.

In addition, the information provided by the company and the opportunities to meet with investors will be orchestrated by a group of enablers. Enablers will include a company's professional advisors (brokers, IR/PR consultants, lawyers, accountants) as well as those that provide the wheels of the market: the regulatory authorities, registrars and regulatory information services.

Investors

Investors can be profiled according to a number of groups based on type, investment criteria (size, sector, SRI) style and orientation. Investor type can be broken into three core characteristics:

- *Institutional* – these are the mainstream fund managers (responsible for investing on behalf of pension funds, mutual funds, insurance companies and major charities). Non-mainstream institutional investors include hedge funds and those who invest based on ethical issues (i.e. traditionally excluded so called 'sin stocks' such as tobacco, guns and alcohol). Both hedge funds and SRI funds are growing in significance and require separate consideration when profiling a company's investor base. In the UK, institutional money tends to be based in one of two centres: London and Edinburgh.

- *Quasi-institutional* – these are discretionary private client stock brokers and wealth management firms who control significant pots of money on behalf of their client base. Quasi-institutional funds are located close to their client base and therefore tend to have greater regional spread than associated with pure institutional players. Regional centres would include: Birmingham, Leeds, Manchester and Liverpool.

- *Retail* – these are individual private clients and employee shareholders, who have traditionally been hard to service and may have been neglected. The arrival of the internet and company intranets as well as the emphasis on fair disclosure and a level playing field for all investors have changed the rules of engagement for this particular niche investor group.

In addition to the above characteristics all investors will have preferred investment strategies based on some of the following:

- *Investment criteria* – does the investor restrict investment according to size (e.g. large-cap, small-cap); quote (e.g. AIM, Main market, International listings); focus on sector (e.g. avoids/prefers mining stocks, technology stocks); SRI criteria (e.g. FTSE4Good)?

- *Style* – Active investors tend to fall into three groups: growth, value and income. However, investors across all three styles will continue to pay attention to revenue and earnings growth, strong cash flow, healthy margins, high returns on assets, equity and investment as well as indicators to support good prospects for continuing improvement.

- *Income investors* – will be particularly concerned with cash flow and growth, both of which will drive dividend policy, hopefully at even higher yields. Most income investors will be looking to achieve a threshold dividend yield or payout ratio. Yield is dividends divided by current stock price. Payout ratio is dividends divided by the price/earnings ratio. When income investors screen companies for potential investment opportunities they will compare the company's dividend yield and payout ratio against the prevailing market average. In order to qualify for inclusion onto the investor's radar screen, the company must be near or above the market average.

- *Growth investors* – will be particularly interested in the trend lines behind revenues, earnings and cash flow profiles. Growth investors are keen to see earnings re-invested in high-growth opportunities; therefore companies attractive to this style of investor are likely to have low yields and payout ratios combined with high price-to-book and price-to-cash flow ratios.

- *Value investors* – are keen to identify good companies that are currently undervalued by the market. Companies in this category may be priced below net asset value, historical pricing levels, may be cyclical, may be in a recovery phase or may be ripe for turnaround intervention. Finally they may simply be 'off-radar' because they do little to engage with market and/or proactively compete for the attention of investors.

■ Orientation – Active investors base their investment strategies on top-down asset allocation and/or bottom-up stock picking. Passive investors track an index and therefore investor relations initiatives in this area are less important as investors are constrained by index weightings and the impact of the buying and selling decisions of more active investors.

Investor targeting

Investor targeting provides the link between financial elements of managing shareholders (the valuation game) and the marketing elements (identifying and understanding the needs of your existing and desired investor base). Companies are increasingly undertaking targeting initiatives as part of a proactive, market-orientated activity, designed to improve both the fair market value of the stock and the stock's efficiency. Marketing a company's stock is no different from marketing its product/service lines – no one would assume there is a universe out there that knows and understands the company – it is the active management of shareholders that develops and populates this universe (target investor group).

Targeting seeks to identify compatibility between an investor's style and the company's investment characteristics and key value drivers. Growth companies need to be matched to growth investors. Income companies need to identify with income styled investors.

There are several ways to profile investors and position the company amongst its ideal investor base. Investor relations strategy is the action plan that leads to this successful union.

Positioning stems from understanding what the investor is looking for (aspirations and expectations), and needs in order to make an informed decision to invest in a company's stock. Research your investors – make sure you know, don't guess, or rely on hearsay from third parties.

Importantly, positioning also needs to be based on reality – get this wrong and the reputation of the company will tainted if not damaged – this will erode investor confidence. Never promise what the business can't deliver. The market neither forgives nor forgets.

Positions can be based both on perception of market needs and on a market opportunity. Perception positioning requires an understanding of both the needs of the market and the company's ability to meet those needs. Market opportunity positioning identifies a gap in the market (e.g. an untapped pool of discretionary money managers) and develops a campaign to attract the attention of this particular target audience. Both approaches will need to be underpinned by a sustainable investor relations campaign.

Once a company has delivered a single position point it can consider building positioning extensions, but it should be careful of diluting its key investor messages. Once the positioning point has been developed the company should consider how to roll out its investor messages, bearing in mind that positioning is a dynamic tool and may need to be rethought as either the company or the market changes (e.g. technology companies that aligned themselves with the dot com boom and were then tarnished by the fallout). Effective positioning will also be dependent upon the company differentiating itself from others competing for the same pools of capital and investor attention. Ultimately positioning the investment opportunity provides a base to communicate the company's ability to meet the needs and expectations of existing and potential investors.

In practice, targeted investor marketing will involve identifying and selecting your prospective investor base, defining its components and segmenting your approach.

CHECKLIST Investor targeting

The following actions will enable a company to define its investment offering in terms of market needs that are clearly defined:

1   Start with defining the type of investor you want – do this in detail.

2   Identify the prospects that fit your investor profile.

3   Devise your engagement campaign.

4   Establish a relationship with key decision makers and influencers (fund managers and analysts).

5   Put in place mechanisms to ensure ongoing dialogue.

6   Be accountable for the plan. Assess its impact and effectiveness in terms of providing greater compatibility between the company and the needs of its investor base.

Measuring IR success

With so many factors influencing share price – not all of them within the control of the person responsible for executing the IR strategy – it is important to focus on the qualitative aspects as well as the quantitative impact of an IR programme.

CHECKLIST Assessing performance

1   Focus on quality and not quantity.

2   Assess changes to the share register over time.

3   Assess improvements to investors' understanding and insight into the business over time – this can be achieved by reviewing the changes made to presentation packs in respect of depth and nature of issues covered.

4   Assess market sentiment and perceptions regarding the investment proposition.

5   Assess shareholder loyalty over time – this can be measured particularly at times of aggressive, hostile interest in the company or if the company needs to go back to the market to raise fresh capital.

Backbone components of the IR calendar

Companies should plan their IR strategy around:

- interim results;
- report and accounts production;
- the AGM;
- market announcements.

They should also for plan complementary events throughout the year and retain some capacity for managing *ad hoc* activities as the need arises. The checklist below itemises the activities that should form the backbone of the IR calendar.

CHECKLIST   The IR calendar

Quarterly, interim and preliminary results

Prelims are an important event in the IR calendar as they provide the first signal to the market of the progress (or otherwise) of the company during the previous reporting period.

Quarterly and interim results act as a refresher to the market and help assess whether the company is on track to deliver what had been previously set out to the market. The meetings held to present these results tend to be led by the chief executive and finance director.

Prelim results will normally be released through a Regulatory Information Service (RIS) at 7.00am on the morning results are due. This is likely to be followed by a series of group and one-on-one meetings during the day. It should be used as an opportunity to gauge market sentiment.

Report and accounts production

This is likely to already be well embedded into the financial reporting calendar of the company. Planning ahead is the key to success and depending upon the year end – a company can assess its report and accounts against those of other companies reporting with similar year ends.

The annual report should meet both statutory requirements and follow best practice – see chapter 7.

Consider posting an electronic version of your report and accounts on the website so that non-shareholders (such as students and researchers) can access information without adding to the costs of the overall mail out.

Work closely with your registrar to ensure mailing lists are up-to-date and accurate – nobody likes to see the post of a dead relative!

Annual General Meetings (AGMs)

The AGM is a statutory requirement and allows shareholders to hear from the horse's mouth a review of activity and to raise any areas of concern.

Factors such as the size and the nature of the company will determine the likely turn out at an AGM – small companies tend to attract smaller numbers of shareholders. Sometimes this is because the AGM may be held off the beaten track – some might say that it is because the refreshments are likely to be thin on the ground compared to some of the arrangements made by larger companies.

If you are likely to have disruptive shareholders you may need to consider security arrangements for the event.

Market announcement

These should be issued in relation to any news which is considered material and could possibly be considered 'inside'.

Market announcements need to be made via an approved Regulatory Information Service (RIS).

Investor meetings

Often these are arranged with core shareholders and influential analysts.

When organising it is important to bear in mind the issues raised above regarding positioning, segmentation, differentiation and targeting – the key is to remain focused.

Investor meetings provide an invaluable opportunity to gather both feedback and market intelligence regarding peer group companies.

Media briefings

A large number of companies will ensure part of the results day is dedicated to media briefings. Depending on how big you are, how interesting you are and what other news you are competing against on a given day will determine the scale and scope of the media coverage relating to the business.

Media briefings tend to be similar to those meetings arranged for analysts, but are likely to be less technically focused – instead journalists will be looking to identify angles that will appeal to their readership – companies can help by thinking about what types of 'hook' they may be able to use to attract the attention of the media.

Site visits

These can prove invaluable to ensuring that analysts in particular understand the key drivers in the business and therefore set about determining a fair market value for the business. Site visits also provide an opportunity to introduce the 'marzipan layer' of a company – senior executives just below board level.

Analyst teach-ins

Briefings where analysts are introduced to the business's key differentiators – this assists analysts to understand the indicators and metrics for the business.

Investor perception studies

Conduct surveys amongst existing and target shareholders to identify current perceptions of the company and management.

These are useful initiatives to undertake as they allow investor expectations to be mapped; provide a focus as to how the investor relations programme may need to evolve in order to change attitudes prevailing in the market; enable a dialogue and relationship to develop outside of the traditional results calendar; correct any misperceptions before they take hold.

Surveys might be conducted on a two to three-year rolling cycle.

Crisis management

A company should have in place a well-documented crisis management plan.

This should be reviewed at least annually and should involve both a designated internal and external team whose prime responsibility is to manage a crisis situation (e.g. hostile takeover, a natural disaster).

This should be linked closely to the risk register established as part of the company's approach to internal controls and risk assessments (including: financial, operational, regulatory and reputational risks).

Best practice communications

IR websites

This is potentially the most efficient and cost-effective way of keeping the investment community up to speed with what is going on within the business. It is a key tool because it provides an accessible platform where information can be updated around the clock and reach out to a global audience. Websites have done much to improve access to information for the private investor. As a result, the costs of traditionally servicing this type of investor have reduced dramatically, whilst the risks of selective disclosure have been reduced.

Web casts/conference calls

Conference calls enable the investment community to participate in presentations despite time differences and geographic separation. Many companies now link their results presentations with conference calls via their IR website platform to reach as many investors as possible. Such web casts and conference calls also benefit from the ability to dynamically link to the website through various archive channels.

Investor newsletters

Newsletters can be in a hard copy and or electronic format. They can be a useful way of communicating with smaller investors, particularly individual private clients and employee shareholders. This type of communication lends itself particularly to situations where a consumer and investor brand can benefit from alignment to reinforce the value proposition to both audiences – who in some cases can be one and the same.

Regulatory environment

Financial Services and Markets Act (FSMA) – UK legislation made effective December 2001, impacting upon the 'selective disclosure' of information, setting out new rules on market abuse and revising the guide on handling inside information. See also chapters 10 and 11 on Internal control

Code of market conduct – contains information relating to the market abuse regime as prescribed by the Financial Services Authority (FSA). The FSMA increased the likelihood of prosecution for market abuse by introducing a new civil offence to augment the existing criminal offences of insider dealing. As a result, the FSA burden of proof was reduced and it now only has to show that an offence has been committed 'on the balance of probability' rather than 'beyond reasonable doubt' as previously required in respect of a criminal prosecution. The new civil offences for market abuse are:

- misuse of information – broadly equivalent to the old insider dealing offence;
- creating a false or misleading impression – relating to market information;
- market distortion – whereby behaviour may distort the market.

Inside information – It is the responsibility of companies and their advisers to determine exactly what this covers in their own particular circumstances. In addition, companies are encouraged to move away from the potential pitfalls of selective disclosure. Specifically:

- briefings to analysts should be opened up to the public – in this respect we have seen many companies making greater use of technology to level the investor playing field – web casts and conference call dial-in facilities have gone some way to alleviating the problem of presenting to a select segment of the market;
- analysts should not be given any preferential treatment by disclosing inside information. If inside information is disclosed inadvertently then a market announcement should be made as soon as is practically possible;

- companies should review their procedures for meetings with analysts to ensure that no inside information is likely to be disclosed;

- companies are encouraged to publish information over the internet but this should not be viewed as a substitute for approved market-wide dissemination of information. Inside information has to be issued to the market via an approved regulatory news service provider (the UKLA maintains a list and vetting procedure for approved RISs).

Shareholder engagement

Activism

The climate for shareholders is increasingly focusing on their role as responsible investors who retain their voting rights to put pressure on companies to behave in certain ways and to be able to express their voice if they are unhappy with the way in which a company is being run. Companies should ensure they understand voting patterns and, where necessary, engage with shareholders on contentious issues.

Corporate social responsibility (CSR)

CSR focuses on the impact that a company's activities has upon all its stakeholders (not just shareholders), society and the environment at large. This initiative is gaining momentum and a number of investors have set up dedicated funds to invest in those companies that have positive track records in this area. This opens up another avenue of investor segmentation and depending upon the type of business the company operates in, new investor segments may open up if a company meets the necessary criteria.

Example: Smaller companies learning to punch above their weight!

- Barriers
  - Inexperienced top teams
  - Inappropriate listings (market/sector)
  - Unattractive free floats and role of founding families
  - Globalisation/fund consolidation
  - Impact of minimum holding levels resulting in unacceptable high shareholdings
  - Investment monitoring costs
- Opportunities
  - Mispricing, therefore opportunity to address misconceptions and achieve more representative market values

- As a small company there exists an opportunity to grow bigger – attract investors who want to take the ride
- Position company as an opportunity to provide further insight/understanding into a company that has an established following (ride on the coat tails)
- Identify smaller company-focused funds
- Identify local private client brokers who may be interested in the company because they are perceived as having a local investor interest and therefore following
- Target those firms who research/invest in similar stocks who may be looking to build expertise within a particular market segment.

- Commitment
  - Ensure top-team support that is prepared to dedicate sufficient time to the cause
  - Ensure visibility and accessibility
  - Embark upon it as an awareness campaign: tell investors what the company is going to do and then ask to go back the following year and let them know what was achieved – no pressure to invest just raise awareness – be prepared to wait and work at it.

CONCLUSION

- The challenge for companies in managing a very necessary relationship with its investor base, is to build on and combine the marketing principles of segmentation, positioning and differentiation in an attempt to develop a consistent 'investor brand' which produces a distinctive investor brand identity.
- Just as brands create value within consumer markets, investor brands are capable of creating value in investor markets: brand appeal increases the brand premiums investors are prepared to pay, leading to greater access to and lower costs of capital.
- Developing an investor brand, will not only stimulate awareness amongst investor audiences but focus the board on those issues that really matter; promoting a common language and understanding of the business – both within (the board) and externally (the investor).

CHAPTER 10

Internal control: management and disclosure of inside information

- Maintaining a sound and effective system of internal controls and risk management
- Compliance with continuing obligations
- Inside Information and the Disclosure Rules
- Market abuse
- Indemnifying directors

Introduction

The original Combined Code introduced the principle that a board of a company should maintain 'a sound system of internal control to safeguard shareholders' investment and the company's assets'. The supporting Code Provisions made it clear that all internal controls are relevant to the principle and included 'financial, operational and compliance controls and risk management'. Such a system should therefore cover how to deal with the unexpected matters which may occur between the regular, diarised board meetings of a company during a year, such as when public announcements need to be made. This chapter examines such continuing obligations, the nature of them, the obligations and potential liabilities arising under them and how the board should address them.

It should be borne in mind that the continuing obligations set out in this chapter are principally applicable to listed companies, but the general principle of having an effective system of internal control to deal with challenges which may arise in day-to-day business applies equally to most companies.

Internal controls

When considering the context of internal control for the purposes of addressing the continuing obligations which may face a company, as stated, such controls should be seen as sensible risk management to protect the company's assets and protect shareholders' investment.

When considering what constitutes 'a sound system of internal control', consideration should be given to the Turnbull Guidance reproduced in Appendix 9. Turnbull notes that 'internal control facilitates the effectiveness and efficiency of operations, helps ensure the reliability of internal and external reporting and assists compliance with laws and regulations'.

In considering how internal controls assist with compliance with laws and regulations (and in this context, compliance with continuing obligations), Turnbull identifies the elements of a sound system of internal control as encompassing the 'policies, processes, tasks, behaviours and other aspects of a company that, taken together:

- facilitate its effective and efficient operation by enabling it to respond appropriately to significant business, operational, financial, compliance and other risks to achieving the company's objectives. This includes the safeguarding of assets from inappropriate use or from loss and fraud and ensuring that liabilities are identified and managed;

- help to ensure the quality of internal and external reporting. This requires the maintenance of proper records and processes that generate a flow of timely, relevant and reliable information from within and outside the organisation; and

- help to ensure compliance with applicable laws and regulations, and also with internal policies with respect to the conduct of business.'

Since listed companies are required to state in their annual report how they have applied the Combined Code main principal, Turnbull suggests that the board should, as a minimum, disclose that there is an 'ongoing process for identifying, evaluating and managing the significant risks faced by the company, that it has been in place for the year under review and up to the date of approval of the annual report and accounts, that it is regularly reviewed by the board and accords with the (Turnbull) guidance'.

When internal control is placed within the context of continuing obligations which a company must adhere to, then processes and policies designed to ensure that information is always up-to-date and accurate and that responses may be made in a timely manner by appropriate, senior personnel within the company immediately come to mind.

The principles behind continuing obligations

The two main principles behind all continuing obligations in the Listing Rules are:

- timely disclosure of all relevant information; and
- equal treatment of shareholders.

The protection afforded to investors by the above two principles ensures that an orderly market in a listed company's securities is maintained, and that all users of the market have simultaneous access to the same information.

The Listing and Disclosure Rules seek to achieve this in a number of ways, but principally through imposing obligations on a listed company to disclose any information necessary to enable the public to appraise the position of the company and to avoid the creation of a false market in its shares.

Consequently, information that would be likely to affect materially the market price of a company's shares must be disclosed without delay, and the internal control processes must ensure that this requirement is always adhered to. In addition, the internal control processes must ensure that the announcements are not inaccurate, misleading, false or deceptive, and do not omit anything likely to affect the import of the information contained in them, otherwise a company may be committing a criminal offence.

These general duties underlie many of the more specific obligations to make announcements which are set out in the Listing Rules.

General disclosure obligations

The Disclosure and Listing Rules require that listed companies must generally disclose by notification to a Regulatory Information Service (RIS) certain matters without delay, including:

- any major new developments in its sphere of activity which are not public knowledge and which may lead to substantial movement in the price of its listed securities;
- a change in the company's financial condition, in the performance of its business or the company's expectation as to its performance which, if made public, would be likely to lead to substantial movement in the price of its listed securities; and
- any impending developments or matters in the course of negotiation where the company has reason to believe that a breach of confidence has occurred or is likely to occur and where such development or matter is such that knowledge of it would be likely to lead to substantial movement in the price of its listed securities.

There are limited exceptions to the general obligation of disclosure, namely:

- a company need not notify to an RIS information about impending developments or matters in the course of negotiation, and (provided that the directors of a company are satisfied that such persons are aware that they must not deal in the company's shares before the relevant information has been made public) may give such information in confidence to a limited category of persons involved in the negotiations. A company may also provide such information in confidence to a statutory or regulatory body (such as the Competition Commission); and

- if the company considers that public disclosure of information might prejudice the company's legitimate interests, the FSA may grant a dispensation from the disclosure requirements. In practice, however, this exception is of little use. The FSA will only grant a dispensation in very limited circumstances and it encourages any company to contact it without delay if it is thought that a situation exists to which such exemption applies.

Announcements are generally made through an RIS. However, if notification to an RIS is required at a time when no RIS is open for business, a company must distribute the relevant information to at least two national newspapers in the UK and to at least two newswire services operating in the UK. The company must then ensure that the information is notified to an RIS for release as soon as it reopens.

CHECKLIST   Specific disclosure obligations

1   The Listing Rules also contain a number of specific disclosure obligations including:

- notification to an RIS (generally, without delay) of various matters concerning its capital, including:

- alterations to its capital structure;

- changes of rights attaching to its shares, the basis of allotment of shares offered generally to the public for cash and of open offers to shareholders;

- the effect (if any) of the issue of further shares on the terms of exercise of rights under options, warrants and convertible securities, and the results of any fresh issue of shares;

2   Notification to an RIS without delay of certain significant interests in its shares disclosed to it in accordance with the Companies Act 1985 and of certain information obtained by it pursuant to s 212 of the Companies Act 1985 or otherwise relating to persons interested in shares.

3   Forwarding to the FSA two copies of all circulars, notices, reports, announcements or other documents to which the Listing Rules apply, at the same time as they are issued, and

forwarding all resolutions passed by the company, other than those concerning ordinary business at an AGM, without delay after the relevant meeting.

4   Notification without delay to an RIS, and not later than 7.30 am on the next business day, of decisions by the board on dividends, profits and other matters requiring announcement.

5   Upon becoming aware that the proportion of any class of its listed equity shares in the hands of the public has fallen below 25% (or such lower percentage as the FSA may have agreed), a company must notify the FSA without delay.

6   An announcement, depending on their size, in relation to certain transactions by a company (e.g. acquisitions and disposals but not transactions of a revenue nature in the ordinary course of business) or (for transactions which are substantial in relation to the size of the company), an announcement, the issue of a circular to shareholders providing details about the transaction, and the prior approval of the transaction by its shareholders.

7   The issue of a circular to shareholders where any transaction is proposed between a listed company (or any of its subsidiaries) and a 'related party', where details are provided about the transaction and prior approval of the shareholders to the transaction is obtained.

8   Notification to an RIS without delay, and not later than the end of the business day following the change or receipt of notice about the change, of any change to the board, including:

   •   the appointment of a new director;

   •   the resignation, removal or retirement of a director; and

   •   any change to the important functions or executive responsibilities of a director.

9   The notification must state the effective date of the change if it is not with immediate effect. If the effective date is not yet known or has not yet been determined, the notification should state this fact, and the company must notify an RIS when the effective date has been decided.

10   In the case of an appointment, the notification must state whether the position is executive or non-executive, and the nature of any specific function or responsibility of the position. In addition, and unless such information has already been disclosed by a company in a prospectus, listing particulars or circular, a company must notify to an RIS, in respect of any newly appointed director, of all directorships held by that director in any other publicly quoted company during the previous five years, together with information on matters such as convictions, bankruptcies, administrations, liquidations or public censures. The information must be notified to an RIS within 14 days of the appointment of the new director becoming effective.

Disclosure rules

The Disclosure Rules contain rules and guidance on listed companies' obligations to disclose and control 'inside information' and notify transactions by 'persons discharging managerial responsibilities'. Such definitions are set out in ss. 96B and 118C of the Financial Services and Markets Act (FSMA).

The main contents of the Disclosure Rules are as follows:

Chapter one: introduction

This chapter deals with the application and purpose of the Disclosure Rules, the procedure to be adopted for modifications to or dispensation from the Disclosure Rules, penalties for breach, market abuse safe harbours and the issuer's obligation to take all reasonable care in notifying information to a RIS.

Chapter two: disclosure and control of inside information by issuers

This chapter contains the general obligation to announce inside information, the circumstances in which disclosure can be delayed or selective disclosures can be made, holding announcements, the obligation to compile and maintain insider lists, publication of inside information on internet sites and the control of inside information.

Chapter three: transactions by persons discharging managerial responsibilities and their connected persons

This chapter replaces the provisions of chapter 16 of the previous Listing Rules regarding requirements to notify directors' transactions and extends the requirements to cover persons discharging managerial responsibilities and their connected persons.

CHECKLIST   Main provisions of the Disclosure Rules

Information gathering and publication

Issuers and persons discharging managerial responsibilities and connected persons are under an obligation to provide to the FSA as soon as possible following a request:

- any information that the FSA considers appropriate to protect investors or ensure the smooth operation of the market; and
- any other information or explanation that the FSA may reasonably require to verify whether the Disclosure Rules are being or have been complied with.

Misleading information

Issuers must take all reasonable care that any information that they give to a RIS is not misleading, false or deceptive and does not omit anything likely to affect the import of the information. Issuers also must not combine a RIS announcement with the marketing of activities in a manner likely to be misleading.

Modification or dispensation of any of the Disclosure Rules

An issuer may apply to the FSA in writing for modification to or dispensation from any of the Disclosure Rules. Such application must normally be made at least five business days before the proposed modification or suspension is to take effect. It should give:

- a clear explanation of why the dispensation or modification is requested;
- details of any special requirements;
- all relevant information that should reasonably be brought to the FSA's attention;
- any statement or information required by the Disclosure Rule for its modification or dispensation; and
- copies of all relevant supporting documents to the application.

This dispensation is only likely to be granted in very limited circumstances.

Notification when a RIS is not open for business

Paragraph 1.3.6R of the Disclosure Rules provides for companies wishing to notify information to a RIS at a time when a RIS is not open for business. However, it should be noted that the FSA guidance specifically states that the fact that a RIS is not open for business is not, in itself, sufficient grounds for delaying the disclosure or distribution of inside information.

Disclosure of inside information

The general disclosure obligation which is now set out in chapter 2 of the Disclosure Rules provides that issuers must notify a RIS as soon as possible of any inside information which directly concerns the issuer, unless paragraph 2.5.1R applies.

Paragraphs 2.2.3 to 2.2.8 of the Disclosure Rules provide guidance on how to identify inside information and establish that inside information is of a precise nature which:

- is not generally available;
- relates directly or indirectly to one or more issuers of qualifying investments or to the qualifying investments themselves;
- would, if generally available, be likely to have a significant effect on the price of the qualifying investments or on the price of related investments.

In determining what information is likely to have a significant effect on price, an issuer should use the *reasonable investor test*, by asking whether the relevant information would be likely to be used by a reasonable investor as part of the basis of his investment decisions and would therefore be likely to have a significant effect on the price of the issuer's financial invest ments.

It should be noted that the reasonable investor test is merely a guide to ascertaining if the information is likely to have a significant price effect if it were made public, and is not a test for inside information in itself.

As a general rule, the more specific the information, then the greater the risk is of the information being inside information.

As soon as possible

Although the Disclosure Rules refer to the disclosure of inside information being 'as soon as possible', which contrasts with the previous requirement of disclosure being 'without delay', the FSA has stated that it does not believe the Disclosure Rules permit an issuer a longer period to make required disclosures to a RIS.

Holding announcements

Paragraph 2.2.9G of the Disclosure Rules provides that where an issuer is faced with an unexpected and significant event, a short delay may be acceptable if necessary to clarify the situation. However, a holding announcement should be made if there is a danger that inside information may leak out before the facts and their impact can be confirmed.

The holding announcement should contain as much detail about the subject matter as possible, the reasons why a fuller announcement could not be made and an undertaking to announce further details as soon as possible.

There is also a requirement to prepare a holding announcement where disclosure is being delayed in accordance with the Disclosure Rules so that an announcement may be released swiftly if there is a breach of confidentiality.

Delaying disclosure

Disclosure of inside information may be delayed to prevent prejudicing its legitimate interests, such as on-going negotiations, where:

- such omission would not be likely to mislead the public;
- the person receiving the information owes the company a duty of confidentiality; and
- the company is able to ensure the confidentiality of the information.

The company must first make the assessment as to whether it has a legitimate interest which would be prejudiced by the disclosure of the inside information in question. However, the FSA has stated that, other than in relation to impending developments or where consent is required in a dual board structure, there are unlikely to be other circumstances when delay would be justified.

Control of inside information

The Disclosure Rules state that companies must have a framework for the control of inside information. The company must:

- establish effective arrangements to deny access to inside information to persons other than those who require it for the exercise of their functions within the issuer; and
- have in place measures to enable public disclosure to be made via a RIS as soon as possible if the company cannot ensure the confidentiality of the inside information.

As part of its control measures, the company should make it clearly known to its employees that any person who does receive inside information and deals in the company's securities may be exposed to various headings of legal liability including the insider dealing offences under Part IV of the Criminal Justice Act 1993 and the civil offence of market abuse under FSMA.

Insider lists

The Disclosure Rules formalise the process required by the Model Code to identify employees with access to inside information.

Companies must compile lists of persons working for them (under a contract of employment or otherwise) with access to inside information relating, directly or indirectly, to the issuer on a regular or occasional basis.

Companies are also required to ensure that persons acting on their behalf or for their account, such as advisers, compile such lists.

Such lists must be kept for five years from the date on which they are drawn up or updated (Rule 2.8.5 Disclosure Rules).

Companies should adopt internal procedures regarding accessibility of sensitive documents. In order to properly manage access to inside information, a company should ensure that no inside information is disclosed in internal publications to all employees.

Where requested, a company must provide an insider list to the FSA as soon as possible.

Transactions by persons discharging managerial responsibilities

The Disclosure Rules require persons discharging managerial responsibilities within a company and their connected persons to disclose to the company transactions conducted on their own account in the shares of the company, or derivatives or any other financial instrument(s) relating to those shares.

Persons discharging managerial responsibilities are:

- the directors of the issuer; and
- senior executives of the issuer who are not directors but who have regular access to inside information relating directly or indirectly to the issuer and the power to make managerial decisions concerning the future developments and business prospects of the issuer.

Connected persons include:

- those connected within the meaning of s. 346 of the Companies Act;
- relatives who have shared the same household as that person for at least 12 months; and
- a body corporate whereby the person discharging managerial responsibilities or a connected person is a director or a senior executive who has the power to make management decisions concerning the future developments and business prospects of the issuer.

As with insider lists, it will be necessary for companies to establish the identity of the relevant individuals and to keep their lists under review to ensure that the correct people within the company understand and comply with their obligations.

Listed companies must notify a RIS of information notified to it by persons discharging managerial responsibilities as soon as possible and no later than the end of the business day following receipt of the information by the company.

Breach of the Disclosure Rules

The FSA may impose a financial penalty on the issuer, a person discharging managerial responsibilities or a connected person, or publish a statement censuring that person, in respect of breaches of the Disclosure Rules.

A financial penalty may be imposed on a former director if the FSA considers that such a person was knowingly concerned in a breach by the issuer.

The FSA may also require the suspension of trading of any financial instrument with effect from such time as it may determine if there are reasonable grounds to suspect non-compliance with the Disclosure Rules.

Market abuse

The market abuse regime is designed to complement the criminal offences of misleading statements and practices under s. 397 of the FSMA and insider dealing under the Criminal Justice Act 1993. The regulations allowing the FSA to exercise their investigatory and regulatory powers are contained in the Code of Market Conduct (CoMC).

The CoMC was made under s. 119 of the Financial Services and Markets Act 2000 and since its implementation in December 2001 has had wide ranging consequences; the CoMC extends to *all* individuals, not just directors and those caught by a company share dealing code – and there is an argument that best practice dictates that companies should draw *all* employees' attention to its provisions.

The CoMC defines 'market abuse' as *behaviour* which occurs in relation to *'qualifying investments'* (including shares and loan stock) traded on a *'prescribed market'*, where such behaviour satisfies one of three specified conditions.

The behaviour must also be likely to be regarded by a regular user of that market, who is aware of the behaviour, as a failure on the part of the person or persons concerned to observe the standard of behaviour reasonably expected of a person in his or their position in relation to the market.

The three specified conditions are:

- *misuse of information* – behaviour (e.g. dealing) is based on information which is not generally available to those using the market but which, if available to a regular user of the market, would or would be likely to be regarded by him as relevant when deciding the terms on which transactions of the kind in question should be effected;

- *false or misleading impression; distortion* – if it is likely to give the regular user of the market a false or misleading impression or to distort the market in the investment in question; or

- *regular user test* – pursuant to this test, even if the other elements of the statutory definition of market abuse are satisfied, the behaviour will not actually amount to market abuse unless it '…is likely to be regarded by a regular user of that market who is aware of the behaviour as a failure on the part of the person or persons concerned to observe the standard of behaviour reasonably expected of a person in his or their position in relation to the market'.

Behaviour encompasses acts of commission and/or omission; it may be by one person alone, or by two persons acting together; and includes acquiring and selling shares, and dissemination of information (including through accepted channels (such as a RIS)).

Any early or selective disclosure of information may amount to the secondary offence of requiring or encouraging another to engage in behaviour which, if engaged in by the person requiring or encouraging, would amount to market abuse. Broadly, early or selective disclosure will be presumed to constitute the secondary offence unless:

- there is a legitimate purpose for making the disclosure; and

- the disclosure is accompanied by a statement that the information is given in confidence, and that the recipient should not base any behaviour in relation to the investment in question which would amount to market abuse on the information until after the information is made generally available.

There are certain 'safe harbours' from the market abuse regime. It should be noted, however, that *there is no blanket safe harbour for compliance with the Listing Rules* (although safe harbours are provided in respect of certain provisions of the Listing Rules – principally, those relating to disclosure of information which is not generally available, content and standard of care applicable to a disclosure, and timing of announcements, documentation and dealings).

The FSA may impose penalties on a company and its directors for market abuse or the 'secondary offence'.

In general, the CoMC allows the FSA very wide investigatory powers with the ability to impose unlimited fines on issuers and individuals based on the balance of probability that an individual or issuer intended to, or did, distort the market. It is true to say that any issuer or individual following the Listing and Disclosure Rules and observing the provisions of their company's share dealing code and the requirements of the Criminal Justice Act are unlikely to be troubled by the conventions contained in the CoMC. However, those operating at the margins need to beware!

Several successful 'prosecutions' have already been made by the FSA using the CoMC. Again, companies will need to demonstrate that they have used their best endeavours to communicate to their employees the implications of getting on the wrong side of the Code of Market Conduct.

What happens if things go wrong? Indemnifying directors and officers

In the context of risk management and control it seems appropriate to discuss the changes brought about in April 2005 to the law governing a company's right to indemnify its directors and officers against certain liabilities.

Before April 2005, companies were permitted to indemnify officers (directors or the company secretary) against any liability for negligence, default, breach of duty or breach of trust *but only* if and when the officer concerned had successfully defended any legal proceedings brought against him/her or if a court granted relief on the grounds that the director had acted honestly and reasonably.

This meant of course that until the outcome of the court case was concluded, it was quite likely that directors would have to fund their defence costs from their own resources.

Changes in the law

Since April 2005, however, companies have been permitted to grant indemnities to their directors where the indemnity is a 'qualifying third-party indemnity'.

Companies will be permitted (but not obliged) to provide a director with funds to meet the cost of:

- defending criminal proceedings or civil proceedings (even if the company itself brings the action); and

- applying for relief from liability under the Companies Act 1985, provided the director would be liable to repay such costs to the company if his defence were unsuccessful or if the court were to refuse his application for relief.

The company *may not* indemnify a director against any liability incurred by the director:

- to the company itself or to an associated company;
- to pay a criminal fine or a regulatory penalty (such as a fine imposed by the FSA);
- incurred in defending criminal proceedings where he is convicted;
- incurred in defending civil proceedings brought by the company, or an associated company, and where judgment is given against him;
- in an unsuccessful application for relief from liability under the Companies Act 1985.

Under the new law, a company may, however, indemnify a director in *civil* proceedings brought by a *third party* (including a regulator, such as the Financial Services Authority or a shareholder) against both the claim itself, and against the cost of defending the proceedings, even if judgment is ultimately given against him, as long as the indemnity does not extend to the payment of criminal fines or regulatory penalties incurred.

If a civil action is brought by the company, however, the indemnity will only be valid if the director successfully defends the claim or the action is settled out of court.

Granting qualifying third-party indemnity provision

Where companies have opted to grant extended indemnities to directors, or to pay directors' defence costs as they are incurred, there is no obligation to obtain shareholder approval *per se*, but the relevant company's articles of associaton must contain appropriate powers to make such grants or payments. The articles will need to be checked and may need to be amended, which would require shareholder approval.

In order to grant the new wider indemnities provided by the Act, companies will need to amend the relevant contractual documentation (e.g. service agreements or letters of appointment) to provide the extended protection, whilst others will have amended their articles of association to reflect the extended provisions. In cases where the indemnity (rather than just the power to grant an indemnity) is contained in the articles, then the extended wording would (as described above) require shareholder approval.

Disclosure

Where a company has chosen to grant a qualifying third-party indemnity provision to its directors, it must disclose that such provision is (or was) in force in the directors' report in its annual report and accounts. This must be done on an annual basis – not just in the year when the indemnity is first provided.

CONCLUSION

- The principle that a board of a company should maintain 'a sound system of internal control to safeguard shareholders' investment and the company's assets underlies much of current regulation and best practice.
- The FSA now has increased powers and the scope of the regulation on handling inside information, Market Abuse etc. is more broadly encompassing and more rigorously and actively enforced.
- More important than ever those companies ensure their risk management systems and controls are robust, and continually reviewed in the light of further regulatory changes.

CHAPTER 11

Internal control: procedures for minimising regulatory risk

Introduction

On 1 July 2005 the new Listing, Prospectus and Disclosure Rules came into force. These replaced the old UKLA Listing Rules and the POS Regulations. The new regime is a result of the UK implementing the EU Market Abuse and the Prospectus Directives. This chapter will explain the internal processes and policies companies should put in place to help ensure that their directors and employees stay the right side of the regulatory line when dealing in the securities of the company and in handling what is now called 'inside' information. Readers should also refer to chapter 10.

Of primary concern to any company should be protection of its corporate reputation. No company would wish to be thought of as a regulatory risk – partly from the viewpoint of commercial sensitivity, but increasingly from the financial penalties associated with a failure to comply with the UK regulatory regime – particularly the Model Code and the FSA's Code of Market Conduct and the EU regulations now embodied in the Listing and Disclosure Rules.

Processes and policies themselves will not prevent a rogue employee from flouting the rules. They will however, provide a degree of protection to the board and to the company where a breach of regulatory Codes by an individual leaves a company open to investigation by the regulators.

Dealing in the shares of the company

The freedom of directors of public quoted companies wishing to deal in the shares of their company is restricted in a number of ways: by statute, common law and the requirements of the Listing Rules.

Company directors, like other individuals, are prohibited from insider dealing by the Criminal Justice Act 1993 (CJA 1993). Under that Act it is a criminal offence for an individual who has information as an insider to deal on a regulated market in securities whose price would be significantly affected if the inside information were made public. It is also an offence to encourage insider dealing and to disclose inside information with a view to others profiting from it.

The policing powers of the CJA were added to under s. 119 of the Financial Services and Markets Act 2000 (FSMA 2000). This piece of legislation required the FSA to produce a Code giving guidance on what does and does not amount to market abuse. The FSA's Code of Market Conduct was brought into effect in December 2001 and draws heavily on insider dealing definitions contained in the 1993 Act.

There have been very few successful prosecutions for insider dealing under the CJA where the test has been one of having to prove *beyond reasonable doubt* (the level of proof required to obtain a conviction in a criminal prosecution) that the offender was involved in insider dealing.

However, the significant difference between the Criminal Justice Act and the FSA's Code of Market Conduct is that the FSA has powers to enforce its Code under the FSMA and impose penalties based on the *balance of probability* that any miscreant it pursues is involved in market abuse. Using this lower burden of proof, the FSA has succeeded in pursuing a significant number of offenders whose cases have resulted in substantial financial penalties being applied (see also chapter 10 which deals with market abuse and the provisions of the Code of Market Conduct in greater detail).

The Listing Rules

It is probably true to say that most regulatory problems faced by companies are caused by a breach of the Disclosure or Listing Rules or a breach of the Code of Market Conduct and the failure of directors and other employees to observe some simple rules.

The Listing Rules require companies to impose on their directors and employee insiders a code of dealing no less exacting that that contained in the Listing Rules. These are contained in the annex to LR9 (the Continuing Obligations) of the Listing Rules – and are more commonly known as the Model Code.

In this chapter we shall refer throughout to 'directors'. However the Model Code makes clear that there are other employees within companies who have access to price sensitive information (now referred to as 'inside information') and that these 'employee insiders' should be treated as if they were directors in terms of their share dealing.

The difference between the two categories is that all board directors are caught automatically by the Model Code, whilst any additional restricted employees (or employee insiders) are individually identified – and should be notified of their status – by the company itself.

The Model Code

The Model Code identifies two broad areas of responsibility: those which fall on the company or issuer; and those aspects that apply to the individual director. There is a further requirement placed on companies to take 'reasonable steps' to secure compliance with their own code of dealing.

As far as the company is concerned, it is required to make all directors aware of their obligations under the Model Code and to maintain written records of requests to deal – and the outcome of those requests.

However, these apparently straightforward requirements belie the procedures that need to be undertaken to provide proof that 'reasonable steps' have been taken by the company to secure compliance with their code of dealing.

The requirements placed on directors are that they must not deal in any securities of the listed company on a short-term basis; in a 'close period' or when in possession of inside information. There is a further requirement for directors to take 'reasonable steps' to ensure that persons connected with them (connected person as defined in s. 96B(2) of the FSMA 2000) do not engage in such dealings.

Perhaps here, companies and individuals should be mindful of recent legislative changes – particularly the Civil Partnership Act 2004. This will almost certainly have the effect of widening the definition of 'connected person'. In any investigation into a breach of the rules involving a potential 'connected person' the FSA is likely to look beyond the strict definition and into the true nature of relationship between employee insiders and those with whom they live.

The Model Code – who is covered?

Who exactly should be covered by a share dealing code? There is interplay here between the Model Code of the Listing Rules and the definitions to be found in the Disclosure Rules. In this respect the reader is referred to in Chapter 10 which deals with the provisions of the Disclosure Rules in more depth.

As noted above, those who will be automatically caught by a company share dealing code are the main board directors; but there are others who will need to be bound by the Model Code.

The FSMA defines these additional employees as those 'persons discharging manage-rial responsibilities' (PDMRs) and 'employee insiders'. A PDMR is defined in the FSMA as a senior executive of an *issuer* who:

- has regular access to *inside information* relating, directly or indirectly, to the *issuer*; and
- has power to make managerial decisions affecting the future development and busi-ness prospects of the *issuer*.

Rule 3.1.2 of the Disclosure Rules requires PDMRs (and their connected persons) to effectively have the same reporting responsibilities as directors; a company is required to announce their transactions to the market (Rule 3.1.4 Disclosure Rules).

An 'employee insider' is any person working for the company, under a contract of employment or otherwise, who has access to inside information relating directly or indirectly to the issuer, whether on a regular or occasional basis (Rule 2.8.1 Disclosure Rules).

It is the responsibility of the *company* to identify the individuals who meet these defini-tions.

Identifying employee insiders

The first step is to prepare a list of such employees – and to keep it up-to-date. Some employees (directors and PDMRs) will always be subject to a company's share dealing code. Others may be added to and deleted from any list maintained by the company on a case-by-case basis, depending on whether they are, for example directly involved in a price-sensitive project.

It is important to note that it is not necessarily seniority alone which will dictate inclusion as an 'employee insider'. Secretarial and support staff with access to confidential project papers or financial results should also be included.

Applying the Model Code

Until recently it has been a common practice for many companies to simply reproduce the Model Code verbatim and circulate it to board members with a memorandum stating that it represents the company's share dealing code. Whilst this (just) meets the requirement to apply a code no less exacting than that contained in the Listing Rules, most companies adopting this policy fail to 'customise' the document to make it specific to themselves.

Company sanctions

Ideally, a company share dealing code will also contain details of the sanctions that will be applied by the company for individuals failing to observe its code. Because of the potential financial and regulatory consequences facing the company, it would not be unusual for companies to treat a breach of their share dealing policy as one of gross misconduct.

Restrictions: Dealing on a short-term basis

Until the publication of the latest Mode Code 'short term' dealing was left to the boards of individual companies to decide and the definitions varied significantly from company to company.

The scope for companies to define 'short term' was eliminated now the latest Model Code wording states baldly:

> An investment with a maturity of one year or less will always be considered to be of a short-term nature.

Restrictions: close periods

The Listing Rules defines a 'close period' as:

> The period of 60 days immediately preceding the preliminary announcement of the *listed company's* annual results (or interims) or, if shorter, the period from the end of the relevant financial year up to and including the time of announcement (such publication).

Additional close periods exist for companies which report on a half-yearly or quarterly basis.

Restrictions: prohibited periods

In addition to preventing directors dealing in the shares of their company during a close period the Model Code also prohibits dealing during a 'prohibited period'. The Model Code defines a prohibited period as any close period, or any period when there exists any matter which constitutes inside information in relation to the company.

Notification

Individuals identified as 'employee insiders' should be formally notified of their status in writing – and a copy of the company's share dealing code provided to them. With the increasing use of corporate intranets – particularly if this is a usual channel of communication with employees – it will be sufficient to direct them to the appropriate online page(s).

However disseminated, the company secretary should obtain a written acknowledgement from individual restricted employees that the code has been received and read. He should also obtain a specific undertaking that the individual(s) so notified will abide by the company's share dealing code requirements that the legal and regulatory implications of mishandling insider information have been clearly understood (Rule 2.8.9 Disclosure Rules).

Significant changes to existing processes should always be notified in writing. The company secretary should seek to obtain written acknowledgements from all directors involved.

CHECKLIST Initial notification letter

The initial notification letter should contain:

- a brief synopsis of the implications of being covered by the company's share dealing code;
- a copy of the code itself;
- details of the sanctions that will be implemented where the code is breached;
- a copy of the document to be completed when requesting permission to trade;
- notification that the individual is responsible for ensuring the code is observed by their 'connected persons';
- an indication of the known 'close periods' leading up to the announcements of results – or the fact that one exists at the time of notification;
- notification that their individual acknowledgement and undertaking will be maintained on file and may be used for regulatory purposes;

- the identity of any person to whom queries should be directed;
- a copy of the letter to sign and return as an acknowledgement from the employee insider.

Acknowledgements

At the time of writing it is not yet required (however, it might now be considered best practice) for the company to request, at the time the employee's acknowledgement letter is returned that the personal details of each director's 'connected persons' should be disclosed. Once obtained, these details should be kept on file and updated from time-to-time.

Monitoring

In all cases consideration should be given to requesting the company registrars to 'flag' the accounts of all directors and connected persons as a check to ensure continuing compliance with the company's share dealing code. Any unexpected or unauthorised movements on these accounts can highlight a failure to comply with company policy and identify the need for further investigation.

Notification of close periods

As a matter of best practice company secretaries should write to all directors at least two weeks ahead of any regular results announcement drawing attention to the fact that a 'close period' will be commencing and that for a period of time any request to deal in the shares of the company will be declined.

Providing sufficient notice to allow individuals to put their financial affairs in order will overcome the need to decline requests for share transactions during the close period.

Managing prohibited periods

Prohibited periods are potentially more difficult to handle. The very fact that it is a 'prohibited period' rather than a 'close period' immediately flags that there is potential insider information surrounding the company. As such, the last thing that needs to happen is to draw attention to the fact by blanket announcing to employees that requests to deal in the securities of the company will be declined!

Instead, a notification should be sent to those individuals directly involved in the price-sensitive project at the outset informing them of their status at that time. In any case the directors will be aware of the standing of any project but it will become important for the company secretary to ensure that he keeps a separate and accurate insider list of the names of other employees and advisers concerned – and the date and timing of their involvement in the project.

Reminders

At least once a year the company secretary should write to each director reminding them that: (a) they are still subject to the provisions of the company's share dealing code; and (b) of their undertaking to comply. It should not be necessary to obtain acknowledgements for an annual reminder, although once again, copies of the letter sent to directors should be kept for regulatory purposes. However, it should be noted that this annual process could provide a suitable opportunity to check and update details of connected persons.

Requests to deal

The other requirement placed on a company is to maintain written records of requests to deal and the outcome of those requests. This is easily achieved by the simple expedient of requiring all directors to complete a document which will elicit the information required.

The request form should also contain a statement to be countersigned by the applicant confirming that the company's code of share dealing has been read and understood and as far as the individual is concerned they are not in possession of any inside information which would prevent them from undertaking the proposed transaction.

The request form should be make it absolutely clear to all that no transaction should be undertaken until written confirmation of clearance has been returned to the director.

Having been completed by the director, the request form should be passed for authorisation to a designated director – and in the case of board member requests this should usually be the chairman. Paragraph 4 of the Model Codes stipulates the individuals from whom clearance to deal must be sought – and in the case of PDMRs and other employee insiders this can be the company secretary.

CHECKLIST Request to deal

A request to deal form should include:

- the name and position of person wishing to deal;
- the name of the registered holders (if different);
- type of transaction to be undertaken (buy/sell/transfer/exercise options);
- the number or value of shares to be transacted;

- a confirmation that the individual is not aware of any inside information which would prevent him from undertaking the transaction;
- a signature.

The 'clearance to deal' permission should make clear:

- the outcome of the request (granted/denied);
- the time and date by which the transaction must be undertaken;
- the identity of the person authorising;
- the process of notifying the outcome of the transaction to the company.

Declining requests

A request form from a board member or PDMR should not be authorised where inside information exists.

The position is slightly less clear for employee insiders. If the individual is genuinely unaware of the existence of the inside information it may still be permissible for him to continue with the transaction. From a regulatory viewpoint the company is covered by the declaration that the individual is unaware of any inside information. However it may be safer for all concerned to avoid the possible element of doubt by declining the request and providing a private explanation to the individual. In this instance the individual has effectively been notified of a prohibited period (see above) and their details will need to be recorded on the insider list for that matter.

Time limits

Under paragraph 5 of the Model Code, companies have to respond to requests to deal within five business days of the request being made. Paragraph 7 requires individuals to deal as soon as possible – and in any event, within two business days of clearance being received.

The authorised request form should be returned to the individual.

Company directors are required to notify changes in their shareholding to the company in order to meet their Company Act requirements. In turn, their notification to the company to changes to their or their 'connected persons' holdings will generate an announcement by the company to the market as required by the Disclosure Rules. The same requirement is now extended to PDMRs. Incidentally, technically the onus is on the connected person to advise the company, although in practice this is likely to be undertaken by the employee insider.

So, for completeness, and to provide an overall audit trail (should it be required) we suggest that *all* employees should be required to report the outcome of their transaction requests within 48 hours of the expiry deadline for dealing.

By requiring all directors and employee insiders to notify the outcome for a request to deal it will complete an audit trail and provide the company secretary with the information he needs to make a market announcement within the timescales set out in the Listing Rules.

In practice then, the company secretary will know within the week whether a director has dealt and, if so, the details of that deal or whether the permission to undertake that transaction has lapsed and no market announcement is required.

CHECKLIST Post-transaction notification

Following a transaction, the notification information from the director should include:

- the name of the director (or PDMR);
- the reason for responsibility to notify;
- the name of the relevant issuer;
- a description of the financial instrument;
- the nature of the transaction (e.g. acquisition or disposal);
- the date and place of the transaction; and
- the price and volume of the transaction.

Alternatively:

- confirmation that the transaction was not undertaken.

Audit trails

Depending upon the number of directors' transactions a company experiences, it may be necessary to maintain a separate system to track outstanding permissions; should an unforeseen event occur, putting the company into a prohibited period, it will be easy to identify those employees who have sought permission to transact share dealing and to withdraw that permission.

Failure to comply with the Model Code

Any breach of the Listing Rules 'opens the door' to a regulatory investigation. The Financial Services and Markets Act 2000 gives powers to the FSA to appoint an investigator in cases where they *believe* a breach of the Listing Rules may have occurred and the subsequent ability to impose financial sanctions on both individuals and issuers where a breach of the Listing Rules *has* occurred.

In attempting to assess the seriousness of any breach of their Listing Rules, the regulators will be examining company's in-house procedures looking for what they refer to as 'systemic weaknesses'. If found, these are likely to increase the sanctions imposed on both the company and any individual offender.

Companies will need to be able to demonstrate that they have taken all reasonable steps to meeting their Model Code requirements. Instances of systemic weakness would include:

- the absence of any written policies or procedures;
- no list of identified 'employee insiders' beyond members of the board;
- no employees notification/acknowledgement letters;
- the absence of properly maintained records of requests to deal (signed and countersigned);
- a lack of clear audit trails.

Penalties

Where a company is found to be in breach of the Listing Rules, the FSA is able to impose unlimited fines on both the company and individual directors. As statutory penalties, these fines will be excluded from any D&O cover and where imposed on an individual they will represent a personal liability.

The FSA has indicated that there will not be a tariff for failing to meet continuing obligation requirements for breach of the Listing Rules. Instead the severity of the fine will be determined by:

- the seriousness of the breach;
- the extent to which it was deliberate or reckless;
- whether the penalty is to be imposed on an individual;
- the conduct of that person before and following the contravention;
- the disciplinary and compliance record and previous guidance provided by the FSA.

Inside information

Throughout this chapter we have talked about 'inside' information. The FSA Disclosure Rules set out the requirements in relation to disclosing, handling and controlling inside information.

The provisions of the Disclosure Rules are dealt with in greater detail in Chapter 10, but it has been the failure on the part of issuers to properly identify, handle and announce inside information which has led to enforcement of these Rules becoming the bread and butter of the FSA's regulatory regime.

The general disclosure obligations which the Disclosure Rules impose upon a company regarding inside information relate to major new developments in the company's sphere of activity which are not public knowledge and which may lead to a substantial movement in the price of its listed securities.

To this extent it is worth repeating here the main principle of the Disclosure Rules: The requirement is that an issuer must notify the market as soon as possible of 'any inside information which directly concerns the issuer'.

Inside information is defined in s. 118C of the FSMA. It is information of a precise nature which:

- is not generally available;
- relates, directly or indirectly, to one or more issuers of the qualifying investments or to one or more of the qualifying investments; and
- would, if generally available, be likely to have a significant effect on the price of the qualifying investments or on the price of related investments.

Information is precise if it:

- indicates circumstances that exist or may reasonably be expected to come into existence or an event that has occurred or may reasonably be expected to occur; and
- is specific enough to enable a conclusion to be drawn as to the possible effect of those circumstances or that event on the price of qualifying investments or related investments.

Announcing inside information

The test is obviously a subjective one – after all what is a 'significant effect on the price of the qualifying investments'?

No definition is given, simply because what might be significant for one company will not be for another. However, some of the factors to be taken into consideration will include the liquidity of the stock; the normal volatility of the sector; the relative importance of the company to the rest of the market, index or sector; and the price of the shares. The Disclosure Rules provide some helpful guidance for issuers on how to assess whether a particular item of information should be considered 'inside' (Rules 2.2.3G – 2.2.8G Disclosure Rules).

However, whether information relating to the company is inside or not is ultimately defined by the *company*. If the board of a company decides (after due consideration) that the information before it is *not* inside, and records the discussions and the decision-making process in reaching its evaluation, there is a defence to any subsequent accusation of failing to meet the requirements of the Disclosure Rules.

Nevertheless, because it is a market test, the board will also need to demonstrate (and record) that they took appropriate advice from the company's advisers – particularly the corporate broker – in reaching their conclusion. If there is any doubt the board should always assume it is safer to make an announcement than not.

Companies should have a framework for handling inside information, with responsibility for communicating with investors, analysts and the press. Such a framework might cover the areas in the checklist below:

CHECKLIST   Framework for handling inside information

- Consistent procedures for determining what information is significant for it to be considered 'inside' and for releasing that information to the market.

- A clear definition of who is responsible for communicating with analysts, investors and the press. Only identified employees should be given responsibility for communicating such information to reduce the chances of unauthorised disclosure.

- Making it known outside of the company about its internal policies on communication, for example a policy including a statement that a company never comments on a market rumour.

- Arrangements to keep inside information confidential until the moment of announcement.

- A structured communications plan with regular updates on the company's trading position and immediate prospects. This practice is especially helpful if market expectations are out of line or there is a long gap between the end of the period and the publication of interim or preliminary results.

- As a general requirement of a company's internal procedures, the market price of its shares should be continually and carefully monitored, especially when circumstances exist where there are impending developments or matters in the course of negotiation which could cause a substantial movement in the market price of its shares.

Invariably, the regulators will reach their view as to whether an item was price sensitive or otherwise with the benefit of hindsight – and knowing the market's reaction when the information is ultimately disclosed. In these circumstances the need for accurate records cannot be overstated!

There are three very straightforward tests to apply to information when endeavouring to decide whether or not it might be price sensitive. They are:

- Is it company or share specific?
- It is knowledge not generally known?
- Would a regular market user expect that information to be announced?

If all three apply, then generally speaking, you are dealing with price-sensitive or inside information.

If the information or project under examination answers 'yes' to all three of these tests, the company should anticipate making an immediate announcement to the market.

The general rule of thumb is to maintain a watching brief for anything that might be considered to be inside information in relation to the company – and to manage it appropriately. To this end it would probably be apposite to have a general discussion at every board meeting and to apply the 'price-sensitive' tests (above) to all issues surrounding the company.

Timing of announcements

However, the most important words in the Disclosure Rules are:

A company must notify a Regulatory Information Service *as soon as possible* …

In practice, the regulators are interpreting this requirement *very* strictly and are imposing significant financial sanctions on directors and issuers who (for whatever reason) delay the announcement of price-sensitive information into the market.

The guidance in the Disclosure Rules also makes it clear that it is not possible to delay the disclosure of financial difficulties just because the disclosure may prejudice financial negotiations; where matters have crystallised, an announcement is required.

Neither is it acceptable to delay an announcement whilst arrangements are made to call a board meeting. If matters within a company have become that urgent, there should already be processes in place to handle the 'unforeseen event' and, if necessary, an emergency sub-committee of the board should have been established and received the appropriate delegated authority to handle such matters.

A new obligation requires issuers to make any information it releases to the market available on its own internet website by the close of business the following day – and to keep it there for at least a year (Rules 2.3.2R & 2.3.5R Disclosure Rules).

Delaying disclosure of inside information

There are, however, some exceptions available to companies wishing to withhold making a market announcement of inside information. A company can (at its own risk) delay the public disclosure of inside information so as not to prejudice its legitimate interests, although in these circumstances, if you are seeking to withhold making a statement, the FSA should be approached as soon as possible – and at a senior level to discuss possible implications.

In any case, if confidentially has been breached the FSA will insist on an immediate announcement. To that end the rules require companies to have to hand at least a holding announcement which could be released immediately pending further announcements (Rules 2.6.2R & 2.6.3G Disclosure Rules).

CHECKLIST Reviewing internal controls

When a company's directors are reviewing its internal controls and processes, they must satisfy themselves that:

- the processes in place are sufficient to achieve the announcement without delay;
- there is sufficient resource available at all times to ensure that the announcement is suitably verified to meet the accuracy standards referred to above;
- appropriate roles for co-ordinating with a company's advisers for the purposes of making announcements are established and well known;
- contingency plans are in place to ensure that there is always a deputy available to make a decision in the event that the person or persons who usually have responsibility are not available;
- the inability to physically convene a full board meeting is not likely to be regarded as warranting a delay in releasing inside information, since most companies can delegate the authority to make 'emergency' announcements to a small number of directors.

Regulatory enforcement

With their enforcement powers, the FSA has not hesitated to flex its regulatory muscle in applying the Rules and implementing the sanctions now available to them; they have tended to focus on the accuracy and timeliness of corporate disclosures – and for the most part the FSA has been content to pursue miscreants through their civil powers. In this regard there is good and bad news: The good news is that the imprisonment penalties available to the criminal court are not available to the FSA; however the bad news for any offender is that the burden of proof required is lower. Any fine imposed (previously capped at £20,000 under the CJA) is – theoretically – unlimited.

However, where the FSA believes that they can secure a criminal conviction it has been decisive in pursuing individuals using the criminal law. In the first case brought under the powers available to the FSA under the FSMA the sentences imposed were significant in terms of imprisonment. Although the sentences were subsequently reduced on appeal, prison terms were served and the criminal convictions remained.

The willingness (and success) of the FSA in using the criminal law has significant consequences for individuals and issuers who find themselves under investigation. There is now the distinct possibility of police arrest, interviews under caution, charge and criminal prosecution for infringements of FSA Rules.

CONCLUSION

There is much that companies can do to guard against inadvertent infringement, whether on a corporate level or by individual employees:

- be fully aware of the Rules and regulations – and ensure that all employees have been informed about their potential liabilities;

- put in place and document as best you can internal policies and procedures which set out your corporate requirements for staying within the regulations – and specify behaviour which will not be tolerated;

- keep accurate records and audit trails in relation to share dealing undertaken by employee insiders and the manner in which inside information is identified and handled.

CHAPTER 12

Reviewing the governance of company pension schemes

Introduction

The pensions industry continues to undergo immense change and challenge. Not only must it respond to the social and economic pressures with which we are all familiar – an aging population, increased life expectancy, decreased levels of return on investments – but, as a result of a number of high profile cases such as *Maxwell* and *Equitable Life*, there is also added pressure on the industry to 'put its house in order', to demonstrate that it runs itself competently and is acting in the best interest of all those whose rely on it for their future prosperity.

In the first two years of this decade, the key drivers of change in the industry were highlighted in successive industry reviews, of which the most relevant to this chapter are Myners Review of Institutional Investment (2001), the Pickering Report (2002) and the review of the Occupational Pensions Regulatory Authority (2002).

One of the key themes which emerged from these reports, and which has since been formalised in the provisions of the Pensions Act 2004, is an increased emphasis on the governance of pension funds and the personal responsibility and accountability of trustees.

The creation of the Pensions Regulator has been a key step in defining and enforcing the new environment for the trustee. The Regulator has made clear that, whilst it sees its role as being in part to help and advise, it also intends to take a proactive enforcement role and to intervene where things are not working as they should.

The responsibilities of a trustee board to its scheme members are in many respects similar to those of the corporate board to its shareholders, and the levels of competency, control and transparency expected from them are increasingly similar.

In the light of these changes, many pension schemes are undertaking a comprehensive review of the way in which their scheme is governed, in much the same way as corporate boards, to ensure that they are operating correctly and to identify any areas which require attention.

This chapter examines the role of the trustee and focuses particularly on those issues which will impact on the governance of the scheme as regulatory changes come into effect. It considers how trustees should approach a review of procedures and performance, and gives practical guidance on some of the key issues which should be considered in such a review. For the practical purposes of this chapter, it is assumed that the trustee is a company.

Key changes in the regulatory environment

In 2001, the findings of the Myners Review were distilled into a set of principles – a new, voluntary, code of conduct for pension schemes.

Whilst more detailed aspects of the code remain best practice guidelines, some of the key recommendations contained in Myners have since been incorporated in the Pensions Act 2004. The Act contains specific requirements relating to areas such as internal controls, information flow between trustee and employer, and trustee knowledge and understanding.

The way in which the industry is regulated has also changed. During 2005 the Pensions Regulator replaced the Occupational Pensions Regulatory Authority (OPRA) as the regulator of work-based pensions in the UK. This new authority has a wider range of powers than its predecessor, and is intended to strengthen regulatory enforcement and to provide increased regulatory guidance and information for pension schemes. Its Codes of Practice, published over 2005 and 2006 provide detailed guidance as to how the well-governed scheme could be expected to comply with key provisions of the Act.

The areas of the new regulatory framework discussed in this chapter are those which particularly affect the role and responsibilities of trustees.

The Pensions Regulator: Codes of Practice

The Pensions Regulator has drafted a number of Codes of Practice, dealing with specific provisions of the Pensions Act. These Codes set out the standards of conduct expected of pension schemes and give guidance as to how a well run scheme might be expected to comply with the relevant legal requirements. Two of these Codes came into force during 2005, with the remainder scheduled for implementation during 2006.

The Codes are not compulsory but, where a scheme chooses not to follow the guidance contained within them, it will need to be able to demonstrate that its alternative approach satisfies relevant legal requirements.

The Regulator also issues on-line guidance, which gives further explanation and is intended to help promote good practice.

The table below summarises the scope of the Codes of Practice and sets out the Pensions Regulator's current implementation timetable (correct at the end of March 2006).

Code of Practice	Summary of scope	(Planned) date for issue of code	Date legislation in force
Code 1 Reporting breaches of the law	Reporting by statutory 'whistleblowers' of certain breaches of the law which affect pension schemes to the Pensions Regulator. (From April 2005 the requirement is extended to include trustees and their advisers and service providers, managers of schemes not set up under trust, and employers sponsoring or participating in work based pension schemes.)	April 2005	In force
Code 2 Notifiable events	Notifying the Pensions Regulator of prescribed events which occur in respect of pension schemes, and in respect of employers who sponsor pension schemes.	June 2005	In force
Code 3 Funding defined benefits	Implementation of the funding arrangements that apply to most private sector occupational pension schemes that provide defined benefits.	Feb 2006	In force

Code of Practice	Summary of scope	(Planned) date for issue of code	Date legislation in force
Reporting late payment of contributions to occupational money purchase schemes (Draft)	Trustees or managers of occupational money purchase schemes to report late payments to the Pensions Regulator in certain circumstances.	May 2006	April 2006
Reporting late payment of contribution to personal pension schemes (Draft)	Managers of personal pension schemes to report late payments to the Pensions Regulator in certain circumstances.	May 2006	April 2006
Member nominated trustees and directors (Draft)	Implementation of arrangements to ensure that at least one-third of the trustees or trustee directors are member-nominated. Definition of reasonable period within which specified steps must be taken.	June 2006	April 2006
Trustee knowledge and understanding (Draft)	Trustees of relevant schemes to have an appropriate body of knowledge and understanding of the law relating to pensions and trusts and the principles relating to the funding of occupational pension schemes and investment of scheme assets.	June 2006	April 2006
Reasonable periods for the purposes of the Occupational Pensions Schemes (Disclosure of Information Regulations 2006).	What constitutes a 'reasonable' period where mentioned in the Disclosure Regulations	October 2006	October 2006

Code of Practice	Summary of scope	(Planned) date for issue of code	Date legislation in force
Early leavers – reasonable periods (Draft)	Trustees or managers duty to provide members who leave schemes after a short period of membership with a statement of their entitlements. Definition of reasonable period within which specified steps must be taken.	May 2006	April 2006
Modification of subsisting rights (Draft)	Exercise of new power to make limited modifications to subsisting rights to benefits under occupational pension schemes whilst protecting the accrued rights of members.	June 2006	April 2006
Internal controls (Draft)	Implementation of the requirement for trustees and managers to have adequate internal controls to ensure that an occupational scheme is administered and managed correctly.	June 2006	December 2005

Scheme funding framework

One of the key benefits to defined benefit schemes contained in the Pensions Act is that it gives them greater freedom and flexibility in developing funding strategies appropriate to their circumstances. The Pensions Act replaces the Minimum Funding Requirement (MFR) for defined benefit schemes with a scheme funding framework. This covers many issues, such as setting a scheme specific Statutory Funding Objective (SFO).

Under the new requirements, which came into effect in February 2006, a defined benefit scheme is required to have, as a minimum, 'sufficient and appropriate assets to cover its technical provisions'. The trustee and employer are expected to negotiate an agreement on this minimum figure and also on the levels of contribution which will be necessary to achieve and maintain it.

Trustees are required to prepare and regularly review a written Statement of Funding Principles, setting out their policy for ensuring that the SFO will be met, highlighting the methods and assumptions to be used, and specifying the period over which any shortfall will be met.

In order to achieve this, trustees will require full and accurate information about the employer's financial standing. There are therefore implications for the flow of information between trustee and employer.

If the trustees and the employer are unable to agree any on of these issues, the matter must be referred to the Pensions Regulator who will have the power to give directions or, if agreement cannot be reached, to impose a schedule of contributions.

The Act also contains a new requirement for trustees of occupational pension schemes to review their Statement of Investment Principles (SIP) at least every three years, replacing the less specific requirement to review the document 'from time to time'.

Employer requirement to consult

With effect from April 2006, the Pensions Act requires employers to consult members of pension schemes on any changes planned to the scheme which will affect future service benefits – for example, a change from defined benefit to defined contribution. The precise requirements will depend on the number of employees in the scheme.

In the light of the requirement for more formal communication, those schemes which have not already done do may wish to consider setting up a liaison committee to help ensure regular and structured communication between employer and scheme members.

Changes to the structure and role of the trustee

Background

The role of the trustee remains unchanged: to manage the pension scheme in line with the scheme's rules and legal requirements, and to hold the scheme's assets in trust on behalf of the scheme members. The detailed way in which this is achieved and the way in which trustees will comply with new regulation, will vary depending on the nature and administrative structure of the scheme concerned. In this chapter we will therefore focus on the collective duties of the trustee board and the high level duties of the individual trustee.

Trustees are normally appointed by the employer or by existing trustees, in accordance with the scheme's governing document and any statutory requirements. Typically, they are drawn from the following groups:

- members of the scheme;
- employees of the company;
- the employer (director of the sponsoring company);

- professional trustees (the Pensions Regulator sees the appointment of independent professional trustees such as lawyers or actuaries as a positive step in introducing expert knowledge and experience – as well as independence – to the board);
- professional trustee companies (since the Maxwell affair, the use of corporate trustees has increased. In this case the fund has a commerical relationship with a company providing trustee services. That company will provide an appropriate person to serve as a representative of the trustee company).

Member-nominated trustees

Under current regulations, a minimum of one-third of trustees should normally be nominated by members of the scheme. In practice, however, the majority of sponsoring companies have been able to opt-out from appointing member-nominated trustees, provided their members agree to this. Companies have felt that opting out allows them the freedom to appoint individuals with a higher level of relevant knowledge and experience as trustees.

The proportion of member-nominated trustees has therefore varied enormously, with scheme members often under-represented or, occasionally, not represented at all.

However, the Pensions Act 2004 removes the opt-out from sponsoring companies, so that from April 2006 all must take steps to appoint at least the minimum proportion of member-nominated and member-*selected* trustees (the relevant Code of Practice to be published in June 2006, will contain guidance on this process). Initially the minimum will be one-third, but this may be increased to 50% by 2009/2010.

The trustee nomination process must involve all active members and pensioners, and the selection process should involve at least some scheme members. Exactly how this will be achieved is not prescribed, but will be determined by each scheme.

The emphasis on the appointment of member-nominated trustees is intended to ensure that the trustee board collectively has a good understanding of, and (perhaps more importantly) takes account of, the views and concerns of scheme beneficiaries.

The introduction of a higher proportion of lay trustees, combined with the new competency requirements, has implications not only for the process of trustee selection, but also for their initial and ongoing training and education.

Trustee knowledge and understanding

A survey conducted for the Myners review, published in 2001, found that:

- 62% of trustees had no professional qualifications in finance or investment;
- more than 50% of trustees received less than three days' training when they became trustees;

- 44% of trustees had not attended any courses since their initial 12 months of trustee-ship; and

- 49% of trustees spent three hours or less preparing for pension investment matters;

- 77% of trustees had no in-house professionals to assist them.

The report concluded that the demands made of pension fund trustees were often 'wholly unrealistic…They are being asked to take crucial investment decisions – yet many lack either the resources or the expertise. They are often unsupported by in-house staff, and are rarely paid'.

The implications for the governance of pension schemes are obvious – and rather worrying! Since the publication of the Myners Report, many changes have been made and trustees are now generally better informed and supported in their role.

However, the government felt that change was not sufficiently rapid or universal and, from April 2006, trustees have had a *statutory duty* to be conversant with their trust deed and rules, statements of investment and funding principles and any other document relating to their scheme's administration. They must also have sufficient understanding of the law relating to pensions and trusts, and the principles relating to funding and investment, to enable them to carry out their duties.

Specifically, the Pensions Regulator states that trustees should have sufficient knowledge and understanding to enable them to:

- increase their own confidence in their ability to carry out their roles;

- know about their powers as well as their duties and responsibilities;

- understand their own schemes, how they work and, in the case of defined benefit (DB) schemes, the importance of the employer covenant;

- understand the advice they are given, enter into discussion with their advisers and participate fully in decision making;

- challenge any of their advisers as appropriate;

- recognise when they need to consult their own or other advisers for particular specialist advice or when they need to consider reselection;

- recognise conflicts of interest and be able to deal with them;

- become familiar with the most important parts of the documentation which sets out the rules governing their schemes.

There is some flexibility in these requirements: trustees are expected to learn only what is appropriate for their particular needs and circumstances, and they are not expected to become experts in investment matters.

However, the Pensions Regulator has stated that it intends as a matter of routine to ask questions of scheme trustees about their learning activities and their knowledge and understanding, and that the responses they give may influence its assessment of the scheme's risk profile. There will be a six-month 'grace period' for new trustees, within which they must achieve the expected standards of knowledge and understanding.

The emphasis on the provision of training and information to trustees must therefore be maintained by all schemes.

Typically this will take the form of:

- induction for new trustees;
- periodic briefings on developments in the pensions industry;
- periodic briefings on legal and regulatory developments;
- regular assessments of trustees' knowledge levels and training requirements;
- provision of ongoing training in line with those requirements identified.

Guidance and training on the trustee role is available from a range of sources.

- The Pensions Regulator offers a number of resources for trustees:
  - a comprehensive guide for trustees which is available from their website on www.thepensionsregulator.gov.uk/trustees/;
  - scope guidance, setting out in detail the areas in which trustees are expected to be knowledgeable, applicable both to Defined Benefit and Defined Contribution schemes. An extract from the Scope for Defined Benefit Schemes with associated defined contribution arrangements is included in this chapter for illustration;
  - an e-learning programme is being prepared at the time of writing.
- Courses for trustees are offered by various industry associations, such as the National Association of Pension Funds (NAPF) and the Pensions Management Institute (PMI), and of course by professional advisers such as lawyers and pensions consultants. Some of these courses will lead to professional qualifications.
- The PMI also provides useful guidance for trustees, including a checklist for new trustees, again available on the Institute's website.
- Both the PMI and NAPF run trustee networks, which offer a range of benefits including seminars, newsletters and training for trustees. Information is available on their respective websites: www.pensions-pmi.org.uk and www.napf.co.uk.

CHECKLIST The scope of knowledge required

The law relating to trusts

1 This includes an understanding of the special nature of a pension trust and the duties, obligations and powers of trustees to operate pension schemes in accordance with the law and with the trust deed and documents.

The law relating to pensions

2 This includes occupational pensions legislation (in outline) and the key provisions of related legislation that affects pension schemes and impacts on the role and activities of trustees.

Investment: defined benefit (DB) and defined contribution (DC) scheme occupational arrangements (including AVCs)

3 This includes the different types of assets available for investment and their characteristics.

Funding: defined benefit (DB) occupational arrangements

4 This includes the principles relating to the funding of occupational DB schemes and the way in which funding is dependent upon the financial circumstances of the sponsoring employer and the value of the liabilities of the scheme.

Contributions: defined benefit (DB) occupational arrangements

5 This includes the principles relating to the funding of occupational DB schemes and the way in which contribution levels are dependent upon the funding of the scheme.

Strategic asset allocation: defined benefit (DB) occupational arrangements

6 This includes the principles relating to the suitability of different asset classes to meet the liabilities of the scheme.

Funding: defined contribution (DC) occupational arrangements (including AVCs)

7 This includes the principles relating to the funding of occupational DC arrangements and the risks borne by scheme members.

Investment choices: defined contribution (DC) occupational arrangements (including AVCs)

8 This includes the principles relating to the choice of investments.

Fund management: occupational defined benefit (DB) and defined contribution (DC) scheme arrangements (including AVCs)

9 This includes the principles of fund management and how performance can be measured

This checklist is taken from the Draft Code of Practice, Trustee Knowledge and Understanding.

Reviewing the trustee board

Background

In the light of the increasing demands made of trustees, and the personal liability which now accompanies the role, many schemes now undertake an annual performance review, in much the same way as corporate boards, to assess whether the people, processes and controls currently in place within the scheme are sufficiently strong, and to improve on any areas of weakness. It also provides an opportunity for trustees to assess their current levels of knowledge and understanding and to identify any training or education requirements. The recommendation to conduct such a review of trustee performance is, of course, contained within the Myners' principles.

The pension trustee board is no different from the corporate board in that its success is dependent on a combination of people and process. Any effective review of trustee performance must therefore focus on those areas which most directly contribute to the board's ability to take informed decisions and to communicate those decisions and the processes underlying them, to their scheme members.

These will include:

- the individual skills and personal qualities of trustees;
- their ability to work together in a culture of openness and trust;
- the structure, processes, controls underlying and supporting their decision-making processes;
- relationships with all stakeholders – the employer, professional advisers, and scheme members.

The key elements of a review of trustee performance, and some of the issues which should be considered, are set out on page 161.

Conducting a performance review

A review of trustee performance should encompass all of the issues outlined earlier in this chapter, and might be structured under headings such as:

- board composition;
- governance of the scheme, including voluntary compliance with Myners' principles;
- approach to investment, including asset allocation and benchmarking;
- relationships and communication with stakeholders.

Some trustees prefer to carry out any review in-house, whilst others choose to seek help from an external service provider. There are advantages to both approaches, and the final decision will depend on a number of factors, such as the perceived importance of an independent approach, available budget and the workload of the Secretary to the Trustee. (See Chapter 5 for detailed advice on the various ways in which a review might be approached.)

The three most common and effective methods of conducting a review discussed in Chapter 5 would be equally applicable in this context and are;

- a structured, round table discussion, which might be led by the chairman or by an external facilitator;

- one-on-one interviews between the chairman and trustees;

- a standard questionnaire, to be completed by all trustees seeking their views on various aspects of their collective performance;

Some schemes choose to appraise the performance of individual trustees at the same time as the collective performance of the board. Others prefer to approach the two as separate exercises. Whatever approach is chosen, the most important aspect of the review is that it should lead to a set of specific action points and objectives for the board and for individual trustees, and that it should be viewed as a practical and constructive exercise.

The following is a guide to the some of the key issues which should be included in a review of trustee performance.

CHECKLIST A review of trustee performance

Board composition

1 Is the composition of the trustee board appropriate?

- Do trustees collectively have an appropriate mix of knowledge and experience?

- Does the trustee board have:

- The correct balance proportion of member-nominated trustees to ensure that the company view does not dominate?

- An appropriate number and mix of independent trustees?

There is a strong argument in favour of benchmarking the board's composition against that of either similar sized schemes or similar size sponsoring companies. Some schemes are already beginning to do this.

2 Has the board established appropriate sub-committees?

- Trustees should consider as part of a general review of the trustee board's composition whether the number and type of sub-committees they have is appropriate to their needs and workload. Whilst an Investment committee is standard (see below), some boards have also set up, for example, an audit committee, and/or a benefits committee.

- The terms of reference for any sub-committee should be set out in writing and reviewed regularly.

Support for trustees

1 Do trustees have:

- Appropriate access to information regarding the pensions industry and investment matters in particular?
- An appropriate level of support from their in-house and/or external advisers?

2 Do trustees receive adequate support from in-house pensions staff?

- Do staff provide a good level of support in areas such as:

  record-keeping;

  providing updates and briefings on the pensions industry?

- Where there is an in-house pensions department, it is important to ensure that the staff are appropriately skilled and qualified in pensions matters, and that there are good communications in place between them and the trustees.

- Are there effective procedures in place to support the relationship? It is a good idea to hold regular meetings between trustees and in-house staff. There should be a formal agenda for this meeting, and discussions should also be minuted.

3 Are trustees remunerated for their work?

- Whilst there seems to be general agreement that independent trustees should be remunerated for their work, there is less commitment to the concept of additional payment for employee trustees. This appears to be viewed in many cases as a voluntary role and one which contributes to the individual's professional development.

- An increasing number of schemes are beginning to undertake regular benchmarking of trustee remuneration – both the levels of remuneration and also the basis on which it is calculated.

4 Do trustees receive appropriate training?

- Initial training

  It is general practice for trustees to receive some initial training on appointment. Trustees should receive thorough induction training covering areas such as the scheme itself, general issues relating to the pensions industry, the responsibilities of trustees, and investment issues.

- Ongoing training

  Best practice is to review training needs regularly and formally and to draw up individual and collective training plans for the year ahead. These might be incorporated into the business plan. There should also be a process for trustees to be kept up-to-date with developments in the pensions industry by their advisers.

Business plan

1   Has the board drawn up a formal business plan?

- Best practice is that all trustees should draw up a formal business plan to prioritise their activities during the year and to allow for measurement of performance against objectives.

- High level objectives for the trustee board might include:
  - ensuring that the scheme's commitments to its members are met;
  - protecting the long-term security of scheme members;
  - maintaining an appropriate balance between cost and risk.

- Additional matters for all schemes should include:
  - regular review of advisers to the scheme;
  - regular review and update of the SIP;
  - regular assessment of trustees' individual and collective performance;
  - training and education for trustees.

- Plans for defined benefit schemes might include:
  - funding and contributions;
  - investment strategy.

- Plans for defined contribution schemes might include:
  - investment choices;
  - member information.

Assessing the performance of advisers to the scheme

1   Some of the issues to consider with regard to professional advisers are:

- Ensuring that there are clearly worded service agreements in place with all advisers, including measurable objectives.

- Advisers' performance should be evaluated against these objectives on a regular and formal basis.

- All advisers and service providers to defined contribution schemes should be subject to particular scrutiny to ensure that they are managing the scheme in all respects for the benefit of the scheme beneficiaries.

Governance and shareholder activism

1   Does the scheme agree with fund managers an approach to governance and shareholder activism?

Some trustees feel that their position on governance issues is largely irrelevant as their percentage holdings in any given company may be rather small. However best practice dictates that *all* schemes should assume responsibility for ensuring that fund managers have an explicit strategy, setting out the circumstances in which they will intervene in a company; the approach they will use in doing so; and how they measure the effectiveness of this strategy.

2   Is the scheme's approach to governance in those companies in which it is invested set out in a written governance policy? If so, this policy should be included in the SIP.

The SIP should also disclose the extent to which social, environmental and ethical considerations are taken into account in the investment strategy, and also the scheme's policy on exercising the rights attached to investments.

3   Does the scheme have clear policies setting out its approach to internal governance issues, including identification and management of potential conflicts of interest?

Asset allocation

1   Do trustees and their advisers consider a full range of strategic investment opportunities?

- No asset class should be excluded without good reason. Where a specific asset class is excluded, the reason for the decision should be clearly and publicly stated.
- When selecting asset classes, trustees should consider only the circumstances of their own fund and their overall investment strategy.

Benchmarking

1   Are the benchmarks agreed with fund managers appropriate to the scheme?

- Trustees should ensure that benchmarks selected encourage optimal performance.
- Trustees should also consider for each asset class invested, whether active or passive management would be more appropriate given the efficiency, liquidity and level of transaction costs in the market concerned.

Transparency and communications

1   Is the SIP regularly and properly maintained?

- The SIP is a key document, setting out and explaining the trustees' approach to investment and their administration of the scheme. It must be regularly reviewed and updated as necessary to reflect any changes in approach.

As a minimum requirement, the SIP should set out:

  - the decision-making process for the scheme and why this structure has been selected;
  - the fund's investment objective;
  - the fund's planned asset allocation strategy, including projected investment returns on each asset class, and how the strategy has been arrived at;

- the mandates given to all the scheme's advisers and managers; and
- the fee structures in place for all advisers and managers, and why this set of structures has been selected.

Best practice would be to include additional information such as:

- Identification and assessment of the main types of risk inherent in an investment strategy, e.g. volatility of market prices; lack of diversification.
- The scheme's position on social, ethical and environmental issues.

The SIP should be available to all scheme members, and trustees are required to report to members its key provisions on a formal, annual basis.

2 Other steps which trustees should take to increase transparency and accountability include:

- Maintaining a formal record of all discussion and decisions taken at meetings of the board and its sub-committee/s.
- Maintaining a formal record of discussions with the sponsor, and all decisions taken.

Relations with members

1 Do trustees have procedures in place for regular dialogue with members?

- A particular point to note for trustees of defined contribution schemes is the need to ensure that all scheme members fully understand the nature and risks of such schemes, and the implications for them as beneficiaries.
- Increasingly, schemes make use of the internet to communicate news and information regarding the pensions industry in general and the scheme in particular to active and retired members. All relevant policies and procedures should be available on the scheme's website, as well as the annual report. An on-line help or enquiry facility linked to the scheme's website can be a particularly useful means of allowing members to raise any questions or concerns with the trustees.

2 Do trustees have procedures in place for regular dialogue with the employer?

- The importance of maintaining good communication with the employer was referred to earlier in the chapter. There should be processes in place for formal discussion and decision making, and a formal record of all discussions should be maintained.

Regular meetings between trustees and nominated representatives of the employer may prove helpful in maintaining dialogue.

Common issues emerging from reviews

Policies and procedures

As might be anticipated, common issues, such as those outlined below, emerge from assessments of trustee performance. 'We do that, we just don't write it down' is a common, but no longer acceptable, observation from trustees! All activities, discussions, decisions, and policies should be clearly and formally documented, not only for the sake of transparency but also to provide an audit trail and to protect the interests of trustees.

Ideally, the output from the performance review will naturally feed into some or all of these documents.

CHECKLIST   Areas which should be documented

- Nomination and selection policy for trustees.
- Policy for identifying and dealing with conflicts of interest.
- Communications strategy setting out the frequency and nature of communication with various stakeholder groups.
- Business plan.
- Governance policy.
- Assessment framework and criteria for the board and for its advisers.
- Objectives and training programmes for individual trustees.
- Administration agreement with the company or with external service providers (a sample agreement can be downloaded from the PMI (www.pensions-pmi.org.uk).

Balance

It is still early days in this new regulatory environment and many trustees are struggling to find an appropriate balance in various areas of their work.

This is particularly the case in relation to the level of dependence on advisers. Trustees are not expected to be experts in legal, actuarial or investment matters, but they are expected to have a sufficient level of knowledge to question and, where necessary challenge, their professional advisers. Assessments have sometimes suggested an over-reliance on external advice and an unwillingness to question that advice.

Identifying an appropriate level of dependence, and taking steps to improve the skills and knowledge base of trustees where necessary will be a continuing objective for many trustee boards.

Feedback from performance reviews also suggests that a balance must be achieved between maintaining a constructive degree of flexibility and complying with the requirement to formalise procedures.

Many trustees are not convinced of the need for a business plan, for example. Others cannot see the value in a governance policy. This is very much a question of changing the culture to bring it more into line with that of the corporate board in terms of transparency and accountability.

Relationship with professional advisers

Many trustees have long-standing relationships with their advisers who have in effect become trusted insiders. This should not allow the relationship to become too 'comfortable'. It should continue to be managed in a formal, transparent and professional way.

A survey conducted by Price Waterhouse Coopers in 2004 (Findings of UK Pension Scheme Governance Survey, March 2004) into the governance of pension scheme found that only 46% of respondents assessed the performance of their advisers against consistent criteria.

A common view appears to be that 'we're very satisfied with the service we're given. If we weren't happy with their performance, then we'd do something about it'. This is no longer sufficient, and there must now be a more formal element to the management of these relationships.

Scope and complexity of the role

There is a strong awareness that the roles of the trustees are becoming increasingly broad and the issues they are required to deal with are increasingly complex. As well as recognising a need to commit more time to their duties, many trustees also see a requirement for:

- more frequent meetings;
- more time to consider issues ahead of meetings and to take advice as necessary;
- increased information flow from in-house or external advisers;
- increased training;
- additional independent/professional trustees;
- additional committees to whom authority for defined elements of the role can be delegated.

CONCLUSION

- The Pensions Act 2004.has significantly increased the emphasis on individual responsibility and liability for trustees.
- Training and education for trustees is more important than ever.
- Trustee boards should review their effectiveness, to ensure that individual skills and knowledge, internal controls, supporting policies and procedures, relationships within the board and with members, advisers and employer, are all appropriate.
- The new Pensions Regulator has greater powers of intervention. Trustees are well advised to ensure their house is in order!

Contents for the Appendices

Appendices 1–6 and 9 are reproduced with permission of the Financial Reporting Council.

Appendix 1
The Combined Code on corporate governance

November 2005

PREAMBLE

1 This Code supersedes and replaces the Combined Code issued by the Hampel committee on Corporate Governance in June 1998. It derives from a review of the role and effectiveness of non-executive directors by Derek Higgs[1] and a review of audit committees[2] by a group led by Sir Robert Smith.

2 The Financial Services Authority has said that it will replace the 1998 Code that is annexed to the Listing Rules with the revised Code and will seek to make consequential Rule changes. There will be consultation on the necessary Rule changes but not further consultation on the Code provisions themselves.

3 It is intended that the new Code will apply for reporting years beginning on or after 1 November 2003.

4 The Code contains main and supporting principles and provisions. The existing Listing Rules require listed companies to make a disclosure statement in two parts in relation to the Code. In the first part of the statement, the company has to report on how it applies the principles in the Code. In future this will need to cover both main and supporting principles. The form and content of this part of the statement are not prescribed, the intention being that companies should have a free hand to explain their governance policies in the light of the principles, including any special circumstances applying to them which have led to a particular approach. In the second part of the statement the company has either to confirm that it complies with the Code's provisions or – where it does not – to provide an explanation. This 'comply or explain' approach has been in operation for over ten years and the flexibility it offers has been widely welcomed both by company boards and by investors. It is for shareholders and others to evaluate the company's statement

5 While it is expected that listed companies will comply with the Code's provisions most of the time, it is recognised that departure from the provisions of the Code may be justified in particular circumstances. Every company must review each provision carefully and give a considered explanation if it departs from the Code provisions.

6 Smaller listed companies, in particular those new to listing, may judge that some of the provisions are disproportionate or less relevant in their case. Some of the provisions do not apply to companies below FTSE 350. Such companies may nonetheless consider that it would be appropriate to adopt the approach in the Code and they are encouraged to consider this. Investment companies typically have a different board structure, which may affect the relevance of particular provisions.

7   Whilst recognising that directors are appointed by shareholders who are the owners of companies, it is important that those concerned with the evaluation of governance should do so with
common sense in order to promote partnership and trust, based on mutual understanding.
They should pay due regard to companies' individual circumstances and bear in mind in particular the size and complexity of the company and the nature of the risks and challenges it
faces. Whilst shareholders have every right to challenge companies' explanations if they are
unconvincing, they should not be evaluated in a mechanistic way and departures from the
Code should not be automatically treated as breaches. Institutional shareholders and their
agents should be careful to respond to the statements from companies in a manner that supports the 'comply or explain' principle. As the principles in Section 2 make clear, institutional
shareholders should carefully consider explanations given for departure from the Code and
make reasoned judgements in each case. They should put their views to the company and be
prepared to enter a dialogue if they do not accept the company's position. Institutional shareholders should be prepared to put such views in writing where appropriate.

8   Nothing in this Code should be taken to override the general requirements of law to treat
shareholders equally in access to information.

9   This publication includes guidance on how to comply with particular parts of the Code: first,
'Internal Control: Revised Guidance for Directors on the Combined Code',[3] which relates to
Code provisions on internal control (C.2 and part of C.3 in the Code); and, second, 'Audit
Committees: Combined Code Guidance', produced by the Smith Group, which relates to the
provisions on audit committees and auditors (C.3 of the Code). In both cases, the guidance
suggests ways of applying the relevant Code principles and of complying with the relevant
Code provisions.

10 In addition, this volume also includes suggestions for good practice from the Higgs report.

11 The revised Code does not include material in the previous Code on the disclosure of directors' remuneration. This is because 'The Directors' Remuneration Report Regulations 2002'[4]
are now in force and supersede the earlier Code provisions. These require the directors of a
company to prepare a remuneration report. It is important that this report is clear, transparent
and understandable to shareholders.

CODE OF BEST PRACTICE

SECTION 1 COMPANIES A. DIRECTORS

A.1 The Board

Main Principle

**Every company should be headed by an effective board, which is collectively responsible for
the success of the company.**

Supporting Principles

The board's role is to provide entrepreneurial leadership of the company within a framework of
prudent and effective controls which enables risk to be assessed and managed. The board should

set the company's strategic aims, ensure that the necessary financial and human resources are in place for the company to meet its objectives and review management performance. The board should set the company's values and standards and ensure that its obligations to its shareholders and others are understood and met.

All directors must take decisions objectively in the interests of the company.

As part of their role as members of a unitary board, non-executive directors should constructively challenge and help develop proposals on strategy. Non-executive directors should scrutinise the performance of management in meeting agreed goals and objectives and monitor the reporting of performance. They should satisfy themselves on the integrity of financial information and that financial controls and systems of risk management are robust and defensible. They are responsible for determining appropriate levels of remuneration of executive directors and have a prime role in appointing, and where necessary removing, executive directors, and in succession planning.

Code provisions

A.1.1 The board should meet sufficiently regularly to discharge its duties effectively. There should be a formal schedule of matters specifically reserved for its decision. The annual report should include a statement of how the board operates, including a high level statement of which types of decisions are to be taken by the board and which are to be delegated to management.

A.1.2 The annual report should identify the chairman, the deputy chairman (where there is one), the chief executive, the senior independent director and the chairmen and members of the nomination, audit and remuneration committees. It should also set out the number of meetings of the board and those committees and individual attendance by directors.

A.1.3 The chairman should hold meetings with the non-executive directors without the executives present. Led by the senior independent director, the non-executive directors should meet without the chairman present at least annually to appraise the chairman's performance (as described in A.6.1) and on such other occasions as are deemed appropriate.

A.1.4 Where directors have concerns which cannot be resolved about the running of the company or a proposed action, they should ensure that their concerns are recorded in the board minutes. On resignation, a non-executive director should provide a written statement to the chairman, for circulation to the board, if they have any such concerns.

A.1.5 The company should arrange appropriate insurance cover in respect of legal action against its directors.

A.2 Chairman and chief executive

Main Principle

There should be a clear division of responsibilities at the head of the company between the running of the board and the executive responsibility for the running of the company's business. No one individual should have unfettered powers of decision.

Supporting Principle

The chairman is responsible for leadership of the board, ensuring its effectiveness on all aspects of its role and setting its agenda. The chairman is also responsible for ensuring that the directors receive accurate, timely and clear information. The chairman should ensure effective communication with shareholders. The chairman should also facilitate the effective contribution of non-executive directors in particular and ensure constructive relations between executive and non-executive directors.

Code provisions

A.2.1   The roles of chairman and chief executive should not be exercised by the same individual. The division of responsibilities between the chairman and chief executive should be clearly established, set out in writing and agreed by the board.

A.2.2[5]   The chairman should on appointment meet the independence criteria set out in A.3.1 below. A chief executive should not go on to be chairman of the same company. If exceptionally a board decides that a chief executive should become chairman, the board should consult major shareholders in advance and should set out its reasons to shareholders at the time of the appointment and in the next annual report.

A.3 Board balance and independence

Main Principle

The board should include a balance of executive and non-executive directors (and in particular independent non-executive directors) such that no individual or small group of individuals can dominate the board's decision taking.

Supporting Principles

The board should not be so large as to be unwieldy. The board should be of sufficient size that the balance of skills and experience is appropriate for the requirements of the business and that changes to the board's composition can be managed without undue disruption.

To ensure that power and information are not concentrated in one or two individuals, there should be a strong presence on the board of both executive and non-executive directors.

The value of ensuring that committee membership is refreshed and that undue reliance is not placed on particular individuals should be taken into account in deciding chairmanship and membership of committees.

No one other than the committee chairman and members is entitled to be present at a meeting of the nomination, audit or remuneration committee, but others may attend at the invitation of the committee.

Code provisions

A.3.1   The board should identify in the annual report each non-executive director it considers to be independent.[6] The board should determine whether the director is independent in character and judgement and whether there are relationships or circumstances which are likely to affect, or could appear to affect, the director's judgement. The board should state its reasons if it determines that a director is independent notwithstanding the existence of relationships or circumstances which may appear relevant to its determination, including if the director:

- has been an employee of the company or group within the last five years;

- has, or has had within the last three years, a material business relationship with the company either directly, or as a partner, shareholder, director or senior employee of a body that has such a relationship with the company;

- has received or receives additional remuneration from the company apart from a director's fee, participates in the company's share option or a performance-related pay scheme, or is a member of the company's pension scheme;

- has close family ties with any of the company's advisers, directors or senior employees;

- holds cross-directorships or has significant links with other directors through involvement in other companies or bodies;

- represents a significant shareholder; or

- has served on the board for more than nine years from the date of their first election.

A.3.2 Except for smaller companies,[7] at least half the board, excluding the chairman, should comprise non-executive directors determined by the board to be independent. A smaller company should have at least two independent non-executive directors.

A.3.3 The board should appoint one of the independent non-executive directors to be the senior independent director. The senior independent director should be available to shareholders if they have concerns which contact through the normal channels of chairman, chief executive or finance director has failed to resolve or for which such contact is inappropriate.

A.4 Appointments to the board

Main Principle

There should be a formal, rigorous and transparent procedure for the appointment of new directors to the board.

Supporting Principles

Appointments to the board should be made on merit and against objective criteria. Care should be taken to ensure that appointees have enough time available to devote to the job. This is particularly important in the case of chairmanships.

The board should satisfy itself that plans are in place for orderly succession for appointments to the board and to senior management, so as to maintain an appropriate balance of skills and experience within the company and on the board.

Code provisions

A.4.1 There should be a nomination committee which should lead the process for board appointments and make recommendations to the board. A majority of members of the nomination committee should be independent non-executive directors. The chairman or an independent non-executive director should chair the committee, but the chairman should not chair the nomination committee when it is dealing with the appointment of a successor to the chairmanship. The nomination committee should make available[8] its terms of reference, explaining its role and the authority delegated to it by the board.

A.4.2 The nomination committee should evaluate the balance of skills, knowledge and experience on the board and, in the light of this evaluation, prepare a description of the role and capabilities required for a particular appointment.

A.4.3 For the appointment of a chairman, the nomination committee should prepare a job specification, including an assessment of the time commitment expected, recognising the need for availability in the event of crises. A chairman's other significant commitments should be disclosed to the board before appointment and included in the annual report. Changes to such commitments should be reported to the board as they arise, and included in the next annual report. No individual should be appointed to a second chairmanship of a FTSE 100 company.[9]

A.4.4 The terms and conditions of appointment of non-executive directors should be made available for inspection.[10] The letter of appointment should set out the expected time commitment. Non-executive directors should undertake that they will have sufficient time to meet what is expected of them. Their other significant commitments should be disclosed to the board before appointment, with a broad indication of the time involved and the board should be informed of subsequent changes.

A.4.5 The board should not agree to a full time executive director taking on more than one non-executive directorship in a FTSE 100 company nor the chairmanship of such a company.

A.4.6 A separate section of the annual report should describe the work of the nomination committee, including the process it has used in relation to board appointments. An explanation should be given if neither an external search consultancy nor open advertising has been used in the appointment of a chairman or a non-executive director.

A.5 Information and professional development

Main Principle

The board should be supplied in a timely manner with information in a form and of a quality appropriate to enable it to discharge its duties. All directors should receive induction on joining the board and should regularly update and refresh their skills and knowledge.

Supporting Principles

The chairman is responsible for ensuring that the directors receive accurate, timely and clear information. Management has an obligation to provide such information but directors should seek clarification or amplification where necessary.

The chairman should ensure that the directors continually update their skills and the knowledge and familiarity with the company required to fulfil their role both on the board and on board committees. The company should provide the necessary resources for developing and updating its directors' knowledge and capabilities.

Under the direction of the chairman, the company secretary's responsibilities include ensuring good information flows within the board and its committees and between senior management and non-executive directors, as well as facilitating induction and assisting with professional development as required.

The company secretary should be responsible for advising the board through the chairman on all governance matters.

Code provisions

A.5.1 The chairman should ensure that new directors receive a full, formal and tailored induction on joining the board. As part of this, the company should offer to major shareholders the opportunity to meet a new non-executive director.

A.5.2 The board should ensure that directors, especially non-executive directors, have access to independent professional advice at the company's expense where they judge it necessary to discharge their responsibilities as directors. Committees should be provided with sufficient resources to undertake their duties.

A.5.3 All directors should have access to the advice and services of the company secretary, who is responsible to the board for ensuring that board procedures are complied with. Both the appointment and removal of the company secretary should be a matter for the board as a whole.

A.6 Performance evaluation

Main Principle

The board should undertake a formal and rigorous annual evaluation of its own performance and that of its committees and individual directors.

Supporting Principle

Individual evaluation should aim to show whether each director continues to contribute effectively and to demonstrate commitment to the role (including commitment of time for board and committee meetings and any other duties). The chairman should act on the results of the performance evaluation by recognising the strengths and addressing the weaknesses of the board and, where appropriate, proposing new members be appointed to the board or seeking the resignation of directors.

Code provision

A.6.1 The board should state in the annual report how performance evaluation of the board, its committees and its individual directors has been conducted. The non-executive directors, led by the senior independent director, should be responsible for performance evaluation of the chairman, taking into account the views of executive directors.

A.7 Re-election

Main Principle

All directors should be submitted for re-election at regular intervals, subject to continued satisfactory performance. The board should ensure planned and progressive refreshing of the board.

Code provisions

A.7.1 All directors should be subject to election by shareholders at the first annual general meeting after their appointment, and to re-election thereafter at intervals of no more than three years. The names of directors submitted for election or re-election should be accompanied by sufficient biographical details and any other relevant information to enable shareholders to take an informed decision on their election.

A.7.2 Non-executive directors should be appointed for specified terms subject to re-election and to Companies Acts provisions relating to the removal of a director. The board should set out to shareholders in the papers accompanying a resolution to elect a non-executive director why they believe an individual should be elected. The chairman should confirm to shareholders when proposing re-election that, following formal performance evaluation, the individual's performance continues to be effective and to demonstrate commitment to the role. Any term beyond six years (e.g. two three-year terms) for a non-executive director should be subject to particularly rigorous review, and should take into account the need for progressive refreshing of the board. Non-executive directors may serve longer than nine years (e.g. three three-year terms), subject to annual re-election. Serving more than nine years could be relevant to the determination of a non-executive director's independence (as set out in provision A.3.1).

B. REMUNERATION

B.1 The level and make-up of remuneration[11]

Main Principles

Levels of remuneration should be sufficient to attract, retain and motivate directors of the quality required to run the company successfully, but a company should avoid paying more than is necessary for this purpose. A significant proportion of executive directors' remuneration should be structured so as to link rewards to corporate and individual performance.

Supporting Principle

The remuneration committee should judge where to position their company relative to other companies. But they should use such comparisons with caution, in view of the risk of an upward ratchet of remuneration levels with no corresponding improvement in performance. They should also be sensitive to pay and employment conditions elsewhere in the group, especially when determining annual salary increases.

Code provisions

Remuneration policy

B.1.1 The performance-related elements of remuneration should form a significant proportion of the total remuneration package of executive directors and should be designed to align their interests with those of shareholders and to give these directors keen incentives to perform at the highest levels. In designing schemes of performance-related remuneration, the remuneration committee should follow the provisions in Schedule A to this Code.

B.1.2 Executive share options should not be offered at a discount save as permitted by the relevant provisions of the Listing Rules.

B.1.3 Levels of remuneration for non-executive directors should reflect the time commitment and responsibilities of the role. Remuneration for non-executive directors should not include share options. If, exceptionally, options are granted, shareholder approval should be sought in advance and any shares acquired by exercise of the options should be held until at least one year after the non-executive director leaves the board. Holding of share options could be relevant to the determination of a non-executive director's independence (as set out in provision A.3.1).

B.1.4 Where a company releases an executive director to serve as a non-executive director elsewhere, the remuneration report[12] should include a statement as to whether or not the director will retain such earnings and, if so, what the remuneration is.

Service contracts and compensation

B.1.5 The remuneration committee should carefully consider what compensation commitments (including pension contributions and all other elements) their directors' terms of appointment would entail in the event of early termination. The aim should be to avoid rewarding poor performance. They should take a robust line on reducing compensation to reflect departing directors' obligations to mitigate loss.

B.1.6 Notice or contract periods should be set at one year or less. If it is necessary to offer longer notice or contract periods to new directors recruited from outside, such periods should reduce to one year or less after the initial period.

B.2 Procedure

Main Principle

There should be a formal and transparent procedure for developing policy on executive remuneration and for fixing the remuneration packages of individual directors. No director should be involved in deciding his or her own remuneration.

Supporting Principles

The remuneration committee should consult the chairman and/or chief executive about their proposals relating to the remuneration of other executive directors. The remuneration committee should also be responsible for appointing any consultants in respect of executive director remuneration. Where executive directors or senior management are involved in advising or supporting the remuneration committee, care should be taken to recognise and avoid conflicts of interest.

The chairman of the board should ensure that the company maintains contact as required with its principal shareholders about remuneration in the same way as for other matters.

Code provisions

B.2.1 The board should establish a remuneration committee of at least three, or in the case of smaller companies[13] two, members, who should all be independent non-executive directors. The remuneration committee should make available[14] its terms of reference, explaining its role and the authority delegated to it by the board. Where remuneration consultants are appointed, a statement should be made available[15] of whether they have any other connection with the company.

B.2.2 The remuneration committee should have delegated responsibility for setting remuneration for all executive directors and the chairman, including pension rights and any compensation payments. The committee should also recommend and monitor the level and structure of remuneration for senior management. The definition of 'senior management' for this purpose should be determined by the board but should normally include the first layer of management below board level.

B.2.3 The board itself or, where required by the articles of association, the shareholders should determine the remuneration of the non-executive directors within the limits set in the articles of association. Where permitted by the articles, the board may however delegate this responsibility to a committee, which might include the chief executive.

B.2.4 Shareholders should be invited specifically to approve all new long-term incentive schemes (as defined in the Listing Rules) and significant changes to existing schemes, save in the circumstances permitted by the Listing Rules.

C. ACCOUNTABILITY AND AUDIT

C.1 Financial Reporting

Main Principle

The board should present a balanced and understandable assessment of the company's position and prospects.

Supporting Principle

The board's responsibility to present a balanced and understandable assessment extends to interim and other price-sensitive public reports and reports to regulators as well as to information required to be presented by statutory requirements.

Code provisions

C.1.1 The directors should explain in the annual report their responsibility for preparing the accounts and there should be a statement by the auditors about their reporting responsibilities.

C.1.2 The directors should report that the business is a going concern, with supporting assumptions or qualifications as necessary.

C.2 Internal Control[16]

Main Principle

The board should maintain a sound system of internal control to safeguard shareholders' investment and the company's assets.

Code provision

C.2.1   The board should, at least annually, conduct a review of the effectiveness of the group's system of internal controls and should report to shareholders that they have done so. The review should cover all material controls, including financial, operational and compliance controls and risk management systems.

C.3 Audit Committee and Auditors[17]

Main Principle

The board should establish formal and transparent arrangements for considering how they should apply the financial reporting and internal control principles and for maintaining an appropriate relationship with the company's auditors.

Code provisions

C.3.1   The board should establish an audit committee of at least three, or in the case of smaller companies[18] two, members, who should all be independent non-executive directors. The board should satisfy itself that at least one member of the audit committee has recent and relevant financial experience.

C.3.2   The main role and responsibilities of the audit committee should be set out in written terms of reference and should include:

- to monitor the integrity of the financial statements of the company, and any formal announcements relating to the company's financial performance, reviewing significant financial reporting judgements contained in them;

- to review the company's internal financial controls and, unless expressly addressed by a separate board risk committee composed of independent directors, or by the board itself, to review the company's internal control and risk management systems;

- to monitor and review the effectiveness of the company's internal audit function;

- to make recommendations to the board, for it to put to the shareholders for their approval in general meeting, in relation to the appointment, re-appointment and removal of the external auditor and to approve the remuneration and terms of engagement of the external auditor;

- to review and monitor the external auditor's independence and objectivity and the effectiveness of the audit process, taking into consideration relevant UK professional and regulatory requirements;

- to develop and implement policy on the engagement of the external auditor to supply non-audit services, taking into account relevant ethical guidance regarding the provision of non-audit services by the external audit firm; and to report to the board, identifying any matters in respect of which it considers that action or improvement is needed and making recommendations as to the steps to be taken.

C.3.3   The terms of reference of the audit committee, including its role and the authority delegated to it by the board, should be made available.[19] A separate section of the annual report should describe the work of the committee in discharging those responsibilities.

C.3.4 The audit committee should review arrangements by which staff of the company may, in confidence, raise concerns about possible improprieties in matters of financial reporting or other matters. The audit committee's objective should be to ensure that arrangements are in place for the proportionate and independent investigation of such matters and for appropriate follow-up action.

C.3.5 The audit committee should monitor and review the effectiveness of the internal audit activities. Where there is no internal audit function, the audit committee should consider annually whether there is a need for an internal audit function and make a recommendation to the board, and the reasons for the absence of such a function should be explained in the relevant section of the annual report.

C.3.6 The audit committee should have primary responsibility for making a recommendation on the appointment, reappointment and removal of the external auditors. If the board does not accept the audit committee's recommendation, it should include in the annual report, and in any papers recommending appointment or re-appointment, a statement from the audit committee explaining the recommendation and should set out reasons why the board has taken a different position.

C.3.7 The annual report should explain to shareholders how, if the auditor provides non-audit services, auditor objectivity and independence is safeguarded

D. RELATIONS WITH SHAREHOLDERS

D.1 Dialogue with Institutional Shareholders

Main Principle

There should be a dialogue with shareholders based on the mutual understanding of objectives. The board as a whole has responsibility for ensuring that a satisfactory dialogue with shareholders takes place.[20]

Supporting Principles

Whilst recognising that most shareholder contact is with the chief executive and finance director, the chairman (and the senior independent director and other directors as appropriate) should maintain sufficient contact with major shareholders to understand their issues and concerns.

The board should keep in touch with shareholder opinion in whatever ways are most practical and efficient.

Code Provisions

D.1.1 The chairman should ensure that the views of shareholders are communicated to the board as a whole. The chairman should discuss governance and strategy with major shareholders. Non-executive directors should be offered the opportunity to attend meetings with major shareholders and should expect to attend them if requested by major shareholders. The senior independent director should attend sufficient meetings with a range of major shareholders to listen to their views in order to help develop a balanced understanding of the issues and concerns of major shareholders.

D.1.2   The board should state in the annual report the steps they have taken to ensure that the members of the board, and in particular the non-executive directors, develop an understanding of the views of major shareholders about their company, for example through direct face-to-face contact, analysts' or brokers' briefings and surveys of shareholder opinion.

D.2 Constructive Use of the AGM

Main Principle

The board should use the AGM to communicate with investors and to encourage their participation.

Code provisions

D.2.1   The company should count all proxy votes and, except where a poll is called, should indicate the level of proxies lodged on each resolution, and the balance for and against the resolution and the number of abstentions, after it has been dealt with on a show of hands. The company should ensure that votes cast are properly received and recorded.

D.2.2   The company should propose a separate resolution at the AGM on each substantially separate issue and should in particular propose a resolution at the AGM relating to the report and accounts.

D.2.3   The chairman should arrange for the chairmen of the audit, remuneration and nomination committees to be available to answer questions at the AGM and for all directors to attend.

D.2.4   The company should arrange for the Notice of the AGM and related papers to be sent to shareholders at least 20 working days before the meeting.

SECTION 2 INSTITUTIONAL SHAREHOLDERS

E. INSTITUTIONAL SHAREHOLDERS[21]

E.1 Dialogue with companies

Main Principle

Institutional shareholders should enter into a dialogue with companies based on the mutual understanding of objectives.

Supporting Principles

Institutional shareholders should apply the principles set out in the Institutional Shareholders' Committee's 'The Responsibilities of Institutional Shareholders and Agents – Statement of Principles',[22] which should be reflected in fund manager contracts.

E.2 Evaluation of Governance Disclosures

Main Principle

When evaluating companies' governance arrangements, particularly those relating to board structure and composition, institutional shareholders should give due weight to all relevant factors drawn to their attention.

Supporting Principle

Institutional shareholders should consider carefully explanations given for departure from this Code and make reasoned judgements in each case. They should give an explanation to the company, in writing where appropriate, and be prepared to enter a dialogue if they do not accept the company's position. They should avoid a box-ticking approach to assessing a company's corporate governance. They should bear in mind in particular the size and complexity of the company and the nature of the risks and challenges it faces.

E.3 Shareholder Voting

Main Principle

Institutional shareholders have a responsibility to make considered use of their votes.

Supporting Principles

Institutional shareholders should take steps to ensure their voting intentions are being translated into practice.

Institutional shareholders should, on request, make available to their clients information on the proportion of resolutions on which votes were cast and non-discretionary proxies lodged.

Major shareholders should attend AGMs where appropriate and practicable. Companies and registrars should facilitate this.

Schedule A: Provisions on the design of performance-related remuneration

1 The remuneration committee should consider whether the directors should be eligible for annual bonuses. If so, performance conditions should be relevant, stretching and designed to enhance shareholder value. Upper limits should be set and disclosed. There may be a case for part payment in shares to be held for a significant period.

2 The remuneration committee should consider whether the directors should be eligible for benefits under long-term incentive schemes. Traditional share option schemes should be weighed against other kinds of long-term incentive scheme. In normal circumstances, shares granted or other forms of deferred remuneration should not vest, and options should not be exercisable, in less than three years. Directors should be encouraged to hold their shares for a further period after vesting or exercise, subject to the need to finance any costs of acquisition and associated tax liabilities.

3 Any new long-term incentive schemes which are proposed should be approved by shareholders and should preferably replace any existing schemes or at least form part of a well considered overall plan, incorporating existing schemes. The total rewards potentially available should not be excessive.

4 Payouts or grants under all incentive schemes, including new grants under existing share option schemes, should be subject to challenging performance criteria reflecting the company's objectives. Consideration should be given to criteria which reflect the company's performance relative to a group of comparator companies in some key variables such as total shareholder return.

5 Grants under executive share option and other long-term incentive schemes should normally be phased rather than awarded in one large block.

6 In general, only basic salary should be pensionable.

7 The remuneration committee should consider the pension consequences and associated costs to the company of basic salary increases and any other changes in pensionable remuneration, especially for directors close to retirement.

Schedule B: Guidance on liability of non-executive directors: care, skill and diligence

1 Although non-executive directors and executive directors have as board members the same legal duties and objectives, the time devoted to the company's affairs is likely to be significantly less for a non-executive director than for an executive director and the detailed knowledge and experience of a company's affairs that could reasonably be expected of a non-executive director will generally be less than for an executive director. These matters may be relevant in assessing the knowledge, skill and experience which may reasonably be expected of a non-executive director and therefore the care, skill and diligence that a non-executive director may be expected to exercise.

2 In this context, the following elements of the Code may also be particularly relevant.

  i) In order to enable directors to fulfil their duties, the Code states that:

   – The letter of appointment of the director should set out the expected time commitment (*Code provision A.4.4*); and

   – The board should be supplied in a timely manner with information in a form and of a quality appropriate to enable it to discharge its duties. The chairman is responsible for ensuring that the directors are provided by management with accurate, timely and clear information (*Code principles A.5*).

  ii) Non-executive directors should themselves:

   – Undertake appropriate induction and regularly update and refresh their skills, knowledge and familiarity with the company (*Code principle A.5 and provision A.5.1*).

   – Seek appropriate clarification or amplification of information and, where necessary, take and follow appropriate professional advice (*Code principle A.5 and provision A.5.2*).

   – Where they have concerns about the running of the company or a proposed action, ensure that these are addressed by the board and, to the extent that they are not resolved, ensure that they are recorded in the board minutes (*Code provision A.1.4*).

   – Give a statement to the board if they have such unresolved concerns on resignation (*Code provision A.1.4*).

3 It is up to each non-executive director to reach a view as to what is necessary in particular circumstances to comply with the duty of care, skill and diligence they owe as a director to the company. In considering whether or not a person is in breach of that duty, a court would take into account all relevant circumstances. These may include having regard to the above where relevant to the issue of liability of a non-executive director.

Schedule C: Disclosure of corporate governance arrangements

The Listing Rules require a statement to be included in the annual report relating to compliance with the Code, as described in the preamble.

For ease of reference, the specific requirements in the Code for disclosure are set out below:

The annual report should record:

- a statement of how the board operates, including a high level statement of which types of decisions are to be taken by the board and which are to be delegated to management (A.1.1);

- the names of the chairman, the deputy chairman (where there is one), the chief executive, the senior independent director and the chairmen and members of the nomination, audit and remuneration committees (A.1 .2);

- the number of meetings of the board and those committees and individual attendance by directors (A.1 .2);

- the names of the non-executive directors whom the board determines to be independent, with reasons where necessary (A.3.1);

- the other significant commitments of the chairman and any changes to them during the year (A.4.3);

- how performance evaluation of the board, its committees and its directors has been conducted (A.6.1);

- the steps the board has taken to ensure that members of the board, and in particular the non-executive directors, develop an understanding of the views of major shareholders about their company (D.1 .2).

The report should also include:

- a separate section describing the work of the nomination committee, including the process it has used in relation to board appointments and an explanation if neither external search consultancy nor open advertising has been used in the appointment of a chairman or a non-executive director (A.4.6);

- a description of the work of the remuneration committee as required under the Directors' Remuneration Reporting Regulations 2002, and including, where an executive director serves as a non-executive director elsewhere, whether or not the director will retain such earnings and, if so, what the remuneration is (B.1 .4);

- an explanation from the directors of their responsibility for preparing the accounts and a statement by the auditors about their reporting responsibilities (C.1 .1);

- a statement from the directors that the business is a going concern, with supporting assumptions or qualifications as necessary (C.1.2);

- a report that the board has conducted a review of the effectiveness of the group's system of internal controls (C.2.1);
- a separate section describing the work of the audit committee in discharging its responsibilities (C.3.3);
- where there is no internal audit function, the reasons for the absence of such a function (C.3.5);
- where the board does not accept the audit committee's recommendation on the appointment, reappointment or removal of an external auditor, a statement from the audit committee explaining the recommendation and the reasons why the board has taken a different position (C.3.6); and
- an explanation of how, if the auditor provides non-audit services, auditor objectivity and independence is safeguarded (C.3.7).

The following information should be made available (which may be met by making it available on request and placing the information available on the company's website):

- the terms of reference of the nomination, remuneration and audit committees, explaining their role and the authority delegated to them by the board (A.4.1, B.2.1 and C.3.3);
- the terms and conditions of appointment of non-executive directors (A.4.4) (see footnote 10 on page 9); and
- where remuneration consultants are appointed, a statement of whether they have any other connection with the company (B.2.1).

The board should set out to shareholders in the papers accompanying a resolution to elect or re-elect:

- sufficient biographical details to enable shareholders to take an informed decision on their election or re-election (A.7.1).
- why they believe an individual should be elected to a non-executive role (A.7.2).
- on re-election of a non-executive director, confirmation from the chairman that, following formal performance evaluation, the individual's performance continues to be effective and to demonstrate commitment to the role, including commitment of time for board and committee meetings and any other duties (A.7.2).

The board should set out to shareholders in the papers recommending appointment or reappointment of an external auditor:

- if the board does not accept the audit committee's recommendation, a statement from the audit committee explaining the recommendation and from the board setting out reasons why they have taken a different position (C.3.6).

Endnotes

1 'Review of the role and effectiveness of non-executive directors', published January 2003.

2 'Audit Committees Combined Code Guidance', published January 2003.

3 'Internal Control: Revised Guidance for Directors on the Combined Code', published by the Financial Reporting Council in October 2005.

4 The Directors' Remuneration Report Regulations 2002, SI No 1986.

5   Compliance or otherwise with this provision need only be reported for the year in which the appointment is made.

6   A.2.2 states that the chairman should, on appointment, meet the independence criteria set out in this provision, but thereafter the test of independence is not appropriate in relation to the chairman.

7   A smaller company is one that is below the FTSE 350 throughout the year immediately prior to the reporting year.

8   The requirement to make the information available would be met by making it available on request and by including the information on the company's website.

9   Compliance or otherwise with this provision need only be reported for the year in which the appointment is made.

10   The terms and conditions of appointment of non-executive directors should be made available for inspection by any person at the company's registered office during normal business hours and at the AGM (for 15 minutes prior to the meeting and during the meeting).

11   Views have been sought by the Department of Trade and Industry by 30 September 2003 on whether, and if so how, further measures are required to enable shareholders to ensure that compensation reflects performance when directors' contracts are terminated: See 'Rewards for Failure': Directors' Remuneration – Contracts, performance and severance, June 2003.

12   As required under the Directors' Remuneration Report Regulations.

13   See footnote 7.

14   See footnote 8.

15   See footnote 8.

16   The Turnbull guidance suggests means of applying this part of the Code.

17   The Turnbull guidance suggests means of applying this part of the Code.

18   See footnote 7.

19   See footnote 8.

20   Nothing in these principles or provisions should be taken to override the general requirements of law to treat shareholders equally in access to information.

21   Agents such as investment managers, or voting services, are frequently appointed by institutional shareholders to act on their behalf and these principles should accordingly be read as applying where appropriate to the agents of institutional shareholders.

22   Available at: www.investmentuk.org.uk/press/2002/20021021-01.pdf

Appendix 2

Sample letter of non-executive director appointment (Higgs guidance)

On [date], upon the recommendation of the nomination committee, the board of [company] ('the Company') has appointed you as non-executive director. I am writing to set out the terms of your appointment. It is agreed that this is a contract for services and is not a contract of employment.

Appointment

Your appointment will be for an initial term of three years commencing on [date], unless otherwise terminated earlier by and at the discretion of either party upon [one month's] written notice. Continuation of your contract of appointment is contingent on satisfactory performance and re-election at forthcoming AGM's. Non-executive directors are typically expected to serve two three-year terms, although the board may invite you to serve an additional period.

Time commitment

Overall we anticipate a time commitment of [number] days per month after the induction phase. This will include attendance at [monthly] board meetings, the AGM, [one] annual board away day, and [at least one] site visit per year. In addition, you will be expected to devote appropriate preparation time ahead of each meeting.

By accepting this appointment, you have confirmed that you are able to allocate sufficient time to meet the expectations of your role. The agreement of the chairman should be sought before accepting additional commitments that might impact on the time you are able to devote to your role as a non-executive director of the company.

Role

Non-executive directors have the same general legal responsibilities to the company as any other director. The board as a whole is collectively responsible for the success of the company. The board:

- provides entrepreneurial leadership of the company within a framework of prudent and effective controls which enable risk to be assessed and managed;
- sets the company's strategic aims, ensures that the necessary financial and human resources are in place for the company to meet its objectives, and reviews management performance; and
- sets the company's values and standards and ensure that its obligations to its shareholders and others are understood and met.

All directors must take decisions objectively in the interests of the company.

In addition to these requirements of all directors, the role of the non-executive director has the following key elements:

- **Strategy** Non-executive directors should constructively challenge and help develop proposals on strategy.

- **Performance** Non-executive directors should scrutinise the performance of management in meeting agreed goals and objectives and monitor the reporting of performance.

- **Risk** Non-executive directors should satisfy themselves on the integrity of financial information and that financial controls and systems of risk management are robust and defensible.

- **People** Non-executive directors are responsible for determining appropriate levels of remuneration of executive directors and have a prime role in appointing, and where necessary removing, executive directors and in succession planning.

Fees

You will be paid a fee of £ [amount] gross per annum which will be paid monthly in arrears, [plus [number] ordinary shares of the company per annum, both of] which will be subject to an annual review by the board. The company will reimburse you for all reasonable and properly documented expenses you incur in performing the duties of your office.

Outside interests

It is accepted and acknowledged that you have business interests other than those of the company and have declared any conflicts that are apparent at present. In the event that you become aware of any potential conflicts of interest, these should be disclosed to the chairman and company secretary as soon as apparent.

[The board of the company have determined you to be independent according to provision A.3.1 of the Code.]

Confidentiality

All information acquired during your appointment is confidential to the company and should not be released, either during your appointment or following termination (by whatever means), to third parties without prior clearance from the chairman.

Your attention is also drawn to the requirements under both legislation and regulation as to the disclosure of price sensitive information. Consequently you should avoid making any statements that might risk a breach of these requirements without prior clearance from the chairman or company secretary.

Induction

Immediately after appointment, the company will provide a comprehensive, formal and tailored induction. This will include the information pack recommended by the Institute of Chartered Secretaries and Administrators (ICSA), available at www.icsa.org.uk. We will also arrange for site visits and meetings with senior and middle management and the company's auditors. We will also offer to major shareholders the opportunity to meet you.

Review process

The performance of individual directors and the whole board and its committees is evaluated annually. If, in the interim, there are any matters which cause you concern about your role you should discuss them with the chairman as soon as is appropriate.

Insurance

The company has directors' and officers' liability insurance and it is intended to maintain such cover for the full term of your appointment. The current indemnity limit is £ [amount]; a copy of the policy document is attached.

Independent professional advice

Occasions may arise when you consider that you need professional advice in the furtherance of your duties as a director. Circumstances may occur when it will be appropriate for you to seek advice from independent advisors at the company's expense. A copy of the board's agreed procedure under which directors may obtain such independent advice is attached. The company will reimburse the full cost of expenditure incurred in accordance with the attached policy.

Committees

This letter refers to your appointment as a non-executive director of the company. In the event that you are also asked to serve on one or more of the board committees this will be covered in a separate communication setting out the committee(s)'s terms of reference, any specific responsibilities and any additional fees that may be involved.

This sample appointment letter has been complied with the assistance of ICSA who have kindly agreed to produce updated guidance on their website www.icsa.org.uk in the future.

Appendix 3
Induction checklist for directors and non-executive directors (Higgs guidance)

Guidance on Induction

Every company should develop its own comprehensive, formal induction programme that is tailored to the needs of the company and individual non-executive directors. The following guidelines might form the core of an induction programme.

As a general rule, a combination of selected written information together with presentations and activities such as meetings and site visits will help to give a new appointee a balanced and real-life overview of the company. Care should be taken not to overload the new director with too much information. The new non-executive director should be provided with a list of all the induction information that is being made available to them so that they may call up items if required before otherwise provided.

The induction process should:

1 Build an understanding of the *nature of the company, its business and the markets in which it operates*. For example, induction should cover:

   - the company's products or services;
   - group structure/subsidiaries/joint ventures;
   - the company's constitution, board procedures and matters reserved for the board;
   - summary details of the company's principal assets, liabilities, significant contracts and major competitors;
   - the company's major risks and risk management strategy;
   - key performance indicators; and
   - regulatory constraints.

2 Build a link with the *company's people* including;

   - meetings with senior management;
   - visits to company sites other than the headquarters, to learn about production or services and meet employees in an informal setting. It is important, not only for the board to get to know the new non-executive director, but also for the non-executive director to build a profile with employees below board level; and
   - participating in board strategy development. 'Awaydays' enable a new non-executive director to begin to build working relationships away from the formal setting of the boardroom.

3 Build an understanding of the *company's main relationships* including meeting with the auditors and developing a knowledge of in particular:

- who are the major customers;
- who are the major suppliers; and
- who are the major shareholders and what is the shareholder relations policy – participation in meetings with shareholders can help give a first hand feel as well as letting shareholders know who the non-executive directors are.

The induction pack

On appointment, or during the weeks immediately following, a new non-executive director should be provided with certain basic information to help ensure their early effective contribution to the company.

ICSA has produced, and undertaken to maintain a guidance note detailing a full list of such matters, on its website www.icsa.org.uk.

Appendix 4
Performance evaluation guidance (Higgs guidance)

Guidance on performance evaluation

The Code provides that the board should undertake a formal and rigorous annual evaluation of its own performance and that of its committees and individual directors. Individual evaluation should aim to show whether each director continues to contribute effectively and to demonstrate commitment to the role (including commitment of time for board and committee meetings and any other duties). The chairman should act on the results of the performance evaluation by recognising the strengths and addressing the weaknesses of the board and, where appropriate, proposing new members be appointed to the board or seeking the resignation of directors. The board should state in the annual report how such performance evaluation has been conducted.

It is the responsibility of the chairman to select an effective process and to act on its outcome. The use of an external third party to conduct the evaluation will bring objectivity to the process.

The non-executive directors, led by the senior independent director, should be responsible for performance evaluation of the chairman, taking into account the views of executive directors.

The evaluation process will be used constructively as a mechanism to improve board effectiveness, maximise strengths and tackle weaknesses. The results of board evaluation should be shared with the board as a whole while the results of individual assessments should remain confidential between the chairman and the non-executive director concerned.

The following are some of the questions that should be considered in a performance evaluation. They are, however, by no means definitive or exhaustive and companies will wish to tailor the questions to suit their own needs and circumstances.

The responses to these questions and others should enable boards to assess how they are performing and to identify how certain elements of their performance areas might be improved.

Performance evaluation of the board

- How well has the board performed against any performance objectives that have been set?
- What has been the board's contribution to the testing and development of strategy?
- What has been the board's contribution to ensuring robust and effective risk management?
- Is the composition of the board and its committees appropriate, with the right mix of knowledge and skills to maximise performance in the light of future strategy? Are inside and outside the board relationships working effectively?
- How has the board responded to any problems or crises that have emerged and could or should these have been foreseen?
- Are the matters specifically reserved for the board the right ones?
- How well does the board communicate with the management team, company employees and others? How effectively does it use mechanisms such as the AGM and the annual report?

- Is the board as a whole up to date with latest developments in the regulatory environment and the market?
- How effective are the board's committees? [Specific questions on the performance of each committee should be included such as, for example, their role, their composition and their interaction with the board.]

The processes that help underpin the board's effectiveness should also be evaluated. For example:

- Is appropriate, timely information of the right length and quality provided to the board and is management responsive to requests for clarification or amplification? Does the board provide helpful feedback to management on its requirements?
- Are sufficient board and committee meetings of appropriate length held to enable proper consideration of issues? Is time used effectively?
- Are board procedures conducive to effective performance and flexible enough to deal with all eventualities?

In addition, there are some specific issues relating to the chairman which should be included as part of an evaluation of the board's performance e.g.:

- Is the chairman demonstrating effective leadership of the board?
- Are relationships and communications with shareholders well managed?
- Are relationships and communications within the board constructive?
- Are the processes for setting the agenda working? Do they enable board members to raise issues and concerns?
- Is the company secretary being used appropriately and to maximum value?

Performance evaluation of the non-executive director

The chairman and other board members should consider the following issues and the individual concerned should also be asked to assess themselves. For each non-executive director:

- How well prepared and informed are they for board meetings and is their meeting attendance satisfactory?
- Do they demonstrate a willingness to devote time and effort to understand the company and its business and a readiness to participate in events outside the boardroom such as site visits?
- What has been the quality and value of their contributions at board meetings?
- What has been their contribution to development of strategy and to risk management?
- How successfully have they brought their knowledge and experience to bear in the consideration of strategy?
- How effectively have they probed to test information and assumptions? Where necessary, how resolute are they in maintaining their own views and resisting pressure from others?
- How effectively and proactively have they followed up their areas of concern?
- How effective and successful are their relationships with fellow board members, the company secretary and senior management? Does their performance and behaviour engender mutual trust and respect within the board?

- How actively and successfully do they refresh their knowledge and skills and are they up-to-date with:
  - the latest developments in areas such as corporate governance framework and financial reporting?
  - the industry and market conditions?
- How well do they communicate with fellow board members, senior management and others, for example shareholders? Are they able to present their views convincingly yet diplomatically and do they listen and take on board the views of others?

Appendix 5
Summary of the principal duties of the nomination committee (Higgs guidance)

There should be a nomination committee which should lead the process for board appointments and make recommendations to the board.

A majority of members of the committee should be independent non-executive directors. The chairman or an independent non-executive director should chair the committee, but the chairman should not chair the nomination committee when it is dealing with the appointment of a successor to the chairmanship.

Duties

The committee should:

- be responsible for identifying and nominating for the approval of the board, candidates to fill board vacancies as and when they arise;

- before making an appointment, evaluate the balance of skills, knowledge and experience on the board and, in the light of this evaluation, prepare a description of the role and capabilities required for a particular appointment;

- review annually the time required from a non-executive director. Performance evaluation should be used to assess whether the non-executive director is spending enough time to fulfil their duties;

- consider candidates from a wide range of backgrounds and look beyond the 'usual suspects';

- give full consideration to succession planning in the course of its work, taking into account the challenges and opportunities facing the company and what skills and expertise are therefore needed on the board in the future;

- regularly review the structure, size and composition (including the skills, knowledge and experience) of the board and make recommendations to the board with regard to any changes;

- keep under review the leadership needs of the organisation, both executive and non-executive, with a view to ensuring the continued ability of the organisation to compete effectively in the marketplace;

- make a statement in the annual report about its activities; the process used for appointments and explain if external advice or open advertising has not been used; the membership of the committee, number of committee meetings and attendance over the course of the year;

- make available its terms of reference explaining clearly its role and the authority delegated to it by the board; and

- ensure that on appointment to the board, non-executive directors receive a formal letter of appointment setting out clearly what is expected of them in terms of time commitment, committee service and involvement outside board meetings.

The committee should make recommendations to the board.

- as regards plans for succession for both executive and non-executive directors;
- as regards the re-appointment of any non-executive director at the conclusion of their specified term of office;
- concerning the re-election by shareholders of any director under the retirement by rotation provisions in the company's articles of association;
- concerning any matters relating to the continuation in office of any director at any time; and
- concerning the appointment of any director to executive or other office other than to the positions of chairman and chief executive, the recommendation for which would be considered at a meeting of the board.

This guidance has been compiled with the assistance of the ICSA who have kindly agreed to produce updated guidance on its website www.icsa.org.uk in the future.

Appendix 6
Guidance on audit committees (Smith guidance)

The following guidance is closely based on Sir Robert Smith's proposed guidance published in January 2003 modified for consistency with the final revised Code

AUDIT COMMITTEES – COMBINED CODE GUIDANCE

1 Introduction

1.1. This guidance is designed to assist company boards in making suitable arrangements for their audit committees, and to assist directors serving on audit committees in carrying out their role.

1.2 The paragraphs in bold are taken from the Combined Code (Section C3). Listed companies that do not comply with those provisions should include an explanation as to why they have not complied in the statement required by the Listing Rules.

1.3 Best practice requires that every board should consider in detail what arrangements for its audit committee are best suited for its particular circumstances. Audit committee arrangements need to be proportionate to the task, and will vary according to the size, complexity and risk profile of the company.

1.4 While all directors have a duty to act in the interests of the company the audit committee has a particular role, acting independently from the executive, to ensure that the interests of shareholders are properly protected in relation to financial reporting and internal control.

1.5 Nothing in the guidance should be interpreted as a departure from the principle of the unitary board. All directors remain equally responsible for the company's affairs as a matter of law. The audit committee, like other committees to which particular responsibilities are delegated (such as the remuneration committee), remains a committee of the board. Any disagreement within the board, including disagreement between the audit committee's members and the rest of the board, should be resolved at board level.

1.6 The Code provides that a separate section of the annual report should describe the work of the committee. This deliberately puts the spotlight on the audit committee and gives it an authority that it might otherwise lack. This is not incompatible with the principle of the unitary board.

1.7 The guidance contains recommendations about the conduct of the audit committee's relationship with the board, with the executive management and with internal and external auditors. However, the most important features of this relationship cannot be drafted as guidance or put into a code of practice: a frank, open working relationship and a high level of mutual respect are essential, particularly between the audit committee chairman and the board chairman, the chief executive and the finance director. The audit committee must be prepared to take a robust stand, and all parties must be prepared to make information freely available to the audit committee, to listen to their views and to talk through the issues openly.

1.8 In particular, the management is under an obligation to ensure the audit committee is kept properly informed, and should take the initiative in supplying information rather than waiting to be asked. The board should make it clear to all directors and staff that they must cooperate with the audit committee and provide it with any information it requires. In addition, executive board members will have regard to their common law duty to provide all directors, including those on the audit committee, with all the information they need to discharge their responsibilities as directors of the company.

1.9 Many of the core functions of audit committees set out in this guidance are expressed in terms of 'oversight', 'assessment' and 'review' of a particular function. It is not the duty of audit committees to carry out functions that properly belong to others, such as the company's management in the preparation of the financial statements or the auditors in the planning or conducting of audits. To do so could undermine the responsibility of management and auditors. Audit committees should, for example, satisfy themselves that there is a proper system and allocation of responsibilities for the day-to-day monitoring of financial controls but they should not seek to do the monitoring themselves.

1.10 However, the high-level oversight function may lead to detailed work. The audit committee must intervene if there are signs that something may be seriously amiss. For example, if the audit committee is uneasy about the explanations of management and auditors about a particular financial reporting policy decision, there may be no alternative but to grapple with the detail and perhaps to seek independent advice.

1.11 Under this guidance, audit committees have wide-ranging, time-consuming and sometimes intensive work to do. Companies need to make the necessary resources available. This includes suitable payment for the members of audit committees themselves. They – and particularly the audit committee chairman – bear a significant responsibility and they need to commit a significant extra amount of time to the job. Companies also need to make provision for induction and training for new audit committee members and continuing training as may be required.

1.12 This guidance applies to all companies to which the Code applies – i.e. UK listed companies. For groups, it will usually be necessary for the audit committee of the parent company to review issues that relate to particular subsidiaries or activities carried on by the group. Consequently, the board of a UK-listed parent company should ensure that there is adequate cooperation within the group (and with internal and external auditors of individual companies within the group) to enable the parent company audit committee to discharge its responsibilities effectively.

2 Establishment and role of the audit committee; membership, procedures and resources

Establishment and role

2.1 The board should establish an audit committee of at least three, or in the case of smaller companies two, members.

2.2 The main role and responsibilities of the audit committee should be set out in written terms of reference and should include:

- to monitor the integrity of the financial statements of the company and any formal announcements relating to the company's financial performance, reviewing significant financial reporting judgements contained in them;

- to review the company's internal financial controls and, unless expressly addressed by a separate board risk committee composed of independent directors or by the board itself, the company's internal control and risk management systems;

- to monitor and review the effectiveness of the company's internal audit function;

- to make recommendations to the board, for it to put to the shareholders for their approval in general meeting, in relation to the appointment of the external auditor and to approve the remuneration and terms of engagement of the external auditor;

- to review and monitor the external auditor's independence and objectivity and the effectiveness of the audit process, taking into consideration relevant UK professional and regulatory requirements;

- to develop and implement policy on the engagement of the external auditor to supply non-audit services, taking into account relevant ethical guidance regarding the provision of non-audit services by the external audit firm;

- and to report to the board, identifying any matters in respect of which it considers that action or improvement is needed, and making recommendations as to the steps to be taken.

Membership and appointment

2.3 All members of the committee should be independent non-executive directors. The board should satisfy itself that at least one member of the audit committee has recent and relevant financial experience.

2.4 The chairman of the company should not be an audit committee member.

2.5 Appointments to the audit committee should be made by the board on the recommendation of the nomination committee (where there is one), in consultation with the audit committee chairman.

2.6 Appointments should be for a period of up to three years, extendable by no more than two additional three-year periods, so long as members continue to be independent.

Meetings of the audit committee

2.7 It is for the audit committee chairman, in consultation with the company secretary, to decide the frequency and timing of its meetings. There should be as many meetings as the audit committee's role and responsibilities require. It is recommended there should be not fewer than three meetings during the year, held to coincide with key dates within the financial reporting and audit cycle[1]. However, most audit committee chairmen will wish to call more frequent meetings.

2.8 No one other than the audit committee's chairman and members is entitled to be present at a meeting of the audit committee. It is for the audit committee to decide if non-members should attend for a particular meeting or a particular agenda item. It is to be expected that the external audit lead partner will be invited regularly to attend meetings as well as the finance director. Others may be invited to attend.

2.9 Sufficient time should be allowed to enable the audit committee to undertake as full a discussion as may be required. A sufficient interval should be allowed between audit committee meetings and main board meetings to allow any work arising from the audit committee meeting to be carried out and reported to the board as appropriate.

2.10 The audit committee should, at least annually, meet the external and internal auditors, without management, to discuss matters relating to its remit and any issues arising from the audit.

2.11 Formal meetings of the audit committee are the heart of its work. However, they will rarely be sufficient. It is expected that the audit committee chairman, and to a lesser extent the other members, will wish to keep in touch on a continuing basis with the key people involved in the company's governance, including the board chairman, the chief executive, the finance director, the external audit lead partner and the head of internal audit.

Resources

2.12 The audit committee should be provided with sufficient resources to undertake its duties.

2.13 The audit committee should have access to the services of the company secretariat on all audit committee matters including: assisting the chairman in planning the audit committee's work, drawing up meeting agendas, maintenance of minutes, drafting of material about its activities for the annual report, collection and distribution of information and provision of any necessary practical support.

2.14 The company secretary should ensure that the audit committee receives information and papers in a timely manner to enable full and proper consideration to be given to the issues.

2.15 The board should make funds available to the audit committee to enable it to take independent legal, accounting or other advice when the audit committee reasonably believes it necessary to do so.

Remuneration

2.16 In addition to the remuneration paid to all non-executive directors, each company should consider the further remuneration that should be paid to members of the audit committee to recompense them for the additional responsibilities of membership. Consideration should be given to the time members are required to give to audit committee business, the skills they bring to bear and the onerous duties they take on, as well as the value of their work to the company. The level of remuneration paid to the members of the audit committee should take into account the level of fees paid to other members of the board. The chairman's responsibilities and time demands will generally be heavier than the other members of the audit committee and this should be reflected in his or her remuneration.

Skills, experience and training

2.17 It is desirable that the committee member whom the board considers to have recent and relevant financial experience should have a professional qualification from one of the professional accountancy bodies. The need for a degree of financial literacy among the other members will vary according to the nature of the company, but experience of corporate financial matters will normally be required. The availability of appropriate financial expertise will be particularly important where the company's activities involve specialised financial activities.

2.18 The company should provide an induction programme for new audit committee members. This should cover the role of the audit committee, including its terms of reference and expected time commitment by members; and an overview of the company's business, identifying the main business and financial dynamics and risks. It could also include meeting some of the company staff.

2.19 Training should also be provided to members of the audit committee on an ongoing and timely basis and should include an understanding of the principles of and developments in financial reporting and related company law. In appropriate cases, it may also include, for example, understanding financial statements, applicable accounting standards and recommended practice; the regulatory framework for the company's business; the role of internal and external auditing and risk management.

2.20 The induction programme and ongoing training may take various forms, including attendance at formal courses and conferences, internal company talks and seminars, and briefings by external advisers.

3 Relationship with the board

3.1 The role of the audit committee is for the board to decide and to the extent that the audit committee undertakes tasks on behalf of the board, the results should be reported to, and considered by, the board. In doing so it should identify any matters in respect of which it considers that action or improvement is needed, and make recommendations as to the steps to be taken.

3.2 The terms of reference should be tailored to the particular circumstances of the company.

3.3 The audit committee should review annually its terms of reference and its own effectiveness and recommend any necessary changes to the board.

3.4 The board should review the audit committee's effectiveness annually.

3.5 Where there is disagreement between the audit committee and the board, adequate time should be made available for discussion of the issue with a view to resolving the disagreement. Where any such disagreements cannot be resolved, the audit committee should have the right to report the issue to the shareholders as part of the report on its activities in the annual report.

4   Role and responsibilities

Financial reporting

4.1   The audit committee should review the significant financial reporting issues and judgements made in connection with the preparation of the company's financial statements, interim reports, preliminary announcements and related formal statements.

4.2   It is management's, not the audit committee's, responsibility to prepare complete and accurate financial statements and disclosures in accordance with financial reporting standards and applicable rules and regulations. However the audit committee should consider significant accounting policies, any changes to them and any significant estimates and judgements. The management should inform the audit committee of the methods used to account for significant or unusual transactions where the accounting treatment is open to different approaches. Taking into account the external auditor's view, the audit committee should consider whether the company has adopted appropriate accounting policies and, where necessary, made appropriate estimates and judgements. The audit committee should review the clarity and completeness of disclosures in the financial statements and consider whether the disclosures made are set properly in context.

4.3   Where, following its review, the audit committee is not satisfied with any aspect of the proposed financial reporting by the company, it shall report its views to the board.

4.4   The audit committee should review related information presented with the financial statements, including the operating and financial review, and corporate governance statements relating to the audit and to risk management. Similarly, where board approval is required for other statements containing financial information (for example, summary financial statements, significant financial returns to regulators and release of price sensitive information), whenever practicable (without being inconsistent with any requirement for prompt reporting under the Listing Rules) the audit committee should review such statements first.

Internal controls and risk management systems

4.5   The audit committee should review the company's internal financial controls (that is, the systems established to identify, assess, manage and monitor financial risks); and unless expressly addressed by a separate board risk committee comprised of independent directors or by the board itself, the company's internal control and risk management systems.

4.6   The company's management is responsible for the identification, assessment, management and monitoring of risk, for developing, operating and monitoring the system of internal control and for providing assurance to the board that it has done so. Except where the board or a risk committee is expressly responsible for reviewing the effectiveness of the internal control and risk management systems, the audit committee should receive reports from management on the effectiveness of the systems they have established and the conclusions of any testing carried out by internal and external auditors.

4.7   Except to the extent that this is expressly dealt with by the board or risk committee, the audit committee should review and approve the statements included in the annual report in relation to internal control and the management of risk.

Whistleblowing

4.8   The audit committee should review arrangements by which staff of the company may, in confidence, raise concerns about possible improprieties in matters of financial reporting or other matters. The audit committee's objective should be to ensure that arrangements are in place for the proportionate and independent investigation of such matters and for appropriate follow-up action.

The internal audit process

4.9   The audit committee should monitor and review the effectiveness of the company's internal audit function. Where there is no internal audit function, the audit committee should consider annually whether there is a need for an internal audit function and make a recommendation to the board, and the reasons for the absence of such a function should be explained in the relevant section of the annual report.

4.10 The need for an internal audit function will vary depending on company-specific factors including the scale, diversity and complexity of the company's activities and the number of employees, as well as cost/benefit considerations. Senior management and the board may desire objective assurance and advice on risk and control. An adequately resourced internal audit function (or its equivalent where, for example, a third party is contracted to perform some or all of the work concerned) may provide such assurance and advice. There may be other functions within the company that also provide assurance and advice covering specialist areas such as health and safety, regulatory and legal compliance and environmental issues.

4.11 When undertaking its assessment of the need for an internal audit function, the audit committee should also consider whether there are any trends or current factors relevant to the company's activities, markets or other aspects of its external environment, that have increased, or are expected to increase, the risks faced by the company. Such an increase in risk may also arise from internal factors such as organisational restructuring or from changes in reporting processes or underlying information systems. Other matters to be taken into account may include adverse trends evident from the monitoring of internal control systems or an increased incidence of unexpected occurrences.

4.12 In the absence of an internal audit function, management needs to apply other monitoring processes in order to assure itself, the audit committee and the board that the system of internal control is functioning as intended. In these circumstances, the audit committee will need to assess whether such processes provide sufficient and objective assurance.

4.13 The audit committee should review and approve the internal audit function's remit, having regard to the complementary roles of the internal and external audit functions. The audit committee should ensure that the function has the necessary resources and access to information to enable it to fulfil its mandate, and is equipped to perform in accordance with appropriate professional standards for internal auditors.[2]

4.14 The audit committee should approve the appointment or termination of appointment of the head of internal audit.

4.15 In its review of the work of the internal audit function, the audit committee should, inter alia:

- ensure that the internal auditor has direct access to the board chairman and to the audit committee and is accountable to the audit committee;
- review and assess the annual internal audit work plan;
- receive a report on the results of the internal auditors' work on a periodic basis;
- review and monitor management's responsiveness to the internal auditor's findings and recommendations;
- meet with the head of internal audit at least once a year without the presence of management; and
- monitor and assess the role and effectiveness of the internal audit function in the overall context of the company's risk management system.

The external audit process

4.16 The audit committee is the body responsible for overseeing the company's relations with the external auditor.

Appointment

4.17 The audit committee should have primary responsibility for making a recommendation on the appointment, reappointment and removal of the external auditors. If the board does not accept the audit committee's recommendation, it should include in the annual report, and in any papers recommending appointment or reappointment, a statement from the audit committee explaining its recommendation and should set out reasons why the board has taken a different position.

4.18 The audit committee's recommendation to the board should be based on the assessments referred to below. If the audit committee recommends considering the selection of possible new appointees as external auditors, it should oversee the selection process.

4.19 The audit committee should assess annually the qualification, expertise and resources, and independence (see below) of the external auditors and the effectiveness of the audit process. The assessment should cover all aspects of the audit service provided by the audit firm, and include obtaining a report on the audit firm's own internal quality control procedures.

4.20 If the external auditor resigns, the audit committee should investigate the issues giving rise to such resignation and consider whether any action is required.

Terms and remuneration

4.21 The audit committee should approve the terms of engagement and the remuneration to be paid to the external auditor in respect of audit services provided.

4.22 The audit committee should review and agree the engagement letter issued by the external auditor at the start of each audit, ensuring that it has been updated to reflect changes in circumstances arising since the previous year. The scope of the external audit should be reviewed by the audit committee with the auditor. If the audit committee is not satisfied as to its adequacy it should arrange for additional work to be undertaken.

4.23 The audit committee should satisfy itself that the level of fee payable in respect of the audit services provided is appropriate and that an effective audit can be conducted for such a fee.

Independence, including the provision of non-audit services

4.24 The audit committee should have procedures to ensure the independence and objectivity of the external auditor annually, taking into consideration relevant UK professional and regulatory requirements. This assessment should involve a consideration of all relationships between the company and the audit firm (including the provision of non-audit services). The audit committee should consider whether, taken as a whole and having regard to the views, as appropriate, of the external auditor, management and internal audit, those relationships appear to impair the auditor's judgement or independence.

4.25 The audit committee should seek reassurance that the auditors and their staff have no family, financial, employment, investment or business relationship with the company (other than in the normal course of business). The audit committee should seek from the audit firm, on an annual basis, information about policies and processes for maintaining independence and monitoring compliance with relevant requirements, including current requirements regarding the rotation of audit partners and staff.

4.26 The audit committee should agree with the board the company's policy for the employment of former employees of the external auditor, paying particular attention to the policy regarding former employees of the audit firm who were part of the audit team and moved directly to the company. This should be drafted taking into account the relevant ethical guidelines governing the accounting profession. The audit committee should monitor application of the policy, including the number of former employees of the external auditor currently employed in senior positions in the company, and consider whether in the light of this there has been any impairment, or appearance of impairment, of the auditor's judgement or independence in respect of the audit.

4.27 The audit committee should monitor the external audit firm's compliance with applicable United Kingdom ethical guidance relating to the rotation of audit partners, the level of fees that the company pays in proportion to the overall fee income of the firm, office and partner, and other related regulatory requirements.

4.28 The audit committee should develop and recommend to the board the company's policy in relation to the provision of non-audit services by the auditor. The audit committee's objective should be to ensure that the provision of such services does not impair the external auditor's independence or objectivity. In this context, the audit committee should consider:

- whether the skills and experience of the audit firm make it a suitable supplier of the non audit service;

- whether there are safeguards in place to ensure that there is no threat to objectivity and independence in the conduct of the audit resulting from the provision of such services by the external auditor;

- the nature of the non-audit services, the related fee levels and the fee levels individually and in aggregate relative to the audit fee; and

- the criteria which govern the compensation of the individuals performing the audit.

4.29 The audit committee should set and apply a formal policy specifying the types of non-audit work:

- from which the external auditors are excluded;
- for which the external auditors can be engaged without referral to the audit committee; and
- for which a case-by-case decision is necessary.
- In addition, the policy may set fee limits generally or for particular classes of work.

4.30 In the third category, if it is not practicable to give approval to individual items in advance, it may be appropriate to give a general pre-approval for certain classes for work, subject to a fee limit determined by the audit committee and ratified by the board. The subsequent provision of any service by the auditor should be ratified at the next meeting of the audit committee.

4.31 In determining the policy, the audit committee should take into account relevant ethical guidance regarding the provision of non-audit services by the external audit firm, and in principle should not agree to the auditor providing a service if, having regard to the ethical guidance, the result is that:

- the external auditor audits its own firm's work;
- the external auditor makes management decisions for the company;
- a mutuality of interest is created; or
- the external auditor is put in the role of advocate for the company.

The audit committee should satisfy itself that any safeguards required by ethical guidance are implemented.

4.32 *The annual report should explain to shareholders how, if the auditor provides non-audit services, auditor objectivity and independence is safeguarded.*

Annual audit cycle

4.33 At the start of each annual audit cycle, the audit committee should ensure that appropriate plans are in place for the audit.

4.34 The audit committee should consider whether the auditor's overall work plan, including planned levels of materiality, and proposed resources to execute the audit plan appears consistent with the scope of the audit engagement, having regard also to the seniority, expertise and experience of the audit team.

4.35 The audit committee should review, with the external auditors, the findings of their work. In the course of its review, the audit committee should:

- discuss with the external auditor major issues that arose during the course of the audit and have subsequently been resolved and those issues that have been left unresolved;
- review key accounting and audit judgements; and
- review levels of errors identified during the audit, obtaining explanations from management and, where necessary the external auditors, as to why certain errors might remain unadjusted.

4.36 The audit committee should also review the audit representation letters before signature by management and give particular consideration to matters where representation has been requested that relate to non-standard issues[3]. The audit committee should consider whether the information provided is complete and appropriate based on its own knowledge.

4.37 As part of the ongoing monitoring process, the audit committee should review the management letter (or equivalent). The audit committee should review and monitor management's responsiveness to the external auditor's findings and recommendations.

4.38 At the end of the annual audit cycle, the audit committee should assess the effectiveness of the audit process. In the course of doing so, the audit committee should:

   – review whether the auditor has met the agreed audit plan and understand the reasons for any changes, including changes in perceived audit risks and the work undertaken by the external auditors to address those risks;

   – consider the robustness and perceptiveness of the auditors in their handling of the key accounting and audit judgements identified and in responding to questions from the audit committees, and in their commentary where appropriate on the systems of internal control;

   – obtain feedback about the conduct of the audit from key people involved, e.g. the finance director and the head of internal audit; and

   – review and monitor the content of the external auditor's management letter, in order to assess whether it is based on a good understanding of the company's business and establish whether recommendations have been acted upon and, if not, the reasons why they have not been acted upon.

5 Communication with shareholders

5.1 The terms of reference of the audit committee, including its role and the authority delegated to it by the board, should be made available. A separate section in the annual report should describe the work of the committee in discharging those responsibilities.

5.2 The audit committee section should include, inter alia:

   – a summary of the role of the audit committee;

   – the names and qualifications of all members of the audit committee during the period;

   – the number of audit committee meetings;

   – a report on the way the audit committee has discharged its responsibilities; and

   – the explanation provided for in paragraph 4.29 above.

5.3 The chairman of the audit committee should be present at the AGM to answer questions, through the chairman of the board, on the report on the audit committee's activities and matters within the scope of audit committee's responsibilities.

Appendix I Specimen terms of reference for an audit committee

Constitution

1 The board hereby resolves to establish a committee of the board to be known as the audit [*and Risk*] committee.

Membership

2 The committee shall be appointed by the board. All members of the committee shall be independent non-executive directors of the company. The committee shall consist of not less than three members. A quorum shall be two members.

3 The chairman of the committee shall be appointed by the board from amongst the independent non-executive directors.

Attendance at meetings

4 The finance director, head of internal audit and a representative of the external auditors shall attend meetings at the invitation of the committee.

5 The chairman of the board, the CEO and other board members shall attend if invited by the committee.

6 There should be at least one meeting a year, or part thereof, where the external auditors attend without management present.

7 The company secretary shall be secretary of the committee.

Frequency of meetings

8 Meetings shall be held not less than [three] times a year, and where appropriate should coincide with key dates in the company's financial reporting cycle.

9 External auditors or internal auditors may request a meeting if they consider that one is necessary.

Authority

10 The committee is authorised by the board to:

(a) investigate any activity within its terms of reference;

(b) seek any information that it requires from any employee of the company and all employees are directed to cooperate with any request made by the committee; and

(c) obtain outside legal or independent professional advice and such advisors may attend meetings as necessary.

Responsibilities

11 The responsibilities of the committee shall be:

(a) to consider the appointment of the external auditor and assess independence of the external auditor, ensuring that key partners are rotated at appropriate intervals;

(b) to recommend the audit fee to the board and preapprove any fees in respect of non audit services provided by the external auditor and to ensure that the provision of non audit services does not impair the external auditors' independence or objectivity;

(c) to discuss with the external auditor, before the audit commences, the nature and scope of the audit and to review the auditors' quality control procedures and steps taken by the auditor to respond to changes in regulatory and other requirements;

(d) to oversee the process for selecting the external auditor and make appropriate recommendations through the board to the shareholders to consider at the AGM ;

(e) to review the external auditor's management letter and management's response;

(f) to review the internal audit programme and ensure that the internal audit function is adequately resourced and has appropriate standing within the company;

(g) to consider management's response to any major external or internal audit recommendations;

(h) to approve the appointment or dismissal of the head of internal audit;

(i) to review the company's procedures for handling allegations from whistleblowers;

(j) to review management's and the internal auditor's reports on the effectiveness of systems for internal financial control, financial reporting and risk management;

(k) to review, and challenge where necessary, the actions and judgements of management, in relation to the interim and annual financial statements before submission to the board, paying particular attention to:

(i) critical accounting policies and practices, and any changes in them,

(ii) decisions requiring a major element of judgement,

(iii) the extent to which the financial statements are affected by any unusual transactions in the year and how they are disclosed,

(iv) the clarity of disclosures,

(v) significant adjustments resulting from the audit,

(vi) the going concern assumption,

(vii) compliance with accounting standards,

(viii) compliance with stock exchange and other legal requirements,

(ix) reviewing the company's statement on internal control systems prior to endorsement by the board and to review the policies and process for identifying and assessing business risks and the management of those risks by the company, and

(i) to consider other topics as defined by the board.

Reporting procedures

12 The secretary shall circulate the minutes of meetings of the committee to all members of the board, and the chairman of the committee or, as a minimum, another member of the committee, shall attend the board meeting at which the accounts are approved.

13 The committee members shall conduct an annual review of their work and these terms of reference and make recommendations to the board.

14 The committee's duties and activities during the year shall be disclosed in the annual financial statements.

15 The chairman shall attend the AGM and shall answer questions, through the chairman of the board, on the audit committee's activities and their responsibilities.

Appendix II

Outline report on the activities of the audit committee

1 Role of the audit committee
- Main responsibilities of the audit committee.

2 Composition of the audit committee
- Members and secretary – names and appointment/resignation dates.
- Appointment process.
- The relevant qualifications, expertise and experience of each member.

3 Resources
- Any dedicated resources available to the committee, internal or bought-in.

4 Meetings
- Number of meetings, and attendance.

5 Remuneration of the members of the audit committee
- Describe the specific policies in relation to the members of the audit committee (or cross-refer to the Directors' Remuneration Report).

Main activities of the committee in the year to xxxx

6 Financial statements
- Describe the activities carried out in order to monitor the integrity of the financial statements.

7 Internal financial control and risk management systems
- Describe the activities carried out in order to review the integrity of the company's internal financial control and risk management systems.

8 External auditors
- Describe the procedures adopted to review the independence of the external auditors, including disclosure of the policy on the provision of non audit services and an explanation of how the policy protects auditor independence.
- Describe the oversight of the external audit process and confirm that an assessment of the effectiveness of the external audit was made.
- Explain the recommendation to the board on the appointment of the auditors and, if applicable, the process adopted to select the new auditor.

9 Internal audit function
- Confirm that a review of the plans and work of the department was carried out. If there is no function explain the committee's consideration of whether there is a need for an internal audit function in accordance with the recommendations of the Turnbull Report.

Appendix III Outline report on the activities of the audit committee

1 Role of the audit committee
   - Main responsibilities of the audit committee.
2 Composition of the audit committee
   - Members and secretary – names and appointment/resignation dates.
   - Appointment process.
   - The relevant qualifications, expertise and experience of each member.
3 Resources
   - Any dedicated resources available to the committee, internal or bought-in.
4 Meetings
   - Number of meetings, and attendance.
5 Remuneration of the members of the audit committee
   - Describe the specific policies in relation to the members of the audit committee (or cross refer to the Directors' Remuneration Report).

Main activities of the committee in the year to xxxx

6 Financial statements
   - Describe the activities carried out in order to monitor the integrity of the financial statements.
7 Internal financial control and risk management systems
   - Describe the activities carried out in order to review the integrity of the company's internal financial control and risk management systems.
8 External auditors
   - Describe the procedures adopted to review the independence of the external auditors, including disclosure of the policy on the provision of non audit services and an explanation of how the policy protects auditor independence.
   - Describe the oversight of the external audit process and confirm that an assessment of the effectiveness of the external audit was made.
   - Explain the recommendation to the board on the appointment of the auditors and, if applicable, the process adopted to select the new auditor.
9 Internal audit function
   - Confirm that a review of the plans and work of the department was carried out. If there is no function explain the committee's consideration of whether there is a need for an internal audit function in accordance with the recommendations of the Turnbull Report.

Appendix 7
ICSA Guidance Note: Terms of reference – remuneration committee

The Combined Code on Corporate Governance (the Combined Code) states that:

'There should be a formal and transparent procedure for developing policy on executive remuneration and for fixing the remuneration packages of individual directors.'[1]

It goes on to state that:

'The board should establish a remuneration committee ... [which] should make available its terms of reference, explaining its role and the authority delegated to it by the board.'[2]

As with most aspects of corporate governance, the above principles make it clear that, not only should companies go through a formal process of considering executive remuneration, but they must be seen to be doing so in a fair and thorough manner. It is, therefore, essential that the remuneration committee is properly constituted with a clear remit and identified authority.

The Combined Code recommends the committee be made up of at least three independent non-executive directors (although two is permissible for smaller companies).[3]

Although not a provision in the Combined Code, the Higgs Report, states as good practice, in its Non-Code Recommendations, that the company secretary (or their designee) should act as secretary to the committee.[4] It is the company secretary's responsibility to ensure that the board and its committees are properly constituted and advised. There also needs to be a clear co-ordination between the main board and the various committees where the company secretary would normally act as a valued intermediary.

The frequency with which the committee needs to meet will vary from company to company and may change from time to time. It is, however, clear that it must meet close to the year end; to review the Remuneration Report which is required to be prepared under the Directors' Remuneration Report Regulations 2002 and be submitted to shareholders with or as part of the company's annual report for their approval at the AGM. We would recommend that the committee should meet at least twice a year in order to discharge its responsibilities properly.

The list of duties we have proposed are those contained within the Summary of Principle Duties Of the Remuneration committee which ICSA helped compile for the Higgs Report and which are now appended to the Combined Code. Some companies may wish to add to this list and some smaller companies may need to modify it in other ways. The Combined Code also states that the chairman of the committee should attend the AGM preparedto respond to any questions that may be raised by shareholders on matters within the committee's area of responsibility.[5]

There is clearly a need for there to be a guiding document for the effective operation of the Remuneration committee. This has led the ICSA to produce this Guidance Note proposing model terms of reference for a Remuneration committee. The document draws on the experience of senior company secretaries and best practice as carried out in some of the country's leading companies.

The Combined Code also requires that the terms of reference of the Remuneration committee, explaining its role and the authority delegated to it by the board, be made available on request and placed on the company's website.[6]

References to 'the committee' shall mean the Remuneration committee. References to 'the board' shall mean the board of directors. The square brackets contain recommendations which are in line with best practice but which may need to be changed to suit the circumstances of the particular organisation.

1   Membership

1.1   Members of the committee shall be appointed by the board, on the recommendation of the nomination committee in consultation with the chairman of the remuneration committee. The committee shall be made up of at least [3] members, all of whom are independent non-executive directors.

1.2   Only members of the committee have the right to attend committee meetings. However, other individuals such as the chief executive, the head of human resources and external advisers may be invited to attend for all or part of any meeting as and when appropriate.

1.3   Appointments to the committee shall be for a period of up to three years, which may be extended for two further three-year periods, provided the director remains independent.

1.4   The board shall appoint the committee chairman who shall be an independent non-executive director. In the absence of the committee chairman and/or an appointed deputy, the remaining members present shall elect one of themselves to chair the meeting.

The chairman of the board shall not be chairman of the committee.

2   Secretary

2.1   The company secretary or their nominee shall act as the secretary of the committee.

3   Quorum

3.1   The quorum necessary for the transaction of business shall be [2]. A duly convened meeting of the committee at which a quorum is present shall be competent to exercise all or any of the authorities, powers and discretions vested in or exercisable by the committee.

4   Meetings

4.1   The committee shall meet [at least twice a year][quarterly on the first Wednesday in each of January, April, July and October] and at such other times as the chairman of the committee shall require.[7]

5   Notice of Meetings

5.1   Meetings of the committee shall be summoned by the secretary of the committee at the request of any of its members.

5.2   Unless otherwise agreed, notice of each meeting confirming the venue, time and date together with an agenda of items to be discussed, shall be forwarded to each member of the committee, any other person required to attend and all other non-executive directors, no later than [5] working days before the date of the meeting. Supporting papers shall be sent to committee members and to other attendees as appropriate, at the same time.

6   Minutes of Meetings

6.1   The secretary shall minute the proceedings and resolutions of all committee meetings, including the names of those present and in attendance.

6.2   Minutes of committee meetings shall be circulated promptly to all members of the committee and, once agreed, to all members of the board, unless a conflict of interest exists.

7   Annual General Meeting

7.1   The chairman of the committee shall attend the annual general meeting prepared to respond to any shareholder questions on the committee's activities.

8   Duties

The committee shall:

8.1   Determine and agree with the board the framework or broad policy for the remuneration of the company's chief executive, chairman, the executive directors, the company secretary and such other members of the executive management as it is designated to consider.[8] The remuneration of non-executive directors shall be a matter for the chairman and the executive members of the board. No director or manager shall be involved in any decisions as to their own remuneration;

8.2   In determining such policy, take into account all factors which it deems necessary. The objective of such policy shall be to ensure that members of the executive management of the company are provided with appropriate incentives to encourage enhanced performance and are, in a fair and responsible manner, rewarded for their individual contributions to the success of the company.

8.3   Review the ongoing appropriateness and relevance of the remuneration policy.

8.4   Approve the design of, and determine targets for, any performance related pay schemes operated by the company and approve the total annual payments made under such schemes.

8.5   Review the design of all share incentive plans for approval by the board and shareholders. For any such plans, determine each year whether awards will be made, and if so, the overall amount of such awards, the individual awards to executive directors and other senior executives and the performance targets to be used.

8.6   Determine the policy for, and scope of, pension arrangements for each executive director and other senior executives;

8.7   Ensure that contractual terms on termination, and any payments made, are fair to the individual, and the company, that failure is not rewarded and that the duty to mitigate loss is fully recognised.

8.8 Within the terms of the agreed policy and in consultation with the chairman and/or chief executive as appropriate, determine the total individual remuneration package of each executive director and other senior executives including bonuses, incentive payments and share options or other share awards.

8.9 In determining such packages and arrangements, give due regard to any relevant legal requirements, the provisions and recommendations in the Combined Code and the UK Listing Authority's Listing Rules and associated guidance.

8.10 Review and note annually the remuneration trends across the company or group.

8.11 Oversee any major changes in employee benefits structures throughout the company or group.

8.12 Agree the policy for authorising claims for expenses from the chief executive and chairman;[9]

8.13 Ensure that all provisions regarding disclosure of remuneration including pensions, as set out in the Directors' Remuneration Report Regulations 2002 and the Combined Code are fulfilled.and

8.14 Be exclusively responsible for establishing the selection criteria, selecting, appointing and setting the terms of reference for any remuneration consultants who advise the committee: and to obtain reliable, up-to-date information about remuneration in other companies. The committee shall have full authority to commission any reports or surveys which it deems necessary to help it fulfil its obligations.

9 Reporting Responsibilities

9.1 The committee chairman shall report formally to the board on its proceedings after each meeting on all matters within its duties and responsibilities.

9.2 The committee shall make whatever recommendations to the board it deems appropriate on any area within its remit where action or improvement is needed.

9.3 The committee shall produce an annual report of the company's remuneration policy and practices which will form part of the company's annual report and ensure each year that it is put to shareholders for approval at the AGM.

10 Other

10.1 The committee shall, at least once a year, review its own performance, constitution and terms of reference to ensure it is operating at maximum effectiveness and recommend any changes it considers necessary to the board for approval.

11 Authority

11.1 The committee is authorised by the board to seek any information it requires from any employee of the company in order to perform its duties.

11.2 In connection with its duties the committee is authorised by the board to obtain, at the company's expense, any outside legal or other professional advice.

October 2003

[1]   The Combined Code on Corporate Governance – July 2003, B.2

[2]   The Combined Code on Corporate Governance – July 2003, B.2.1

[3]   A smaller company is defined as one which is below the FTSE 350 throughout the year immediately before the reporting year.

[4]   Review of the role and effectiveness of non-executive directors, January 2003 para 11.30

[5]   The Combined Code on Corporate Governance – July 2003 D.2.3

[6]   The Combined Code on Corporate Governance – July 2002 A.4.1

[7]   The frequency and timing of meetings will differ according to the needs of the company.
Meetings should be organised so that attendance is maximised (for example by timetabling
them to coincide with board meetings).

[8]   Some companies require the remuneration committee to consider the packages of all executives at or above a specified level, such as those reporting to a main board director, while
others require the committee to deal with all packages above a certain figure.

[9]   It is suggested that the more common arrangement is for the chairman of the board to authorise the chief executive's expenses and for the chairman of the remuneration committee to
authorise the chairman's claims. An alternative would be for the committee to authorise the
expenses of both.

Appendix 8
ICSA Guidance Note: Voting at general meetings

Introduction

Historically, voting at AGMs has tended to be conducted on a show of hands. Following the disruption of a number of high profile shareholder meetings, however, some companies now deal with some or all resolutions on a poll. Other companies, particularly those with a dual listed companies structure, may be required to hold votes on a poll so that the votes of the members of both companies can be added together to obtain the final result.

Neither system is generally 'right' or 'wrong' but there does appear to be some confusion as to whether one is fairer or more democratic than the other. In this Guidance Note we have attempted to explain the advantages and disadvantages of each system of voting and provide some suggestions as to how to overcome some of the problems that are frequently encountered. Whilst the Guidance Note is primarily aimed at listed companies, and we refer to 'companies' and 'shareholders' throughout, most of the comments and principles involved equally apply to unlisted plcs, private companies and other, such as non-profit, organisations.

1   Show of hands

1.1   Advantages:

- A vote on a show of hands enables a company to deal with an issue there and then, thus it tends to be much quicker and can avoid unnecessary paperwork and extra cost.

- The result of the vote is instantly available.

- It is seen specifically to involve or 'enfranchise' those shareholders who attend the meeting and who like to vote in this way so that they can show publicly how they feel about an issue, especially if they are unhappy about something. This applies particularly to private shareholders who may feel overwhelmed by the much larger holdings of institutional shareholders.

1.2   Disadvantages:

The unprepared company can be taken by surprise should a poll be demanded. This can lead to confusion, significant embarrassment and disruption to the proceedings.

In a show of hands one shareholder effectively has one vote and it can be quite easy for a small group to influence the outcome. When a single interest group wants to do this it often distributes a few shares between a number of individuals, usually giving them just one share each. In a poorly attended AGM a group of such individuals can override a smaller number of shareholders even though the latter may represent a much higher number of shares.

This 'one shareholder one vote' situation has led some to consider the show of hands to be undemocratic. Shareholders who cannot attend the meeting may feel disfranchised and that their vote will not count believing, erroneously, that proxies are ignored unless a poll is called. The chairman will usually have been appointed as proxy by a number of shareholders and as such will normally be under an obligation to call for a poll[1] if the show of hands produces a result at odds with the overall views of shareholders, including those who have lodged proxy forms. In these circumstances it might be considered even more important that sufficient proxies are lodged to ensure that the chairman is aware of the weight of shareholder opinion.

In a close vote the decision as to whether or not the resolution is passed can be subjective unless an accurate count is taken.

2 Polls

2.1 Advantages:

- This is often seen to be a more transparent method of voting as shareholder votes are seen to be counted according to the number of shares held.

- A poll does produce an exact and definitive result; It saves disruption (and possible embarrassment) from unexpected calls for a poll.

- As companies are obliged to disclose 'proxy votes' under the Combined Code,[2] it can be less misleading to disclose the results of a poll, that is the actual vote taken after due discussion and consideration of the subject matter, than the proxy position as at, typically, 48 hours before the meeting;

2.2 Disadvantages:

- A poll will involve more time and paperwork, as it usually requires distributing and collecting voting cards.

- Extra time will also be required to count the votes.

- Shareholders present at the meeting, particularly those with small holdings, may feel disfranchised and overwhelmed by the larger shareholdings of Institutional shareholders.

- If all resolutions are to be taken on a poll, smaller (mainly individual), shareholders may consider it pointless for them to attend.

- Although the outcome of a poll may be calculated fairly quickly, the actual result may not be known until some time after the meeting has been concluded.

3 Preparing for a poll

If a vote is to be taken on a show of hands it is always advisable to be prepared for the fact that a poll may be demanded. For example:

- Shareholder question cards can be sent out in advance to try to assess which are the most likely topics on which a poll might be demanded; Decide before the meeting how poll cards are to be distributed, votes collected and counted and the results announced.

- Ensure that the chairman is primed with a suitable script to deal with the situation so that he (or she) is not taken completely by surprise; Unwanted demands for a poll can sometimes be pre-empted by having the chairman deal with potentially controversial topics in his speech; Ensure that a basic form of poll card is available.

- Ensure that some form of 'ballot box' is available if needed to collect the poll cards.

- One point worth noting is that the chairman's authority to call for a poll would normally derive from the company's articles or, as mentioned above, by virtue of his (or her) being appointed proxy by the requisite number of shareholders. A check on the articles is therefore recommended just to clarify the situation.

If a poll is intended to be held on some or all resolutions, companies may take certain steps before and during the meeting in order to ensure that shareholders attending the meeting do not feel aggrieved by the lack of opportunity to vote on a show of hands:

- The notice of meeting, or a letter from the chairman sent with it, can explain that some or all of the votes at the meeting will be taken on a poll and give the reasons why this is being done. This helps to manage shareholders' expectations.

- Poll cards are usually given out to shareholders as they arrive, or personalised ones may be incorporated into the proxy form or admission card to be brought to the meeting by shareholders. This can save time at, and aid the smooth running of, the meeting.

- The chairman's script should repeat the reasons for the poll and should describe the process clearly.

- The chairman can encourage shareholders to complete their poll cards as each resolution is proposed, in the same way that they would vote on a show of hands.

- Alternatively, the chairman may still allow shareholders to express their views on a show of hands. This will clearly have no substance but may be considered of value to 'include' the shareholders attending. The result can be announced along the lines of 'The show of hands indicates general approval, subject of course to the results of the poll'. Shareholders may then complete the poll card after each resolution or at the end of the meeting. In this way those attending the meeting (and the company) are able to gauge the feeling of those present, even though this may not be representative of the views of all shareholders whose votes are then counted in the final poll result.

For most straightforward meetings the outcome of a poll can be calculated quickly although the detailed results may take longer. There may be issues if the business is controversial and the vote expected to be close. For example corporate representatives or proxies may turn up on the day of the meeting, perhaps without the proper paperwork showing their authority, and wishing to amend their previously lodged proxy vote. Strict application of the law and the company's articles can deal with these situations, even though they are likely to cause some delay.

There are electronic poll voting systems now available where shareholders press a button on a handset to indicate their vote and the results, combined with the proxies already received, are displayed on screen shortly after. As far as we are aware the current systems do not, however, enable a shareholder to split their vote. Thus a poll card will still be required by shareholders wishing to vote some shares 'for' and some 'against' the resolution. Also, there may be a few shareholders who are not comfortable with the new technology in which case they should be given the opportunity to on a poll card, although experience to date has not shown this to be a significant problem. This electronic method offers a neat, if partial, solution but may be less economic for smaller companies;

If a poll is being held it is important that shareholders at the meeting have adequate opportunity to express their views on any matter before the meeting and to ask questions. The majority of questions at AGMs are asked on the resolution to receive the report and accounts as this allows questions to be asked about any aspect of the company's business.

Many companies encourage shareholders to ask all questions at this stage, so that the formal business of voting then moves reasonably swiftly. To ensure that all shareholders have been able to express their views it is best practice for the chairman to check that there are no further questions on each specific resolution as it is proposed. This should, however, not be an opportunity for repetition if the issues were adequately covered at the general question and answer session.

If a company is aware that there are several major topics on which it is likely to face questions it may choose to divide up the question and answer session by subject; for example, questions on the report and accounts and the business generally, questions on a proposed new share plan and questions on a contentious development in its business (which may not be on the agenda).

It is not always possible to direct questions at AGMs into a particular pattern and the chairman's handling of them is important to ensure there is adequate debate while not allowing a minority of shareholders present to dominate or disrupt the proceedings.

The draft Companies Bill suggested that independent scrutineers should be appointed to cover the whole proxy process if shareholders demanded it in advance of the meeting.[3] This can, however, add significantly to the cost.

Normal practice is for the registrars to act as scrutineers and sign off on the result for the chairman. Alternatively the company may use an outside firm of accountants (whether or not it is the company's auditors will depend on the policy on the auditors providing non-audit services). Other bodies, such as the Electoral Reform Society, may also be called upon. At the moment the decision rests with the company but, unless special circumstances apply, there does not appear to be much to be gained by incurring the additional cost of using external firms other than the company's professional registrars.

4 Announcing the results

It may be possible for the results of a poll to be announced at the meeting but many of the shareholders may have left the meeting by that stage. It is recommended that companies display the results on their website as soon as these are available and listed companies should issue the results in a regulatory announcement to the market. Some may also choose to publish the results in one or two national newspapers but, if this is intended, space should be booked in advance.

Some listed companies who hold votes on a show of hands also issue an announcement of the results, simply to say that all resolutions were passed. In this case the number of votes would not be released. It should be noted, however, that, where a resolution is passed by a show of hands the Combined Code now requires companies to count all proxies and to indicate both the level of proxies cast for and against the resolution and the number of abstentions.[4]

5 Conclusion

In conclusion, it would not be appropriate to label one method as 'right' or 'better' and the other as 'wrong' or 'inferior' as each method can be valid in particular circumstances.

For many small companies and for those who have low shareholder attendance at their AGMs, with little prospect of disruption, there may be no great case for moving to a poll vote on all resolutions; however, as mentioned above, companies should always be prepared for one, just in case it is called for.

Many large companies now find it convenient to use a poll vote as it can aid the smooth running of the meeting and gives greater transparency to voting figures. If handled well, both ahead of and at the meeting, shareholders who actually attend need not be made to feel disenfranchised.

1   See ICSA Guidance Note *Pols – Chairman's Obligations*.

2   *The Combined Code on Corporate Governance* July 2003 provision D.2.1

3   White Paper *Modernising Company Law – Draft Clauses* CM 5553-11 July 2002, s165

4   *The Combined Code on Corporate Governance* July 2003 prov.D.2.1

'The information given in this Guidance Note, is provided in good faith with the intention of furthering the understanding of the subject matter. Whilst we believe the information to be accurate at the time of publication, ICSA and its staff cannot however accept any liability for any loss or damage occasioned by any person or organisation acting or refraining from action as a result of any views expressed therein. If the reader has any specific doubts or concerns about the subject matter they are advised to seek legal advice based on the circumstances of their own situation.'

Appendix 9

Internal control: Guidance for directors on the Combined Code (The Turnbull guidance)

Preface

Internal Control: Guidance for Directors on the Combined Code (The Turnbull guidance) was first issued in 1999. In 2004, the Financial Reporting Council established the Turnbull Review Group to consider the impact of the guidance and the related disclosures and to determine whether the guidance needed to be updated.

In reviewing the impact of the guidance, our consultations revealed that it has very successfully gone a long way to meeting its original objectives. boards and investors alike indicated that the guidance has contributed to a marked improvement in the overall standard of risk management and internal control since 1999.

Notably, the evidence gathered by the Review Group demonstrated that respondents considered that the substantial improvements in internal control instigated by application of the Turnbull guidance have been achieved without the need for detailed prescription as to how to implement the guidance. The principles-based approach has required boards to think seriously about control issues and enabled them to apply the principles in a way that appropriately dealt with the circumstances of their business. The evidence also supported the proposition that the companies which have derived most benefit from application of the guidance were those whose boards saw embedded risk management and internal control as an integral part of running the business.

Accordingly, the Review Group strongly endorsed retention of the flexible, principles-based approach of the original guidance and has made only a small number of changes.

This however does not mean that there is nothing new for boards to do or that some companies could not make more effective use of the guidance. Establishing an effective system of internal control is not a one-off exercise. No such system remains effective unless it develops to take account of new and emerging risks, control failures, market expectations or changes in the company's circumstances or business objectives. The Review Group reiterates the view of the vast majority of respondents in emphasising the importance of regular and systematic assessment of the risks facing the business and the value of embedding risk management and internal control systems within business processes. It is the board's responsibility to make sure this happens. Boards should review whether they can make more of the communication opportunity of the internal control statement in the annual report. Investors consider the board's attitude towards risk management and internal control to be an important factor when making investment decisions about a company. Taken together with the Operating and Financial Review, the internal control statement provides an opportunity for the board to help shareholders understand the risk and control issues facing the company, and to explain how the company maintains a framework of internal controls to address these issues and how the board has reviewed the effectiveness of that framework.

It is in this spirit that directors need to exercise their responsibility to review on a continuing basis their application of the revised guidance.

Turnbull Review Group October 2005

One – Introduction

The importance of internal control and risk management

1   A company's system of internal control has a key role in the management of risks that are significant to the fulfilment of its business objectives. A sound system of internal control contributes to safeguarding the shareholders' investment and the company's assets.

2   Internal control (as referred to in paragraph 19) facilitates the effectiveness and efficiency of operations, helps ensure the reliability of internal and external reporting and assists compliance with laws and regulations.

3   Effective financial controls, including the maintenance of proper accounting records, are an important element of internal control. They help ensure that the company is not unnecessarily exposed to avoidable financial risks and that financial information used within the business and for publication is reliable. They also contribute to the safeguarding of assets, including the prevention and detection of fraud.

4   A company's objectives, its internal organisation and the environment in which it operates are continually evolving and, as a result, the risks it faces are continually changing. A sound system of internal control therefore depends on a thorough and regular evaluation of the nature and extent of the risks to which the company is exposed. Since profits are, in part, the reward for successful risk-taking in business, the purpose of internal control is to help manage and control risk appropriately rather than to eliminate it.

Objectives of the guidance

5   This guidance is intended to:
   * reflect sound business practice whereby internal control is embedded in the business processes by which a company pursues its objectives;
   * remain relevant over time in the continually evolving business environment; and
   * enable each company to apply it in a manner which takes account of its particular circumstances.

   The guidance requires directors to exercise judgement in reviewing how the company has implemented the requirements of the Combined Code relating to internal control and reporting to shareholders thereon.

6   The guidance is based on the adoption by a company's board of a risk-based approach to establishing a sound system of internal control and reviewing its effectiveness. This should be incorporated by the company within its normal management and governance processes. It should not be treated as a separate exercise undertaken to meet regulatory requirements.

Internal control requirements of the Combined Code

7 Principle C.2 of the Code states that 'The board should maintain a sound system of internal control to safeguard shareholders' investment and the company's assets'.

8 Provision C.2.1 states that 'The directors should, at least annually, conduct a review of the effectiveness of the group's system of internal control and should report to shareholders that they have done so. The review should cover all material controls, including financial, operational and compliance controls and risk management systems'.

9 Paragraph 9.8.6 of the UK Listing Authority's Listing Rules states that in the case of a listed company incorporated in the United Kingdom, the following items must be included in its annual report and accounts:

- a statement of how the listed company has applied the principles set out in Section 1 of the Combined Code, in a manner that would enable shareholders to evaluate how the principles have been applied;

- a statement as to whether the listed company has:

  - complied throughout the accounting period with all relevant provisions set out in Section 1 of the Combined Code; or

  - not complied throughout the accounting period with all relevant provisions set out in Section 1 of the Combined Code and if so, setting out:

    (i) those provisions, if any, it has not complied with,

    (ii) in the case of provisions whose requirements are of a continuing nature, the period within which, if any, it did not comply with some or all of those provisions, and the company's reasons for non-compliance.

10 The Preamble to the Code makes it clear that there is no prescribed form or content for the statement setting out how the various principles in the Code have been applied. The intention is that companies should have a free hand to explain their governance policies in the light of the principles, including any special circumstances which have led to them adopting a particular approach.

11 The guidance in this document applies for accounting periods beginning on or after 1 January 2006, and should be followed by boards of listed companies in:

- assessing how the company has applied Code Principle C.2;

- implementing the requirements of Code Provision C.2.1; and

- reporting on these matters to shareholders in the annual report and accounts.

12 For the purposes of this guidance, internal controls considered by the board should include all types of controls including those of an operational and compliance nature, as well as internal financial controls.

Groups of companies

13 Throughout this guidance, where reference is made to 'company' it should be taken, where applicable, as referring to the group of which the reporting company is the parent company.

For groups of companies, the review of effectiveness of internal control and the report to the shareholders should be from the perspective of the group as a whole.

The Appendix

14 The Appendix to this document contains questions which boards may wish to consider in applying this guidance.

Two – Maintaining a sound system of internal control

Responsibilities

15 The board of directors is responsible for the company's system of internal control. It should set appropriate policies on internal control and seek regular assurance that will enable it to satisfy itself that the system is functioning effectively. The board must further ensure that the system of internal control is effective in managing those risks in the manner which it has approved.

16 In determining its policies with regard to internal control, and thereby assessing what constitutes a sound system of internal control in the particular circumstances of the company, the board's deliberations should include consideration of the following factors:

- the nature and extent of the risks facing the company;
- the extent and categories of risk which it regards as acceptable for the company to bear;
- the likelihood of the risks concerned materialising;
- the company's ability to reduce the incidence and impact on the business of risks that do materialise; and
- the costs of operating particular controls relative to the benefit thereby obtained in managing the related risks.

17 It is the role of management to implement board policies on risk and control. In fulfilling its responsibilities management should identify and evaluate the risks faced by the company for consideration by the board and design, operate and monitor a suitable system of internal control which implements the policies adopted by the board.

18 All employees have some responsibility for internal control as part of their accountability for achieving objectives. They, collectively, should have the necessary knowledge, skills, information, and authority to establish, operate and monitor the system of internal control. This will require an understanding of the company, its objectives, the industries and markets in which it operates, and the risks it faces.

Elements of a sound system of internal control

19 An internal control system encompasses the policies, processes, tasks, behaviours and other aspects of a company that, taken together:

- facilitate its effective and efficient operation by enabling it to respond appropriately to significant business, operational, financial, compliance and other risks to achieving the company's objectives. This includes the safeguarding of assets from inappropriate use or from loss and fraud and ensuring that liabilities are identified and managed;

- help ensure the quality of internal and external reporting. This requires the maintenance of proper records and processes that generate a flow of timely, relevant and reliable information from within and outside the organisation;

- help ensure compliance with applicable laws and regulations, and also with internal policies with respect to the conduct of business.

20 A company's system of internal control will reflect its control environment which encompasses its organisational structure. The system will include:

- control activities;

- information and communications processes; and

- processes for monitoring the continuing effectiveness of the system of internal control.

21 The system of internal control should:

- be embedded in the operations of the company and form part of its culture;

- be capable of responding quickly to evolving risks to the business arising from factors within the company and to changes in the business environment; and

- include procedures for reporting immediately to appropriate levels of management any significant control failings or weaknesses that are identified together with details of corrective action being undertaken.

22 A sound system of internal control reduces, but cannot eliminate, the possibility of poor judgement in decision making; human error; control processes being deliberately circumvented by employees and others; management overriding controls; and the occurrence of unforeseeable circumstances.

23 A sound system of internal control therefore provides reasonable, but not absolute, assurance that a company will not be hindered in achieving its business objectives, or in the orderly and legitimate conduct of its business, by circumstances which may reasonably be foreseen. A system of internal control cannot, however, provide protection with certainty against a company failing to meet its business objectives or all material errors, losses, fraud, or breaches of laws or regulations.

Three – Reviewing the effectiveness of internal control responsibilities

24 Reviewing the effectiveness of internal control is an essential part of the board's responsibilities. The board will need to form its own view on effectiveness based on the information and assurances provided to it, exercising the standard of care generally applicable to directors in the exercise of their duties. Management is accountable to the board for monitoring the system of internal control and for providing assurance to the board that it has done so.

25 The role of board committees in the review process, including that of the audit committee, is for the board to decide and will depend upon factors such as the size and composition of the board; the scale, diversity and complexity of the company's operations; and the nature of the significant risks that the company faces. To the extent that designated board committees carry out, on behalf of the board, tasks that are attributed in this guidance document to the board, the results of the relevant committees' work should be reported to, and considered by, the

board. The board takes responsibility for the disclosures on internal control in the annual report and accounts.

The process for reviewing effectiveness

26 Effective monitoring on a continuous basis is an essential component of a sound system of internal control. The board cannot, however, rely solely on the embedded monitoring processes within the company to discharge its responsibilities. It should regularly receive and review reports on internal control. In addition, the board should undertake an annual assessment for the purposes of making its public statement on internal control to ensure that it has considered all significant aspects of internal control for the company for the year under review and up to the date of approval of the annual report and accounts.

27 The board should define the process to be adopted for its review of the effectiveness of internal control. This should encompass both the scope and frequency of the reports it receives and reviews during the year, and also the process for its annual assessment, such that it will be provided with sound, appropriately documented, support for its statement on internal control in the company's annual report and accounts.

28 The reports from management to the board should, in relation to the areas covered by them, provide a balanced assessment of the significant risks and the effectiveness of the system of internal control in managing those risks. Any significant control failings or weaknesses identified should be discussed in the reports, including the impact that they have had, or may have, on the company and the actions being taken to rectify them. It is essential that there be openness of communication by management with the board on matters relating to risk and control.

29 When reviewing reports during the year, the board should:

- consider what are the significant risks and assess how they have been identified, evaluated and managed;
- assess the effectiveness of the related system of internal control in managing the significant risks, having regard in particular to any significant failings or weaknesses in internal control that have been reported;
- consider whether necessary actions are being taken promptly to remedy any significant failings or weaknesses; and
- consider whether the findings indicate a need for more extensive monitoring of the system of internal control.

30 Additionally, the board should undertake an annual assessment for the purpose of making its public statement on internal control. The assessment should consider issues dealt with in reports reviewed by it during the year together with any additional information necessary to ensure that the board has taken account of all significant aspects of internal control for the company for the year under review and up to the date of approval of the annual report and accounts.

31 The board's annual assessment should, in particular, consider:

- the changes since the last annual assessment in the nature and extent of significant risks, and the company's ability to respond to changes in its business and the external environment;

- the scope and quality of management's ongoing monitoring of risks and of the system of internal control, and, where applicable, the work of its internal audit function and other providers of assurance;

- the extent and frequency of the communication of the results of the monitoring to the board (or board committee(s)) which enables it to build up a cumulative assessment of the state of control in the company and the effectiveness with which risk is being managed;

- the incidence of significant control failings or weaknesses that have been identified at any time during the period and the extent to which they have resulted in unforeseen outcomes or contingencies that have had, could have had, or may in the future have, a material impact on the company's financial performance or condition; and

- the effectiveness of the company's public reporting processes.

32 Should the board become aware at any time of a significant failing or weakness in internal control, it should determine how the failing or weakness arose and reassess the effectiveness of management's ongoing processes for designing, operating and monitoring the system of internal control.

Four – The board's statement on internal control

33 The annual report and accounts should include such meaningful, high-level information as the board considers necessary to assist shareholders' understanding of the main features of the company's risk management processes and system of internal control, and should not give a misleading impression.

34 In its narrative statement of how the company has applied Code Principle C.2, the board should, as a minimum, disclose that there is an ongoing process for identifying, evaluating and managing the significant risks faced by the company, that it has been in place for the year under review and up to the date of approval of the annual report and accounts, that it is regularly reviewed by the board and accords with the guidance in this document.

35 The disclosures relating to the application of Principle C.2 should include an acknowledgement by the board that it is responsible for the company's system of internal control and for reviewing its effectiveness. It should also explain that such a system is designed to manage rather than eliminate the risk of failure to achieve business objectives, and can only provide reasonable and not absolute assurance against material misstatement or loss.

36 In relation to Code Provision C.2.1, the board should summarise the process it (where applicable, through its committees) has applied in reviewing the effectiveness of the system of internal control and confirm that necessary actions have been or are being taken to remedy any significant failings or weaknesses identified from that review. It should also disclose the process it has applied to deal with material internal control aspects of any significant problems disclosed in the annual report and accounts.

37 Where a board cannot make one or more of the disclosures in paragraphs 34 and 36, it should state this fact and provide an explanation. The Listing Rules require the board to disclose if it has failed to conduct a review of the effectiveness of the company's system of internal control.

38 Where material joint ventures and associates have not been dealt with as part of the group for the purposes of applying this guidance, this should be disclosed.

Five – Appendix

Assessing the effectiveness of the company's risk and control processes

Some questions which the board may wish to consider and discuss with management when regularly reviewing reports on internal control and when carrying out its annual assessment are set out below. The questions are not intended to be exhaustive and will need to be tailored to the particular circumstances of the company.

This Appendix should be read in conjunction with the guidance set out in this document.

Risk assessment

- Does the company have clear objectives and have they been communicated so as to provide effective direction to employees on risk assessment and control issues? For example, do objectives and related plans include measurable performance targets and indicators?

- Are the significant internal and external operational, financial, compliance and other risks identified and assessed on an ongoing basis? These are likely to include the principal risks identified in the Operating and Financial Review.

- Is there a clear understanding by management and others within the company of what risks are acceptable to the board?

Control environment and control activities

- Does the board have clear strategies for dealing with the significant risks that have been identified? Is there a policy on how to manage these risks?

- Do the company's culture, code of conduct, human resource policies and performance reward systems support the business objectives and risk management and internal control system?

- Does senior management demonstrate, through its actions as well as it policies, the necessary commitment to competence, integrity and fostering a climate of trust within the company?

- Are authority, responsibility and accountability defined clearly such that decisions are made and actions taken by the appropriate people? Are the decisions and actions of different parts of the company appropriately co-ordinated?

- Does the company communicate to its employees what is expected of them and the scope of their freedom to act? This may apply to areas such as customer relations; service levels for both internal and outsourced activities; health, safety and environmental protection; security of tangible and intangible assets; business continuity issues; expenditure matters; accounting; and financial and other reporting.

- Do people in the company (and in its providers of outsourced services) have the knowledge, skills and tools to support the achievement of the company's objectives and to manage effectively risks to their achievement?

- How are processes/controls adjusted to reflect new or changing risks, or operational deficiencies?

Information and communication

- Do management and the board receive timely, relevant and reliable reports on progress against business objectives and the related risks that provide them with the information, from inside and outside the company, needed for decision-making and management review purposes? This could include performance reports and indicators of change, together with qualitative information such as on customer satisfaction, employee attitudes etc.

- Are information needs and related information systems reassessed as objectives and related risks change or as reporting deficiencies are identified?

- Are periodic reporting procedures, including half-yearly and annual reporting, effective in communicating a balanced and understandable account of the company's position and prospects?

- Are there established channels of communication for individuals to report suspected breaches of law or regulations or other improprieties?

Monitoring

- Are there ongoing processes embedded within the company's overall business operations, and addressed by senior management, which monitor the effective application of the policies, processes and activities related to internal control and risk management? (Such processes may include control self-assessment, confirmation by personnel of compliance with policies and codes of conduct, internal audit reviews or other management reviews.)

- Do these processes monitor the company's ability to re-evaluate risks and adjust controls effectively in response to changes in its objectives, its business, and its external environment?

- Are there effective follow-up procedures to ensure that appropriate change or action occurs in response to changes in risk and control assessments?

- Is there appropriate communication to the board (or board committees) on the effectiveness of the ongoing monitoring processes on risk and control matters? This should include reporting any significant failings or weaknesses on a timely basis.

- Are there specific arrangements for management monitoring and reporting to the board on risk and control matters of particular importance? These could include, for example, actual or suspected fraud and other illegal or irregular acts, or matters that could adversely affect the company's reputation or financial position.

Glossary

AGM Annual general meeting of a company.

audit committee A committee of the board of directors, with responsibility for a range of audit-related issues, and in particular the conduct of the external audit and the company's relationship with its auditors.

audit report Report for shareholders produced by the external auditors on completion of the annual audit, and included in the company's published annual report and accounts.

auditor independence Relationship between the external auditors and a client company, whereby the auditors are able to exercise their independent professional judgement, and where their judgement will not be influenced by the closeness of the relationship with the client company or by matters of self-interest.

authorised share capital The maximum amount of share capital that a company is permitted to issue. A company's authorised share capital is stated in its memorandum of association, and can be increased only if the shareholders agree, normally (in the case of public companies) by ordinary resolution in a general meeting.

board committee A committee established by the board of directors, with responsibility for a particular aspect of the board's affairs. For example, audit committee, remuneration/compensation committee and nominations committee.

Cadbury Code A code of corporate governance, published by the Cadbury committee in the UK in 1992 (and since superseded).

Combined Code The UK code on corporate governance, which applies to UK listed companies. It is a voluntary code rather than a regulatory requirement. However, the UK Listing Rules require listed companies to disclose in their annual report the extent of their compliance or non-compliance with the Code. The Code was revised in 2003.

compliance statement A statement by a listed company of whether it has complied with the requirements of the national code of corporate governance, and if not, in what ways has it failed to do so. In the UK, listed companies are required by the Combined Code to include a compliance statement in their annual report and accounts.

corporate social responsibility (CSR) Responsibility shown by a company (or other organisations) for matters of general concern to the society in which it operates, such as protection of the environment, health and safety, and social welfare.

directors' report A report by the board of directors to the shareholders, contained in the annual report and accounts of the company and containing mainly statutory disclosures of information.

external audit Statutory annual audit of a company by independent external auditors.

fiduciary duty A duty of a trustee. The directors of a company are given their powers in trust by the company, and have fiduciary duties towards the company.

financial statement A statement containing financial information. The main financial statements by a company are the balance sheet and profit and loss account in the annual report and accounts. Other financial statements include a cash flow statement, and the balance sheet and profit and loss account in a company's published interim or quarterly accounts.

general meeting A meeting of the equity shareholders of a company, either an annual general meeting (AGM) or an Extraordinary General Meeting. Public companies are required to hold an AGM.

Greenbury Report Report in the UK in 1995 by the Greenbury committee, focusing mainly on corporate governance issues related to directors' remuneration.

Hampel committee Committee set up in the UK to continue the review of corporate governance practices in the UK, following the Cadbury and Greenbury committee Reports. The Hampel committee suggested that the recommendations of all three committees should be integrated into a single code of corporate governance, which was published in 1998 as the Combined Code.

Higgs Report The 2003 UK-government commissioned review into the role and effectiveness of non-executive directors.

independence Free from the influence of another individual (or individuals) and free from conflicts of interest.

insider dealing Dealing in the shares of a company by an individual who has knowledge of undisclosed 'insider information' (price-sensitive information) that comes from an 'inside source'. In the UK, insider dealing is a criminal offence under Part V of the Criminal Justice Act 1993.

institutional investor An organisation or institution that invests funds of clients, savers or depositors. The main institutional investors are pension funds, insurance/life assurance companies, investment trust companies and organisations such as unit trusts and open-ended investment companies ('OEICs'). Institutional investors are the main investors in shares in the leading stock markets of the world. In the UK, most institutional investors are members of an 'industry association', such as the Association of British Insurers and the National Association of Pension Funds. These make best practice recommendations to their members.

internal control statement A statement by the board of directors of a listed company to the shareholders on internal control, and contained in the company's annual report and accounts. This statement is a requirement of the combined Code in the UK.

internal controls Control measures within an organisation that are intended to ensure the safeguarding of the organisation's assets and the prevention or detection of fraud or error.

majority shareholder A shareholder holding a majority of the equity shares in a company and so having a controlling interest in the company. (A majority shareholder has the voting power to remove directors from the board, and so can control the board.)

market abuse A civil offence under the Financial Services and Markets Act 2000, for which an individual can be fined by the Financial Services Authority. Market abuse occurs when an individual distorts a market in investments, creates a false or misleading impression of the value or price of an investment or misuses relevant information before it is published. (In effect, this is similar to insider trading, but it is a civil offence, rather than a criminal offence, and the burden of proof is lower.)

Model Code A Code that applies restrictions on share dealings that go beyond the restrictions imposed by law, for example the insider dealing legislation. Its aim is to ensure that directors, relevant employees and 'connected persons' do not abuse price-sensitive information, especially in a period leading up to the announcement of results by the company (a 'close period'). Listed companies must apply a code of conduct that is at least as stringent as the Model Code.

Myners Report A UK report into the role and responsibilities of institutional investors.

nomination committee A committee of the board of directors, with responsibility for identifying potential new members for the board of directors. Suitable candidates are recommended to the main board, which then makes a decision about their appointment.

operating and financial review (OFR) A report by a company, written in simple English and contained in the company's annual report and accounts, giving a description of the company's operations and financial performance and position for the year under review. At the time of writing, operational and financial reviews are voluntary statements, but larger companies might in the future be required by law to publish them.

price-sensitive information Undisclosed information that, if made generally known, would be likely to have an effect on the share price of the company concerned.

proxy vote A vote delivered by an individual (a proxy) on behalf of a shareholder, in the shareholder's absence. The absent shareholder gives instructions to the proxy on how to vote (although might give the proxy discretion in deciding how to vote).

remuneration policy The policy of a company on the remuneration of its senior executives, including basic salary and all incentive-related elements and severance payment terms. The remuneration policy might be formulated by the remuneration committee, and shareholders might be invited to vote to approve the policy at the company AGM.

remuneration committee A committee of the board of directors, with responsibility for deciding remuneration policy for top executives and the individual remuneration packages of certain senior executives, for example all the executive directors.

senior independent director An independent non-executive director, recognised as the senior individual amongst the non-executives.

share options Instruments giving their holder the right (but not the obligation) to subscribe for shares in a company at a predetermined price (the exercise price). When issued, share options are usually exercisable at any time after a given future date, up to a final date when they eventually lapse. If the company share price rises, an option holder stands to make an immediate profit by exercising share options and buying shares at the exercise price and selling them at the current market price.

shareholder activism A term that refers to (1) the considered use by institutional investors of their rights as shareholders, by voting against the board of directors at general meetings (or threatening to vote against the board); and (2) active dialogue with the boards of companies, to influence decisions by the board.

Smith Report The 2003 Report by an FRC-appointed group into the role and responsibilities of audit committees.

stakeholder A stakeholder group is an identifiable group of individuals or organisations with a vested interest. Stakeholder groups in a company include the shareholders, the directors, senior executive management and other employees, customers, suppliers, the general public and (in the case of many companies) the government. The nature of their interests differs between stakeholder groups. Issues in corporate governance are which stakeholder group interests should predominate and to what extent can the interests of the different groups be met or reconciled.

sustainability reporting A report by a socially responsible company on its social, ethical, health and safety and environmental policies and procedures. It might also refer more specifically to environmental reporting, with a focus on how the company is following the business options with the least-damaging effect on the environment.

Table A In the context of UK company law, standard articles of association (company constitution) that a company can adopt (and amend as necessary). In practice, the articles of association of most UK companies are based on the Table A articles.

total shareholder return The total returns in a period earned by the company's shareholders, consisting normally of the dividends received and the gain (or minus the fall) in the share price during the period. The returns might be expressed as a percentage of the share value, (e.g. the share price at the start of the period).

Turnbull Report A report of the Turnbull committee in the UK, giving listed companies guidance on how the directors should carry out their responsibility for the internal control system, as required by the Combined Code.

unitary (one-tier) board A board structure where the organisation has just a single board of directors. This consists of executive directors and (in the case of listed companies and also many other public companies and some private companies) non-executive directors. A unitary board structure is used by companies in many countries, including the US and UK.

Directory

Web resources
Association of British Insurers: www.abi.org.uk
Business for Social Responsibility: www.bsr.org
Council of Institutional Investors (US): www.cii.org
Department of Trade and Industry: www.dti.gov.uk
Financial Reporting Council: www.frc.org.uk
Financial Services Authority: www.fsa.gov.uk
Global Corporate Governance Forum: www.gcgf.org
Institute for Business Ethics: www.ibe.org.uk
Institute of Chartered Secretaries and Administrators: www.icsa.org.uk
Institute of Directors: www.iod.co.uk
International Corporate Governance Network: www.icgn.org
Investor Relations Society: www.ir-soc.org.uk
London Stock Exchange: www.londonstockexchange.com
National Association of Pension Funds: www.napf.co.uk and www.votingissues.com
New York Stock Exchange: www.nyse.com
Organisation for Economic Cooperation and Development: www.oecd.org
Panel on Takeovers and Mergers: www.thetakeoverpanel.org.uk
Pensions Investments Research Consultants Limited: www.pirc.co.uk/
Pensions Management Institute www.pensions-pmi.org.uk
Pensions Regulator www.thepensionsregulator.gov.uk

Further reading
ICSA Publications (available from ICSA Publishing: www.icsapublishing.co.uk)
Armour, D. (2004) *The ICSA Company Secretary's Checklists*, 5th edition
Armour, D. (2006) *The ICSA Company Secretary's Handbook*, 6th edition
Bruce, M. (2003) *The ICSA Directors' Guide* 2nd edition
Cooper, B. *(2006) The ICSA Handbook of Good Boardroom Practice* 2nd edition
Copnell, T. (2005) *The ICSA Audit Committee Guide*
Coyle, B. (2005) *The ICSA Corporate Governance Handbook*
Martin, D. (2005) *One Stop Company Secretary*
O'Hare, S. (2006) The ICSA Remuneration Committee Guide
Walmsley, K .*Company Secretarial Practice*, Looseleaf

Codes, guidelines and reports

Association of British Insurers (2001) *Disclosure Guidelines on Socially Responsible Investment* (available at www.abi.org.uk)

Association of British Insurers (2002) *Guidelines on Executive Remuneration* (available at www.abi.org.uk)

Cadbury Committee on the Financial Aspects of Corporate Governance (1992) *Report of the Committee on the Financial Aspects of Corporate Governance: The Code of Best Practice*, Gee Publishing

Combined Code on Corporate Governance (October 2005) Financial Reporting Council available at www.frc.org.uk

DTI Consultation document '"Rewards for Failure": Directors' Remuneration – Contracts, Performance and Severance', (2003): www.dti.gov.uk/cld/4864rewards.pdf

Greenbury Study Group (1995) *Report on Directors' Remuneration*, Gee Publishing

Hampel Committee on Corporate Governance (1998) *Committee on Corporate Governance: Final Report*, Gee Publishing

Hermes Pensions Management (1998, updated 2001) *Statement on Corporate Governance and Voting Policy* (available at www.hermes.co.uk)

Hermes Pensions Management (2002) *The Hermes Principles* (available at www.hermes.co.uk)

Higgs Report (2003) *The Role and Effectiveness of Non-Executive Directors* Department of Trade and Industry (available at www.dti.gov.uk)

Institutional Shareholders Committee (2002) *Responsibilities of Institutional Shareholders and Agents – Statement of Principles* (available at www.abi.org.uk)

Myners, Paul (2001) *Institutional Investment in the UK: A Review*, HM Treasury available at www.hm-treasury.gov.uk/media//843F0/31.pdf

National Association of Pension Funds (2001) *Corporate Governance Policy* (available at www.napf.co.uk)

Pensions Investments Research Consultants Ltd (2003) *Shareholder Voting Guidelines* (available at www.pirc.co.uk)

Smith Review Panel (2003) *Audit Committees: Combined Code Guidance* Financial Reporting Council (original version available at www.frc.org.uk; updated version included in the October 2005 Combined Code)

Turnbull Working Party (1999) *Internal Control: Guidance for Directors on the Combined Code* Croner CCH (available in pdf format via www.icaew.co.uk and also included in the October 2005 Combined Code)

Index